AF687059

Smart Capital

-The Formula for Globalizing Mid-market Enterprises

Smart Capital = RWA × Stablecoin × (Tri-Market Listing: IPOs + STO) × (OpCo + NewCo)

V3.2

Aug 17th, 2025

By Wilson Liu
Founder, Chairman & CEO of ETAO International
Founding Partner of WSHP Capital
Former AVP, New York Stock Exchange (NYSE)

The Strategic Operating System for Global Capitalization

This handbook is not only a strategic framework for valuation enhancement and capital integration.

It is a standardized, exportable operating system for the international capital elevation of Chinese mid-sized enterprises.

It serves as a capital solution, a market strategy framework, and a reference model for industrial policy, with high commercial value for broad replication, execution, and implementation.

Foreword

Over the course of my 35-year journey in the global capital markets, I have witnessed countless companies make the pivotal leap from regional operations to the international stage. And I've come to understand deeply that those who truly achieve capital elevation, industrial synergy, and global deployment are not only driven by technological innovation — they are distinguished by a profound grasp of capital logic and the strategic use of financial instruments.

As the former Chairman and Audit Committee Chair of NASDAQ-listed Visionary Holdings Inc., I have led strategic transformations across AI, life sciences, and green energy sectors. I've also had the privilege of serving as an advisor and board member for various international think tanks, philanthropic platforms, and foundations, working in collaboration with institutions like the United Nations and the World Health Organization to promote global justice and sustainable investment.

It is precisely because of this experience that, upon reading the Capital Strategy Handbook for Internationalization of Innovative Biopharma Enterprises, I was struck by how this is far more than a "technical guide to capital operations." It is a systematic, forward-looking playbook for capital transformation.

This handbook is the work of my esteemed friend, Mr. Wilson Liu, Founder and Chairman of ETAO International. Drawing upon over two decades of Wall Street experience in capital markets, Wilson integrates expertise in AI healthcare, biotech, and cross-border M&A to present highly actionable solutions — including the NewCo model, RWA tokenization structures, and PIPE financing with strategic exit mechanisms. These frameworks are not only designed for the hundreds of mid-sized Chinese companies struggling to grow beyond the 2-billion-RMB valuation ceiling, but they also offer a globally applicable template for capital uplift.

Wilson is a true practitioner-thinker with global financial acumen. As the Founding Partner of WSHP Capital and the visionary leader behind ETAO, he has led numerous successful SPACs, PIPE deals, and acquisitions. More importantly, he remains committed to bridging capital with industry to help enterprises break through valuation bottlenecks and achieve international expansion. His strategic thinking, global vision, and cultural depth are vividly reflected in this work.

I sincerely recommend this book to all entrepreneurs, investors, financial advisors, policymakers, and platform institutions committed to enterprise growth, capital integration, and international listing. It is both a practical field manual and a strategic roadmap worthy of repeated study.

May this book be your guiding light on the journey toward the global capital markets.

Dr. William Chai
Former Chairman, Visionary Holdings Inc. (NASDAQ: GV)
Founding Partner, Global Citizen Action Platform (GCAP)
Honorary PhD in Global Philanthropic Management
Senior Advisor, Global Innovation Center
Toronto, Aug 2025

Author's Preface

A Staircase Fall and the Birth of Smart Capital

On an ordinary afternoon of June 18, 2025, I was at home in the United States when I went downstairs to retrieve some documents. I missed a step on the way to the basement and fell hard, severely injuring my lower back. In an instant, the pain ripped me away from the rhythm of daily life. The following weeks were agonizing—I could hardly sleep at night, alternating between prayer, painkillers, and deep contemplation. It was during this forced stillness that I found myself revisiting the questions that had long troubled me:

- Why do so many mid-sized Chinese tech companies hit a valuation ceiling of RMB 2 billion and stall?
- Why do companies with real transactions, cash flow, and innovation struggle to receive fair global valuation?
- Why, even today, with PE, Hong Kong IPOs, and SPACs all facing headwinds, have we not built a scalable, replicable capital strategy specifically for mid-sized private enterprises?

In early July 2025, I traveled to Brown University on the East Coast for academic exchange. Each day, I walked the beautiful campus and quietly continued writing this book. During that period, my body gradually healed, and my mind found clarity in Rhode Island's ocean breeze and academic atmosphere. On the morning of July 18, in a spotless meeting room at Brown's Watson Institute for International and Public Affairs, while looking out at a vast green lawn, a formula suddenly flashed into my mind:

Smart Capital = RWA × Stablecoin × (Tri-Market Listing： IPOs +STO) × (OpCo + NewCo)

It was more than just an elegant financial structure—it was a multidimensional, actionable model. It blended cross-border experience between China and the U.S., token-based capital architecture, and timely policy alignment. It wasn't an abstract idea, but a strategic roadmap for international capital elevation—verifiable by data, executable by structure, and compliant with regulation.

I quickly wrote down each variable in my notebook:

- RWA represents transferable future income—license agreements, medical data, or AI models.
- Stablecoins serve as the bridge between global LPs and digital capital.
- Tri-market listing refers to Hong Kong's liquidity platform, U.S. tech valuation systems,

and policy-backed Middle East financial channels.

- And the (OpCo + NewCo) structure is the operational bridge for asset unbundling, value reassessment, and token-based pricing.

This book was born from that moment. It is not only a distillation of my 30 years in capital markets, but a **practical guide for mid-sized Chinese innovation firms** struggling to leap from RMB 2 billion to 10 billion in value. I titled it:

Smart Capital-The Formula for Globalizing Mid-market Enterprises

While it begins by focusing on the medical and AI sectors, it can be extended to new materials, green energy, and high-end manufacturing.

Its core mission is:

To provide mid-sized companies with a systematic, executable, and globally compliant capital framework for outbound growth—connecting international investors and unlocking valuation.

I am now strangely grateful for that fall on the staircase—for the pain, the pause, and the prayer that allowed me to finally "hear" the formula that had lived in my mind for years. Smart capital is not financial wizardry. It is a language of global capital consensus.

It is a pathway to billion-dollar valuations.

And most importantly, it is a key for mid-sized Chinese firms to step boldly onto the world stage.

How to Use This Book – Smart Capital？

This book covers a broad and in-depth system of concepts and tools, including valuation strategy, cross-border structuring, tokenization mechanisms, PIPE financing, ESG disclosure, and more. To help readers of different roles navigate the content effectively, we recommend the following reading paths:

Entrepreneurs / Founders

Focus: Strategic logic + practical pathways + real-world case studies

- Chapter 1: The Smart Capital Formula and Valuation Amplification Logic
- Chapter 6: Why Smart Capital Is the Ultimate Valuation Amplifier for Mid-market Firms
- Chapter 20: SPAC + HK Spinoff + STO Hybrid Strategy
- Chapter 25: Real-World Application of the Smart Capital Formula

Recommended to read alongside Chapter 36 (Tri-Market Listing Timeline) and the "12-Step Global Capital Elevation Roadmap."

Investors / LPs / Fund Managers

Focus: Asset structuring + target company evaluation toolkits

- Chapters 7–11: RWA design logic, valuation models, and tokenization frameworks
- Chapter 14: Feasibility of Stablecoins as RWA Pricing & Liquidity Intermediaries
- Chapter 16: How Digital Capital Enhances Valuation Liquidity
- Chapters 32–38: Complete toolkits including PIPE agreement templates, ESG disclosure, investor FAQs, and pitch deck structure

Highly recommended: Appendix II – Chinese-English Glossary of Key Financial and Legal Terms, useful for cross-border communication and concept alignment.

Lawyers / Financial Advisors (FA) / Consulting Teams

Focus: Legal structuring + compliance pathways + implementation checklists

- Chapters 21–24: Strategic value of NewCo structures, asset revaluation, and legacy shareholder exit planning
- Chapter 33: NewCo Formation Flowchart and Legal Checklist

- Chapter 34: RWA + Token Compliance Guide (Reg D / Reg S)
- Chapter 35: ESG Disclosure Templates (IFRS / SASB Format)
- Chapters 39–41: Bilingual Strategic Cooperation Agreement Templates + On-chain Governance Diagrams

Can be used as a Pre-IPO standard execution checklist or for preparing client-facing capital structure proposals.

Preface

At a time when the global economic order is being restructured and technology industries are deeply integrated, China stands at a historic turning point—transitioning from a "manufacturing powerhouse" to a "capital-driven nation." While a number of leading enterprises have successfully entered international capital markets, there remain hundreds of mid-sized innovative companies in China, each with technical potential yet constrained by valuation ceilings, financing bottlenecks, governance limitations, and global branding challenges.

The *Handbook of Capital Strategy for Internationalization of Innovative Biopharma Enterprises* was written precisely to address this "mid-market growth gap." It offers a practical and replicable pathway for capital elevation and systematically maps out the strategic architecture spanning legacy equity restructuring, NewCo modeling, PIPE financing, ESG disclosure, RWA tokenization, and dual-market arbitrage across HKEX and NASDAQ.

This handbook is intended for, but not limited to:

- Founders and executives of Chinese mid-sized enterprises seeking global expansion;
- Financial advisors (FA), lawyers, and investors focused on Pre-IPO, PIPEs, and M&A deals;
- Policymakers and economic development zone leaders;
- EMBA/DBA faculty, scholars, and researchers at business schools;
- Young entrepreneurs who view capital markets as accelerators of business growth.

For these audiences, this handbook serves as both a "capital operations manual" and a "strategic blueprint." By combining frameworks, case studies, and actionable toolkits, it modularizes and systematizes the complexities of international capital access, significantly lowering execution barriers for practitioners.

The book's author, Mr. Wilson Liu, brings over 20 years of experience on Wall Street. He previously served as an audit director at the New York Stock Exchange (NYSE), where he became the first Chinese national appointed to a core regulatory position in the institution's history. Throughout his career, he has led dozens of cross-border M&A transactions, PIPE financings, and SPAC listings. He currently serves as Chairman and CEO of ETAO International (a NASDAQ-listed company) and Managing Partner of WSHP Capital, with a mission to facilitate the capital transformation and brand ascension of China's mid-sized tech enterprises globally.

In this book, he introduces groundbreaking concepts such as the NewCo model, the "One Body, Two Wings" strategic framework, and RWA + Token capital structures. Drawing from his real-world practice in AI healthcare, digital health, and biotech, Liu presents a deeply insightful view of China's industrial capital upgrading trend.

We firmly believe that once Chinese mid-sized enterprises master the ability to "capitalize themselves," they will gain pricing power, narrative influence, and industry leadership on the global stage.

This book was written for exactly that moment—for enterprises ready to rise in this new era.

Disclaimer

The contents of this book are intended solely for academic research, educational training, and strategic reference. Nothing herein constitutes investment advice, an offer to sell securities, a solicitation of financing, or legal counsel.

All company case studies, market data, and financing pathways discussed are compiled from publicly available sources and are provided strictly for educational purposes. They do not represent the views or endorsements of the author or publisher, nor should they be interpreted as investment recommendations.

Historical events, financial data, and market size information cited in this book may change over time and may no longer be accurate at the time of reading. While reasonable efforts have been made to ensure accuracy, no guarantee of completeness or timeliness is provided. Readers must independently verify and exercise their own judgment.

References to external works (including but not limited to *Currency Wars*, Marx, Drucker, and other scholarly or public discourse) are cited or derived from publicly available sources. Copyrights belong to the original authors or publishers. This book provides academic commentary only and does not imply endorsement or rejection of the referenced viewpoints.

Any contract templates, structural diagrams, or procedural guides included are illustrative only and must not be used as substitutes for professional advice from licensed attorneys, accountants, or financial advisors.

Discussions of "conspiracy theories," "philosophical comparisons," or "religious/cultural analyses" are presented solely as academic reflections on public discourse. They do not reflect the personal stance of the author, nor should they be interpreted as discriminatory or prejudicial.

All opinions expressed in this book are solely those of the author in a personal capacity and do not represent the positions of any company, institution, or organization with which the author is or has been affiliated.

By using this book, you acknowledge and accept that you assume full responsibility and risk.

Author Biography

Author: Wilson Liu

Founder, Chairman & CEO of ETAO International Group Inc. (Since 2017)

Professional Background:

With over 20 years of experience on Wall Street, Wilson Liu has held key positions at leading global financial institutions, including:

- J.P. Morgan
- Core regulatory roles at the New York Stock Exchange
- Reuters
- PricewaterhouseCoopers (PwC)
- Citibank
- an Auditor in Charge at Morgan Stanley

Entrepreneurial Achievements:

- Founder of Growing Pains Solution
- Founder of WSHP Capital
- Founder & President of Wall Street HuangPu Center
- Co-founder of Beijing CSII Software Technology Co., Ltd. (Stock Code: 300663)
    - Over 4,000 employees
    - Participated in and helped drive the early rollout of online banking in China in 1999

Public Company & Capital Markets Experience:

- Former CFO of Apollo Solar Energy, a NASDAQ-listed company
- Led the merger and Nasdaq listing of ETAO and MCAE SPAC, with a combined valuation of USD 1 billion
- Led the IPO of ADOC Acquisition Corp, raising USD 90 million
    - One of the earliest SPAC IPOs led by a Chinese executive globally
- Extensive hands-on experience in M&A, PIPE financing, and NASDAQ listings

Publications & Thought Leadership:

- Author of over 10,000 classical Chinese poems and more than a dozen books spanning culture, philosophy, history, and religion

- Creator of "The 12-Lecture Fast Track to NASDAQ", hailed as one of the most practical capital market courses for public company executives
- *Smart Capital – The Formula for Globalizing Mid-market Enterprises* is designed to offer entrepreneurs and investors a practical roadmap to global capital and is included in Appendix II.

Education & Certifications:

- Holds two Master's degrees from Baruch College, City University of New York (CUNY):
    - M.S. in Computer Information Systems (1997)
    - M.S. in Accounting (2003)
- Dual certified as a CPA (Certified Public Accountant) and CFA (Chartered Financial Analyst)
- Microsoft Certified Solutions Developer (MCSD)
    - One of the first 500 recipients personally certified by Bill Gates in 1997

Photographic Highlights of the Author's Journey

Milestones on the Capital Journey

These photographs capture defining moments in Wilson Liu's professional and academic journey—bridging Wall Street, global capital markets, and cross-border healthcare. Each image reflects not only a career milestone but also a piece of the intellectual path that inspired *From Competition to Non-Competition*.

1. At the New York Stock Exchange (NYSE) — 2005

Wilson Liu serving in the Regulatory & Compliance Division as AVP.
A historic role as the **first American-Chinese regulatory officer** in the NYSE's core compliance team, overseeing IPO listings, governance rules, and market integrity.

2. Leading ADOC SPAC IPO on NASDAQ — 2020

Wilson Liu directing the successful listing of **ADOC**, raising **USD 90 million**.
This moment marked not only the culmination of two decades of Wall Street experience but also the beginning of a new era of **structural finance and SPAC-driven value creation**.

3. ETAO International NASDAQ Listing Ceremony — March 3, 2023

Wilson Liu with **Dr. David Wu, President of Baruch College**, and fellow alumni, celebrating ETAO International's NASDAQ debut.
This event bridged Wilson's academic alma mater with his entrepreneurial journey—demonstrating the link between scholarship, capital innovation, and enterprise building.

Together, these three photographs trace a continuous arc:
from **regulation and governance (NYSE)** → to **structural innovation and capital raising (ADOC SPAC)** → to **cross-border healthcare listing and global leadership (ETAO International).**

They are not just memories—they are **structural anchors of a career dedicated to designing trust, structure, and value creation.**

Event –Wilson Liu at New York Stock Exchange (NYSE) – Serving in Regulatory Role, 2005

Event – Wilson Liu leading the ADOC IPO on NASDAQ, Raising USD 90M through SPAC, in November 2020

Event –Wilson Liu with Baruch College President David and Fellow Alumni at the ETAO International NASDAQ Listing Ceremony on March 3, 2023

Contents

Professional Endorsement

The ***Smart Capital - The Formula for Globalizing Mid-market Enterprises*** stands out as a highly structured, forward-looking, and actionable strategy guide. Unlike generic narratives about "going global," this book addresses the real challenges faced by Chinese mid-sized enterprises in valuation, financing structures, and cross-border investor engagement, offering clearly executable solutions.From a business logic perspective, the book demonstrates the following strengths:

1. Complete Pathway with Closed-Loop Design

It lays out a comprehensive roadmap from asset packaging to equity structuring, valuation anchoring, capital raising, regulatory compliance, and multi-market exits. The proposed model — *NewCo + PIPE + Token + ESG* — represents a structural innovation blending traditional financing tools with digital asset mechanisms.

2. Highly Replicable Toolkits

With bilingual templates, strategic agreements, investor FAQs, ESG disclosure guides, and token economics frameworks, this handbook offers a ready-to-use toolkit for founders, investment bankers, legal counsel, and LPs.

3. Aligned with Global Capital Trends

The insights on valuation arbitrage between NASDAQ and HKEX, combined with case studies on sovereign wealth funds from the Gulf (e.g., G42, Mubadala), position this book at the frontier of China's global capital integration.

4. Unique Strategic Perspective

Rather than focusing solely on technical financing steps, the book takes a holistic view of how Chinese mid-sized innovators can amplify their global market relevance through legal, financial, and strategic positioning.

In summary, this is not just a "manual for fundraising"—it is a tactical playbook for capital elevation, a strategic framework for international expansion, and a powerful toolset for those navigating the next generation of cross-border growth.

I highly recommend this book to founders, investors, advisors, and capital market professionals. — Dr. Wang - Capital Markets Strategist | Chief Advisor to Chinese Overseas IPOs | Former IB Managing Director

Part I: Smart Capital Formula & Structural Overview

Introduces the "Smart Capital" formula and its foundational logic, analyzing Wall Street's capital structure, global capital trends, and valuation pitfalls faced by mid-sized enterprises. Constructs a replicable capital uplift model using concepts such as RWA, Tokens, and NewCo to initiate a theoretical framework for internationalization.

Chapter 1: Smart Capital: Overview of the Formula, Logic and Framework

Who Controls Wall Street?

Wall Street, a mere 0.7 miles (approximately 1.1 kilometers) long, embodies the soul of global finance.

This short street, beginning at Broadway and ending at the edge of the East River, is neither the longest street in New York nor its most prosperous commercial district. Yet, it has become the symbolic epicenter of the global capital order. Beneath its cobbled stones runs a three-century evolution of financial systems; between its buildings stand the New York Stock Exchange, the New York Fed, and the historic site of the Morgan banking empire—early temples of the modern financial empire.

On this one-kilometer stretch, the tides of wealth, the rise and fall of asset bubbles, the fate of national credit and currency—all have quietly been decided. Every inch of pavement seems etched with echoes of crashes, mergers, and crises.

In this short street, trillions in capital have surged and vanished; a few short steps have witnessed centuries of financial order rise and fall. I have spent three decades walking these streets, striving to decipher the logic behind its operations.

This is Wall Street—narrow in appearance, yet unfathomably deep.

I. The Conspiracy Theory Version: Jewish Banking Clans, the Illuminati, and Wall Street Control

In China's financial literacy journey, one cannot overlook a phenomenon-level figure—Song Hongbing.

A graduate of the University of International Business and Economics who later studied and worked in Washington, D.C., Song published his *Currency Wars* book series in 2007. Written in a sensational yet accessible tone, it unveiled a hidden global financial power structure. The book claimed that world finance is not the product of free markets but rather a monetary printing network controlled by a handful of international banking families.

Why did *Currency Wars* explode in popularity in China?

The book quickly topped bestseller lists and triggered countless discussions, imitations, and even official scrutiny over the following decade. The reasons behind its appeal include:

1. **Outlet for social anxiety –** Amid economic transition pains, currency depreciation, and a real estate bubble, China's middle class grew uneasy about "the invisible hand."

2. **Cognitive satisfaction through deconstruction –** The book's claims, such as "the Rothschilds control central banks" and "the Federal Reserve is not a government entity," provided readers with a sense of "unveiled truth."

3. **Resonance with nationalist narratives –** The underlying crisis consciousness, alleging that "Western finance manipulates China's destiny," aligned with popular national rejuvenation themes.

Beyond Academia: The Pedagogical Value of Conspiracy Narratives

Though *Currency Wars* faced harsh academic criticism for lacking evidence and logical coherence, from a mass communication perspective, it introduced millions of Chinese readers to concepts like the Federal Reserve, fiat currency, and the gold standard.
As one financial writer put it: "*Currency Wars* may not be accurate, but for many Chinese, it was their first financial literacy class."

Summary: In an era of information asymmetry, conspiracy theories often represent the public's intuitive resistance to opaque power structures.

In a world where Wall Street is seen as the "central nervous system of global capital," Song's work resonated with Chinese concerns about international financial opacity. By using simplified logic, concrete family names, and mysterious storytelling, he reframed a complex financial system as a global wealth-manipulation scheme—and thus dominated cultural discourse.

He may not mark the end of financial science, but he was certainly the beginning of public financial awakening.

I came to the U.S. in the summer of 1994 for study and work, spending nearly five years at the New York Stock Exchange and later serving in three of the world's top four investment banks, including JPMorgan, Citibank, and Morgan Stanley.

Regarding "who controls Wall Street," aside from Song Hongbing's "Rothschild-Fed" narrative, many conspiracy theories have persisted over the years:

- Some claim a "Jewish financial cabal" controls both the Fed and Wall Street, citing names like the Rothschilds, George Soros, and Guggenheim.
- Others believe secret societies like the Illuminati or Freemasons orchestrate global financial turbulence to engineer cycles of wealth redistribution.
- Online discourse includes extreme narratives such as *The Financial New World Order* or *How Jews Control the World Economy*.

While these theories lack empirical support and often contain racial bias and hate speech, they reveal a deep public anxiety over excessive capital concentration and opaque rule-making.

II. Systems and Structures: Wall Street as a Financial Control Network

Wall Street is more than a physical street in Lower Manhattan; it symbolizes the financial central nervous system of the U.S. and the world.
It comprises a network of exchanges (like NYSE and Nasdaq), investment banks, hedge funds, regulators (like the SEC and Federal Reserve), and credit rating agencies. This forms a complex "capital system network."

In my view, this structural network isn't controlled by a single force, but rather functions through the interplay of rules, leverage, and compliance systems. It reflects *institutional power*, not *individual domination*.

III. Capital Oligarchy: The "Invisible Empire" of Asset Management Giants

Despite Wall Street's apparent diversity, real control over shareholder and voting power is increasingly concentrated among a few asset management giants:

- BlackRock – With over $10 trillion in assets under management, it's often referred to as the "shadow central bank."
- Vanguard – A passive investment giant with control over governance rights in hundreds of listed companies.
- State Street – One of the global "Big Three" in ETFs alongside the above two.

These institutions, through "passive investment + long-term holdings," wield real influence over corporate boards, M&A decisions, and executive compensation—effectively becoming the silent rulers behind the façade of "capital democracy."

IV. Conclusion: Capital Concentration + Information Asymmetry ≠ Conspiracy

Wall Street indeed reflects structural power concentration, where a few super-financial institutions guide global capital flows and market sentiment. But their control stems from institutional advantages, technological pathways, and regulatory arbitrage—not from secret meetings in locked rooms.

What we must truly guard against is not "conspiracy," but the erosion of fairness and transparency when capital escapes oversight and narrative control becomes monopolized.

Philosophical Prelude: Jewish Capital Intelligence — From Deconstruction to Reconstruction

A Comparative Reflection on Jewish Intellectual Giants: Karl Marx and Peter F. Drucker, and the Rise of the Smart Capital Formula

Throughout the history of modern capital thought, two intellectual giants of Jewish descent—Karl Marx and Peter F. Drucker—respectively represent the deconstructive force and the constructive wisdom of capital theory.

Marx exposed the exploitative essence of capital, aiming to dismantle the system through class struggle. Drucker, on the other hand, sought to redefine the relationship between capital and organization by centering management and knowledge, making the operation of capital more efficient and humane.

Both thinkers embody the systemic thinking, structural insight, and expressive power characteristic of Jewish intellectual culture: one shook the old order, the other built a new paradigm.

The proposal of Smart Capital emerges precisely from the dialectic tension between Marx and Drucker, seeking a third path—not revolution, but systemic optimization.
It recognizes structural imbalances, yet emphasizes that these can be restructured through capital design, corporate governance, and digital tools.

As illustrated by the core formula of this book:

Smart Capital = RWA × Stablecoin × (Tri-Market Listing： IPOs + STO) × (OpCo + NewCo)

This is not just a capital engineering framework, but also a philosophical blueprint—empowering mid-sized enterprises to break free from structural traps and reposition themselves in the global value chain.

The author takes a path from deconstruction to construction to reconstruction, standing on the shoulders of giants and addressing pain points from the perspective of Chinese private entrepreneurs.

The goal is not for this book to become a bestseller like *Currency Wars*, but rather that:

This formula may not be loud in voice, but it aims to become the leverage point for unlocking trillions in capital—and a real solution to the pain points of Chinese entrepreneurs.

Comparing Two Jewish Giants: Karl Marx vs. Peter F. Drucker

Though Karl Marx and Peter F. Drucker lived in different eras and held fundamentally different political ideologies, both had Jewish backgrounds and made lasting impacts in the fields of capital, social structures, and organizational management. Their legacies represent two extreme yet complementary paths of Jewish wisdom in capital theory.

I. "The Double Mirror of Capital" from a Jewish Perspective

Aspect	**Karl Marx**	**Peter Drucker**
Background	Jewish ancestry; father converted to Christianity; Marx was atheist	Jewish heritage; parents converted to Lutheranism; deeply influenced by Jewish culture
Representative Role	Founder of socialism/communism theory	Father of Modern Management
Core View on Capital	Capital = tool of exploitation; capitalism destined to collapse	Capital = system of resource allocation; must be optimized via management
Analytical Approach	Deconstructing capitalist structures of exploitation	Constructing capitalist systems of productivity and efficiency
Major Works	*Das Kapital*, *The Communist Manifesto*, *On the Jewish Question*	*The Practice of Management*, *Innovation and Entrepreneurship*, *Managing for the Future*
Historical Positioning	Vanguard of radical structuralism; awakening the proletariat	Advocate of practical managerialism; promoting efficiency and corporate responsibility

II. How Do Jewish Thinkers Excel in Capital Thought? Three Key Strengths:

1. Systemic Structural Analysis

- Marx masterfully uncovered the systematic links between capital, labor, commodity, and surplus value, pioneering historical materialism.

- Drucker built internal organizational models such as matrix management and the concept of the knowledge worker.

Jewish culture's emphasis on logic, textual interpretation, and structuralism contributes to a sustained advantage in philosophy and economic analysis.

2. Interdisciplinary Synthesis and Foresight

- Marx integrated philosophy, political economy, sociology, and history.
- Drucker combined history, social psychology, behavioral science, and business management.

The Jewish educational tradition values classical liberal arts (Torah + philosophy + science), enabling thinkers to construct theories with predictive foresight.

Torah (תּוֹרָה) is the most sacred and central scripture in Judaism. In Hebrew, it means "law", "teaching", or "guidance".

3. Linguistic Expression and Idea Dissemination

- Marx's *Communist Manifesto* is a pinnacle of political rhetoric—sharp, evocative, and mobilizing.
- Drucker's writing is precise and logically elegant, widely adopted in Harvard Business School case teaching.

The ability to articulate complex economic issues in terms of "morality + structure + humanity" is a core competitive edge for Jewish thinkers in shaping capital discourse.

Conclusion: Two Complementary Modes of "Jewish Capital Wisdom"

Model	**Core Mission**	**Representative Applications**
Marxian	Deconstruct capital's oppressive structures	Left-wing ideologies, labor unions, class revolution
Druckerian	Construct capital's organizational efficiency	Modern management, corporate governance, ESG models

Systemic structural thinking, interdisciplinary synthesis, and expressive communication are essential for ethnic Chinese to stand out on the global stage.

The Smart Capital Formula introduced here is a humble spark—intended to inspire outstanding Chinese minds and catalyze deeper innovation in the realm of global capital theory.

From Karl Marx to Peter F. Drucker and to Smart Capital Formula

About Karl Marx (1818–1883)

Karl Marx was a German philosopher, economist, political theorist, and revolutionary socialist, best known for his critical analysis of capitalism and his foundational role in developing Marxist theory. His work has profoundly influenced political ideologies, economics, sociology, and labor movements worldwide.

Major Book: *Das Kapital* (Capital: Critique of Political Economy)

- First published: Volume I in 1867 (Volumes II and III were published posthumously by Friedrich Engels)
- Focus: An in-depth analysis of capitalist production, the mechanics of labor and capital, the surplus value system, and the inevitable contradictions within capitalism.

Key Ideas Related to Productivity

1. Labor Theory of Value

- Marx built upon the classical economists (e.g., Adam Smith and David Ricardo), arguing that labor is the source of all value.
- Productivity is a function of human labor applied to nature through tools and capital.
- Value arises not from exchange, but from human labor embedded in goods.

2. Surplus Value (Mehrwert)

- Surplus value is the difference between the value produced by labor and the wages paid to laborers.
- It is the core of capitalist profit and exploitation.
- Formulaically, it can be expressed as:
  Surplus Value = Total Value Produced – Wages Paid

3. Capital (C) and Labor (L)

- Marx distinguishes between:
  - Constant Capital (C): machinery, tools, raw materials—do not create new value but transfer their value.
  - Variable Capital (L): human labor—the only source of new value.

Hence, in simplified terms:

Productivity (P) = L + C,
But only labor (L) generates net new value.

4. Alienation of Labor

- In capitalist systems, workers are alienated from:
  - The product of their labor
  - The act of production itself
  - Their own human potential
  - Other workers (due to competition)
- This alienation reduces human labor to a commodity, stifling both creativity and productivity in a holistic sense.

5. Historical Materialism

- Productivity and social structures evolve based on material (economic) conditions, especially the means and relations of production.
- The history of society is the history of class struggles, primarily over control of productive forces.

Marx's View of Productivity in Capitalism

- Productivity under capitalism is increased to maximize surplus value, not to meet social needs.
- Technological advancements are driven by the need to reduce labor costs, increase output, and intensify exploitation.
- However, Marx predicted that this would eventually lead to crises, unemployment, and a collapse of the capitalist system.

Legacy

- Marx's insights laid the foundation for:
  - Socialist and communist thought
  - Labor rights movements
  - Critiques of inequality and global capitalism
- His productivity model highlighted the central role of labor, later expanded by thinkers like Peter Drucker with the Knowledge Economy (adding K: Knowledge as a productivity factor).

Peter F. Drucker (1909–2005): Overview

Peter F. Drucker, known as the "Father of Modern Management," was an Austrian-American thinker who made lasting contributions as a management theorist, economist, social philosopher, author, and advisor. He profoundly influenced the development of modern business management, organizational theory, and the rise of the knowledge-based economy in the 20th century.

Selected Major Works

Chinese Title	Original English Title	Year Published
《管理的实践》	The Practice of Management	1954
《管理：任务、责任、实践》	Management: Tasks, Responsibilities, Practices	1973
《创新与企业家精神》	Innovation and Entrepreneurship	1985
《21 世纪的管理挑战》	Management Challenges for the 21st Century	1999
《后资本主义社会》	Post-Capitalist Society	1993

Core Concept: The Knowledge Economy

1. Knowledge as the Key Factor of Production

Drucker argued that humanity had evolved from an agricultural economy to an industrial economy, and was now entering the era of the knowledge economy, where:

"Knowledge, not capital or labor, is the most important factor of production today."

The traditional formula P = L + C (Productivity = Labor + Capital) was no longer sufficient to explain modern economic productivity. In the mid-to-late 20th century, Drucker proposed that Knowledge (K) should be added to the formula:

P = L + C + K
Productivity = Labor + Capital + Knowledge

This formula was not merely theoretical—it responded directly to the transformation of real-world economic structures.

2. The Rise of Knowledge Workers

- Drucker believed that future organizations must center around Knowledge Workers—individuals who rely on intellectual rather than physical labor, and who possess high levels of autonomy and creativity.
- The focus of business would shift from merely achieving "efficiency" to enhancing knowledge output and management capability.

3. Knowledge Management

- Knowledge is a flowing asset that must be effectively organized, shared, innovated, and converted into competitive advantage.
- A key task of organizations is to institutionalize individual knowledge, turning it into replicable and scalable productivity.

4. Organizational Purpose and Social Responsibility

- Drucker emphasized that enterprises should not be seen merely as "profit machines," but rather as purpose-driven organizations with broader social responsibilities.
- He advocated for organizations to clarify their "Why" (purpose of existence), not just their "How" (means of operation).

Theoretical Evolution and Significance of P = L + C + K

Evolution of the Productivity Formula

Generation	Formula	Thinker	Background & Significance
First	P = L + C	Karl Marx (19th century)	Emphasized labor and capital as dual forces in industrial capitalism
Second	P = L + C + K	Peter Drucker (20th century)	Introduced "Knowledge" as the third driver, signifying the rise of the knowledge economy

Generation	Formula	Thinker	Background & Significance
Third	P = L + C + K + A (AI)	Modern thinkers (no unified author)	Adds Artificial Intelligence as an emerging and scalable productivity force

Real-World Applications

- Enterprises now place increasing value on intangible assets in valuation and strategic planning, such as intellectual property, data, and talent.
- Leading companies like Google, Apple, and Alibaba no longer rely primarily on physical assets, but on their knowledge base and data infrastructure.
- The role of managers has shifted from controlling processes to activating knowledge and inspiring innovation.

Selected Quotes from Peter Drucker

"The most valuable asset of a 21st-century institution will be its knowledge workers and their productivity."

"The purpose of a business is to create a customer."

Conclusion: Drucker and Modern Capital Structures

Drucker's contribution went beyond the idea that "knowledge is the new capital." He helped global businesses and organizations understand a new logic of productivity and how to unlock the value of knowledge through management.

His formulation—P = L + C + K—offers a solid theoretical foundation for redefining asset structures today, and helps us better understand emerging concepts like tokenization and RWA (Real World Asset) digitization.

Extending the Legacy of Karl Marx and Peter F. Drucker to Wilson Liu's Smart Capital Formula

Smart Capital = RWA × Stablecoin × (Tri-Market Listing: IPOs + STO) × (OpCo + NewCo)

1. From Marx's P = L + C: Labor and Capital as Dual Engines of Productivity

Karl Marx's model, P = L + C, laid the foundation for understanding how labor (L) and capital (C) jointly contribute to productivity. He emphasized that while capital (machinery, raw materials) transfers existing value, only labor creates new value. His focus on surplus value and the exploitation of labor remains a fundamental critique of capitalist production.

In the context of Smart Capital, Marx's emphasis on production structure inspires the role of OpCo (Operating Company), which embodies traditional productive assets, labor-intensive operations, and real-world cash flows—the backbone of value creation.

2. From Drucker's P = L + C + K: Entering the Knowledge Economy

Peter Drucker extended Marx's model by adding Knowledge (K) as the third factor of productivity. In his formula, P = L + C + K, Drucker recognized that knowledge workers, innovation, and intangible assets (IP, data, algorithms) had become more valuable than physical assets in the 21st century.

This idea directly informs the NewCo (New Corporate Structure) in the Smart Capital formula. NewCo captures offshore structuring (e.g., Cayman entities), token governance models, and knowledge-intensive digital assets like AI algorithms, license rights, and clinical data—representing the evolution from capital to cognitive capital.

3. Integrating the Digital Age: Tokenization and Stablecoins

Wilson Liu advances this lineage by incorporating tokenized Real World Assets (RWA) and stablecoins—new digital tools for representing value, transferring rights, and settling cross-border investments.

- RWA echoes Marx's concept of concrete productive value but expresses it via digital means (e.g., license income, IP rights).
- Stablecoins serve as the modern equivalent of monetary capital (C), but with programmable, borderless, and decentralized properties.

4. Tri-Market Listing Strategy: Enhancing Capital Liquidity

Unlike Karl Marx, who focused on institutional critique of capital, and distinct from Peter F. Drucker, who emphasized internal structure and management efficiency within enterprises, **Wilson Liu**'s "Smart Capital" strategy centers on the design and coordination of **global capital access pathways**—specifically, how mid-sized enterprises can gain **liquidity, valuation power, and strategic exit rights** within the global capital system through structural arrangements.

The so-called **Tri-Market Listing Mechanism** refers to enterprises establishing interconnected pathways across three capital hubs:

- **U.S. Nasdaq** (CeFi strong regulation),
- **Hong Kong HKEX** (valuation anchor),
- **Middle East ADGM / DIFC** (regulatory innovation zones).

This structure enables **cross-jurisdictional, cross-valuation, and cross-currency** capital flows, accelerating transaction speed and diversifying pricing mechanisms.

Within this framework:

- **IPO** (Initial Public Offering) symbolizes **CeFi** (Centralized Finance)—a system of trust-based pricing under audit, disclosure, and regulatory scrutiny.
- **STO** (Security Token Offering), by contrast, represents **DeFi** (Decentralized Finance)—a freer form of capital formation driven by blockchain smart contracts and consensus mechanisms, unlocking the potential of emerging asset classes.

Together, they embody a **dual-track capital integration philosophy**:

Tri-Market Listing = IPO + STO = CeFi + DeFi = Stability + Innovation

The Smart Capital strategy does not take sides with or against any system. Rather, it seeks to **build a bridge between two financial worlds**:

- Drawing upon the **compliance and credibility** of centralized finance,
- While embracing the **flexibility and innovation** of decentralized finance.

This hybrid architecture not only echoes Drucker's vision of "organizations adapting to a global environment," but also establishes a **future-oriented framework of capital sovereignty**—empowering enterprises to gain **self-pricing power, self-liquidity, and self-determined exit strategies** in a rapidly shifting global landscape.

5. The Unified Formula: Smart Capital as a 21st Century Capital Architecture

Marx gave us the original structure of productivity. Drucker revealed the power of knowledge and intangible assets. Liu integrates both into a programmable, tokenized, and borderless architecture:

Smart Capital = RWA × Stablecoin × (Tri-Market Listing: IPOs + STO) × (OpCo + NewCo)

This formula provides a replicable framework for mid-sized companies, especially in sectors like healthcare and AI, to leap into global capital markets through a combination of:

- Tangible and intangible asset integration
- Legal-compliant token structures
- Cross-border fundraising and listing mechanisms

It is the embodiment of financial evolution: from industrial capital → knowledge capital → digital smart capital.

This book carries a bold and ambitious vision—
not only to profoundly change the world, like the twelve classic works in history that have shaped the course of capital (see Appendix III),
but also to ensure that the "Smart Capital Formula" exerts a lasting and far-reaching influence, just as the twelve great economic formulas have done throughout history.

List of the Most Important 12 Economic Formulas in History

Serial	Formula	Description	Economist / Origin
1	**P = L + C**	Productivity = Labor + Capital	Karl Marx (19th century)
2	**P = L + C + K**	Productivity = Labor + Capital + Knowledge	Peter Drucker (20th century)
3	**MV = PQ**	Money Supply × Velocity = Price Level × Output (Quantity Theory of Money)	Irving Fisher (1911)
4	**Y = C + I + G + (X - M)**	National Income (GDP) = Consumption + Investment + Government Spending + Net Exports	Keynesian Macroeconomics
5	**π = R - C**	Profit = Revenue - Cost	Classical Economics
6	**GDP Deflator = (Nominal GDP / Real GDP) × 100**	Measures price inflation	National Income Accounting
7	**ΔY = 1 / (1 – MPC) × ΔG**	Keynesian Multiplier: Change in income = Multiplier × Change in Government Spending	John Maynard Keynes
8	**r = (1 + i) / (1 + π) - 1**	Real Interest Rate = Nominal Interest Rate adjusted for inflation	Irving Fisher
9	**g = s / θ**	Harrod–Domar Growth Model: Growth = Savings rate / Capital-output ratio	Roy Harrod & Evsey Domar
10	**S = I**	Savings = Investment (in closed economy, long-run equilibrium)	Classical Economics
11	**L = f(W/P)**	Labor Supply as a function of real wages	Neoclassical Labor Theory
12	**E[π] = πe**	Rational Expectations Hypothesis: Expected inflation equals actual inflation (in long run)	Robert Lucas

Smart Capital Formula Upgrade: Synergy Loop × Multiplier Effect

1. Two Formula Structures & Logical Positioning

Dimension	↔ Formula (Synergy Loop)	× Formula (Multiplier Effect)
Expression	Smart Capital = RWA ↔ Stablecoin ↔ Tri-Market Listing ↔ (OpCo + NewCo)	Smart Capital = RWA × Stablecoin × (Tri-Market Listing: IPOs + STO) × (OpCo + NewCo)
Symbol Meaning	↔ means "is empowered by and empowers"	× means "Multiplicative Effect," where all factors are indispensable
Logic	Emphasizes cyclical synergy and ecosystem closure	Emphasizes quantitative amplification and mathematical rigor
Scenarios	Strategic blueprints, structural diagrams, partner communications	Investor roadshows, valuation models, financial forecasts
Pros	Easy to understand, strong narrative appeal	Quantifiable, ideal for investor pitches
Cons	Lacks mathematical precision	Less interactive and ecosystem-oriented

2. Integrated Formula: Internal Synergy × External Multiplier

Smart Capital = (RWA ↔ Stablecoin ↔ Tri-Market Listing: IPOs + STO ↔ (OpCo + NewCo)) × Synergy Multiplier Effect

Core Synergy Loop (↔):

1. RWA provides a foundation of real assets → Stablecoins grant global liquidity
2. Stablecoins reduce cross-border capital costs → Tri-market listing adds a liquidity premium
3. Tri-market listing boosts valuation → OpCo + NewCo provide business and structural support

4. OpCo + NewCo tokenize assets → RWA value is further enhanced

The four elements form a closed loop, each empowering the others.

External Multiplier (×):
Each module not only empowers but also amplifies the others; removing one significantly reduces the overall effect.

3. Synergy Multiplier Effect Formula & Example

Formula:

Synergy Multiplier Effect=(1+αRWA)×(1+αStablecoin)×(1+αTri−Market)×(1+α Structural Synergy)−1

Example Assumption:

- RWA value uplift: +50% (α = 0.5)
- Stablecoin capital efficiency: +30% (α = 0.3)
- Tri-market listing premium: +40% (α = 0.4)
- Structural synergy optimization: +20% (α = 0.2)

Result:

(1.5)×(1.3)×(1.4)×(1.2)=3.276

Synergy Multiplier Effect ≈ **3.28**

4. Suggested Visual Layout

- **Left:** Four-node synergy loop diagram (RWA → Stablecoin → Tri-Market Listing → OpCo + NewCo → back to RWA)
- **Right:** × formula and Synergy Multiplier Effect calculation box
- **Center Slogan:**
  "Internal Synergy Loop, External Multiplier—The Structural Magic of Smart Capital"

5. Investor Pitch Script Suggestion

"Our Smart Capital model integrates RWA, stablecoins, tri-market listings, and structured corporate operations into a closed-loop synergy (↔), and applies a multiplier effect (×) to amplify valuations. When all four core modules work in full synergy, the multiplier effect is around 3.28, meaning we can achieve over triple the valuation in the capital markets on the same asset base."

Chapter 2: The Genesis and Practical Logic of the Smart Capital Formula

On Acrostic Poetry: A Symphony of Inspiration and Structural Beauty

Acrostic poetry, also known as "hidden-word" or "embedded-line" poetry, is a unique literary form in which specific words or phrases are hidden within the first characters (or designated positions) of each line. It not only emphasizes meter and rhyme but also combines ingenuity with symbolism, representing a sophisticated blend of linguistic artistry and emotional expression. Every acrostic poem is a meticulous arrangement of the author's intent and logic—a seamless fusion of content and form.

I am deeply passionate about this ancient and dynamic poetic style. Over the past thirty years, I have composed thousands of acrostic poems across a wide range of themes and formats, including:

- Personal names: Poems dedicated to friends, entrepreneurs, and team members, subtly embedding blessings and admiration;
- Company names: Verses written for businesses to convey brand spirit and strategic vision;
- Place names: Geographical tributes that express cultural heritage and emotional connection;
- Idioms and classical phrases: Skillful integration of traditional expressions with contemporary meaning;
- Major events: Poetic reflections that capture the spirit of significant moments and inner transformation.

In my view, acrostic poetry is more than a linguistic game—it is an aesthetic of structure and a projection of the soul. It parallels my Smart Capital Formula: both involve embedding complex elements within a structured framework, conveying profound meaning through refined, elegant form.

Below is an example I composed, using the theme "How a company generates value." As illustrated in the chart, the highest level of business strategy lies in the integration of capital and elite resources. Thus, the pursuit of a Smart Capital Formula has been my lifelong mission during three decades on Wall Street.

A Prayer-Inspired Acrostic Poem by Wensheng (Wilson Liu)

Inspired by the Holy Spirit at the only Chinese Christian Church in Rhode Island

Worshiping Buddha and God seeking shelter,
Praise to my Heavenly Father standing higher.
Merging wealth, the Shell Coin we acquire,
Money is not all — the Lamb is our Shepherd entire.
Fingers interlocked, eyes brimming with tearful fire,
Great grace and ceremony — who shall redeem the mire?
Layered structure revealed, divine and clear,
Step by step, the Lord makes each flower appear.

An acrostic praise poem by Wilson Liu (文勝悟道体藏头诗)

礼佛拜神求庇护,
赞我天父站高处,
赚为兼并贝壳币,
钱非萬能羔羊牧,
十指紧扣泪满目,
大恩大典谁救赎,
层级结构很清晰,
次第花开神做主。
文勝悟道体藏头诗礼赞聖靈感动于罗德岛华人唯一基督教会

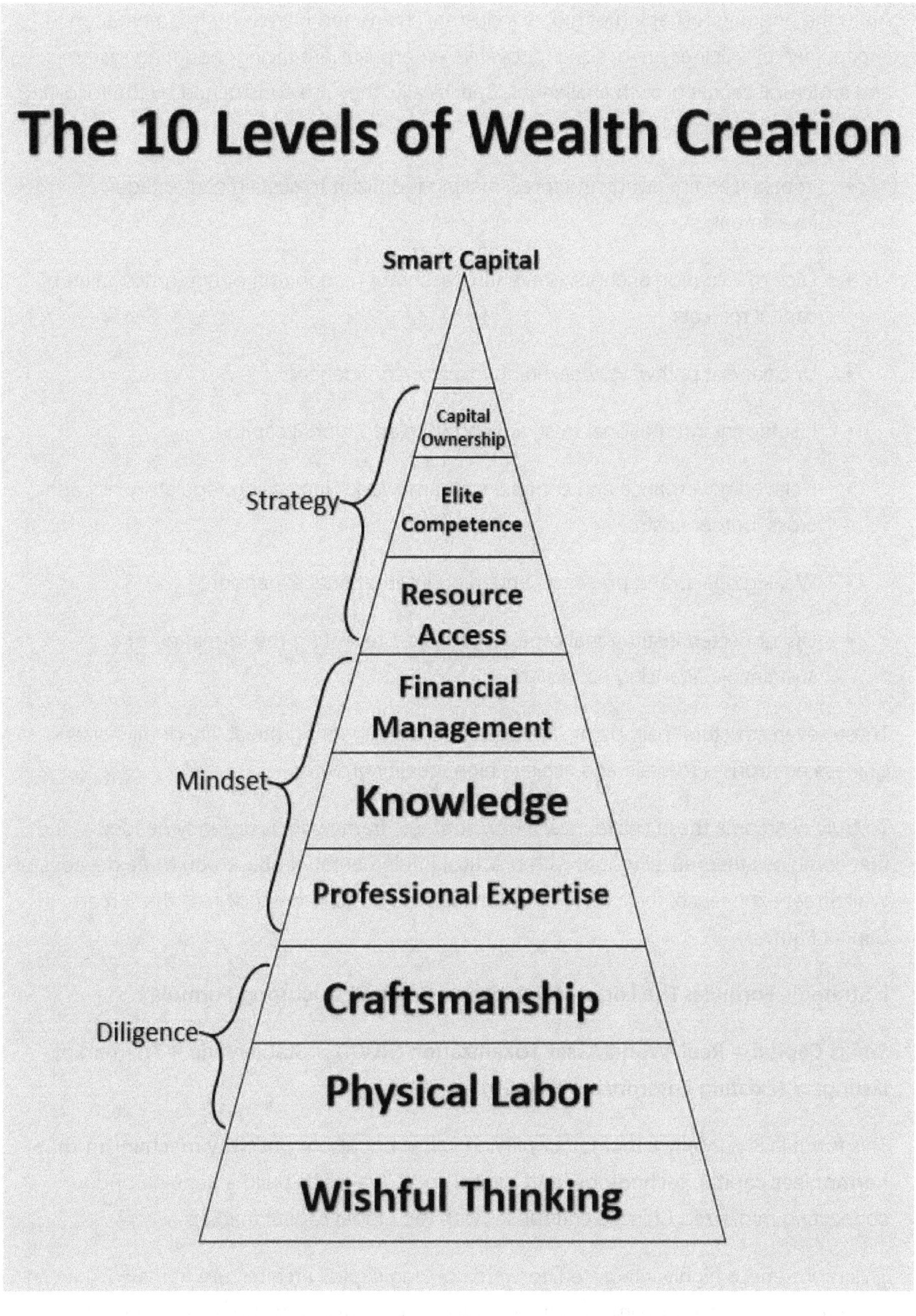

Diagram of the Ten Levels of Making Money

Amid the ongoing reshaping of global industrial chains and increasing fragmentation in capital markets, Chinese mid-sized innovative enterprises are facing mounting systemic and structural capital growth challenges. Specifically, they are constrained by the following seven core pain points:

- Imbalanced financing structures, making it difficult to sustain early-stage investment;
- Lack of valuation anchors, preventing accurate recognition of enterprise value by capital markets;
- Unclear exit pathways, weakening investor confidence;
- Insufficient international trust, limiting access to global capital;
- Delayed governance and compliance frameworks, increasing regulatory risk and cross-border costs;
- Weak global brand presence, impeding international expansion;
- Disconnected institutional capital channels, preventing the formation of a sustainable financing ecosystem.

These seven structural pain points are systematically hindering the ability of mid-sized Chinese enterprises to scale and achieve high-quality growth.

To truly overcome these challenges, a new strategic framework is urgently needed—one that combines theoretical insight with practical implementation. Based on three decades of Wall Street experience, the author proposes a strategic solution known as the "Smart Capital Pathway."

I. Strategic Formula: The Logic of the “Smart Capital Structuring Formula”

Smart Capital = Real-World Asset Tokenization (RWA) × Stablecoins × Tri-market Listings × (Existing Enterprise + NewCo)

This formula is not only a tool for amplifying value, but also a **pathway mechanism that harmonizes capital, technology, and global trust**. It aims to build a genuine bridge connecting mid-sized Chinese enterprises with the global capital markets.

This represents a highly integrated, forward-looking capital architecture framework. It can be validated across four commercial dimensions: **strategic logic, financial structure, feasibility, and capital market trends**.

1. Formula Breakdown and Business Implications:

Component	Meaning & Strategic Value
Real-World Assets (RWA)	Tokenizing core assets (e.g., equity, IP, orders, receivables) onto blockchain to form digital capital units with clear valuation and tradability.
Stablecoins	Act as low-volatility cross-border capital carriers (e.g., USDC, HKD-pegged tokens) to facilitate settlement and compliance in digital capital pools, overcoming traditional FX and control constraints.
Tri-Market Listings *(HKEX + NASDAQ + Middle East)*	Combine Hong Kong's regulatory recognition, NASDAQ's tech valuation premium, and sovereign-backed capital from the Middle East to achieve valuation arbitrage and flexible exits.
Existing Enterprise + NewCo Model	Preserve the operating path and valuation base of the main entity, while NewCo carries new valuation logic, tokenized assets, digital architecture, and financing/exit channels—creating a "dual-track capital strategy."

2. Validation of Strategic Logic (By Module):

Module	Commercial Justification
RWA × Stablecoin	Tokenized real-world assets are an emerging global trend. Combining RWA with stablecoins enables financing, liquidity, and programmable coordination, ideal for Pre-IPO and OTC markets.
Tri-market Listing	HKEX offers compliance credibility; NASDAQ offers premium tech valuation; the Middle East (e.g., G42, Tadawul) provides strategic capital. Together: valuation arbitrage, liquidity upgrade, and diversified exit paths.

Module	Commercial Justification
Existing Enterprise + NewCo	NewCo enables asset bundling, old share restructuring, PIPE funding, token issuance, license-out deals—reducing valuation pressure on the core company while boosting capital access. Widely adopted in SPAC, AI, and biotech projects.

3. Feasibility and Technical Toolkits:

- **Token protocols:** ERC1400 (compliant security tokens), ERC3643, Chainlink Proof-of-Reserve support cross-chain verification and auditability
- **Stablecoin examples:** Circle USDC, Hong Kong DUSD, Middle East Dinar-backed stablecoins already piloting RWA-based settlements
- **Tri-market architecture:** Realized via SPACs, dual-sovereign setups (HK–Cayman, DE–Cayman, or ADGM-based structures)
- **NewCo implementation:** NewCos can be established in Cayman/BVI/ADGM to hold old shares, receive PIPE investments, issue tokens, and structure exits via license-outs or SPAC mergers

4. Supporting Cases and Trend Validation:

Example / Trend	Key Takeaways
Backed Finance, Ondo Finance	Demonstrated RWA tokenization + stablecoin redemption mechanisms
HK virtual asset pilot + GBA token funds	Piloting closed-loop structures combining digital assets + HKEX + cross-border stablecoins
G42 investment in BGI Genomics	Validated the capital synergy between Middle East sovereign funds and Chinese tech assets
Dual-entity models in Chinese listings	Separating NewCo to host AI, token, and license assets for independent valuation boosts

Conclusion: This formula holds strong commercial logic and innovative capital design value

Smart Capital = RWA × Stablecoin × Tri-market Listings × (OpCo + NewCo)

This is not just a theoretical framework—it synthesizes the **liberalization of global capital, the digitalization of assets, valuation arbitrage models, and modular growth strategies**, providing a **blueprint for next-gen FA systems, cross-border fundraising strategies, LP communications, and investment promotion initiatives**.

II. Capital Solution Structure: The "NewCo + PIPE + Token + ESG" Four-in-One Model

This handbook proposes a **four-part capital leap framework**, integrating:

1. **NewCo** – as the operating platform that absorbs legacy assets and builds new governance;
2. **PIPE** – uses Reg D / Reg S formats to bring in qualified USD investors;
3. **Token** – partial tokenization of asset rights to digitize capital flows and design incentive systems;
4. **ESG** – embedded into IFRS/SASB reporting standards to meet global LP transparency demands.

This model goes beyond just financing—it emphasizes **holistic design across assets, governance, and exit**.

III. The "One Core, Two Wings" Strategic Execution Model

To enhance the replicability and cross-border adaptability of the above solution, we recommend the "**One Core, Two Wings**" path:

- **One Core**:
  Use **NewCo** as the central platform to restructure assets, optimize governance, and enable capital entry via PIPE.
- **Two Wings**:
  - **Left Wing**: Connect to industrial resources — via legacy shareholders, industry funds, government parks, and local partners to ensure landing and data integration.
  - **Right Wing**: Link to international capital — via family offices, PIPE funds, strategic buyers, investment banks, and BD teams to ensure global brand positioning and exit readiness.

IV. Capital Leap Pathway Map

Old Shareholder Restructuring → NewCo Setup → PIPE Investment

→ International Compliance → Brand Expansion → Strategic BD

→ Offshore IPO / M&A Exit

This pathway provides a **closed-loop, executable capital transformation roadmap**, beginning with asset structuring and ending with valuation amplification and global exit. It's particularly suited for **tech-driven companies lacking capital leverage**.

V. Commercial Value Summary

1. **System-level breakthrough**: Goes beyond isolated financing—integrates asset, capital, compliance, brand, market, and exit.
2. **Replicable path**: Standardized, trainable, promotable model that FAs, funds, and governments can deploy.
3. **Multi-party applicability**:
   - For enterprises: a roadmap for global capital integration;
   - For FAs: a turnkey capital structuring toolkit;
   - For local governments: a platform for investment attraction;
   - For funds: a framework to identify and package emerging targets.
4. **Dual-language adaptability**: Ready-to-use bilingual templates for LP communications, IB outreach, and regulatory disclosures.

This chapter lays the core strategic foundation for the entire handbook. In the chapters that follow, we will delve into PIPE structures, token valuation logic, ESG disclosures, and real-world internationalization scenarios, gradually building a global capital operating system for mid-sized innovative enterprises.

Understand the Enhanced version of Smart Capital Formula from Economic Perspectives

Smart Capital = RWA × Stablecoins × (Triple Listing IPOs + STO) × (OpCo + NewCo)

This enhanced version of the Smart Capital Structuring Formula captures a **next-generation capital formation framework** that integrates traditional corporate structures with digital financial innovation and global capital market access. Let's break it down component by component and analyze the **economic rationale and systemic impact**.

1. RWA – Real-World Asset Tokenization

Definition:

The process of digitally representing real-world assets (e.g., real estate, equity, receivables, IP, carbon credits) on a blockchain via tokens.

Economic Impact:

- **Liquidity Transformation**: Converts illiquid assets into tradable digital instruments.
- **Fractional Ownership**: Lowers investment thresholds and democratizes access to high-value assets.
- **Reduced Transaction Costs**: Smart contracts reduce reliance on intermediaries (Coase's transaction cost theory).
- **Improved Transparency & Risk Pricing**: Blockchain-enabled audit trails improve market trust.

Economic Insight: Tokenizing RWAs increases **capital productivity** by unlocking previously dormant asset value, increasing both asset turnover and investment velocity.

2. Stablecoins – Settlement Infrastructure for Digital Capital

Definition:

Digital tokens pegged to fiat currencies (e.g., USD, RMB) used for payments, settlement, and cross-border transactions.

Economic Impact:

- **Medium of Exchange in Tokenized Ecosystems**: Enables real-time, borderless trade and capital flows.

- **Reduces Currency Frictions**: Particularly valuable in cross-border listings and token offerings.
- **Monetary Innovation in Developing Markets**: Provides a stable store of value where fiat is volatile.

Economic Insight: Stablecoins act as the **"digital grease"** for tokenized capital machinery — reducing friction and time lag in capital movement, thereby lowering opportunity costs and transaction latency.

3. (Triple Listing IPOs + STO) – Hybrid Capital Market Entry

A. IPOs with Triple Listings (Nasdaq + HKEX + SSE/STAR Market)

Definition:
Simultaneous or sequential listings on three major global stock exchanges — providing access to investors in USD, HKD, and RMB markets.

Economic Benefits:

- **Diversification of Capital Sources**: Institutional capital (US), retail & family office capital (HK), policy & state funds (China).
- **Valuation Arbitrage**: Firms can benefit from different pricing multiples in each market (e.g., AI firms valued higher in Nasdaq, healthcare in Hong Kong, deep-tech in STAR Market).
- **Currency Diversification**: Raises funds in multiple currencies, improving FX hedging.
- **Regulatory Hedging**: Regulatory exposure is diversified across jurisdictions, reducing systemic risk.

Economic Insight: Triple listings apply **portfolio theory to capital raising** — optimizing valuation, reducing funding volatility, and increasing global investor reach.

B. STO (Security Token Offering)

Definition:
Blockchain-native fundraising method where digital tokens are issued directly to investors.

Economic Benefits:

- **Decentralized Capital Formation**: Bypasses intermediaries like underwriters and VC firms.

- **Global Retail Access**: Anyone with internet and crypto access can invest.
- **Community Governance & Incentives**: Especially valuable for Web3 and network-based business models.

Economic Insight: STOs represent **permissionless innovation in financial intermediation**, enabling the rise of **"tokenized public goods"** and agile capital markets.

4. (OpCo + NewCo) – Structural Capital Design

OpCo (Operating Company)

- **Definition:** The mature, existing enterprise with proven operations, assets, and revenue.
- **Role:** Anchors credibility, provides underlying cash flow and asset backing for capital raising.

NewCo (New Company)

- **Definition:** A newly incorporated entity, often offshore (e.g., BVI, Cayman, Singapore) used for listings, JV, token issuance, or R&D ventures.
- **Role:** Offers structural flexibility, regulatory arbitrage, and scalability for new capital strategies (e.g., IPO, SPAC, STO).

Economic Insight: This dual-entity structure separates **core operating risk from capital innovation risk**, enabling **dynamic capital structuring** with limited liability and global mobility.

Integrated Economic Model of "Smart Capital"

Layer	**Economic Role**
RWA	Converts tangible assets into **liquid, investable capital units**
Stablecoins	Reduces settlement friction, enhances **cross-border monetary efficiency**
Triple IPO + STO	Enables **valuation optimization** and **regulatory diversification**
OpCo + NewCo	Provides **operational stability + structural agility**

Strategic & Macroeconomic Implications

For Companies:

- Lowers capital raising barriers.
- Attracts multi-region investors.
- Enhances capital structure flexibility.
- Reduces dependency on traditional VC/private equity.

For Investors:

- Global access to high-growth enterprises via multiple channels (equity & tokens).
- Opportunity for arbitrage across markets and instruments.
- Tokenized assets increase transparency and liquidity.

For Policymakers:

- Encourages cross-border capital flow.
- Aligns with RMB internationalization (via STAR or Shanghai listings).
- Stimulates regulated digital finance innovation.

Conclusion (From Economics Perspective)

Smart Capital is a programmable, multi-layered capital architecture designed to unlock global liquidity, optimize valuation across jurisdictions, and align operational value with capital strategy.

It reflects the **convergence of TradFi + DeFi + global market theory** — empowering mid-sized, high-potential enterprises to leap from local champions to global capital players.

Chapter 3: Valuation Bottlenecks and Capital Misconceptions of Chinese Mid-market Enterprises

Before starting this book, ask myself the following three questions:

1. Between China and the United States, which country currently hosts the most Global Fortune 500 companies?

- As of 2024, the United States leads with 139 Global 500 companies; China (including HK/Macau/Taiwan) has 133.
- Roughly 70% of Chinese Fortune 500 companies are state-owned, contributing ~78% of revenue and ~89% of total assets.
- In contrast, U.S. firms on the list are more innovation- and consumer-driven, dominated by sectors like tech, finance, and healthcare.

2. What is the Strategic Role of SMEs, Especially Mid-Sized Firms, in China's Economy?

- Employment Engine: SMEs create over 60% of China's urban jobs, forming the base of economic stability.
- Innovation Drivers: Mid-sized firms act as agile platforms for transforming R&D into commercial products.
- Structural Bridge: They serve as connectors between micro firms and state-owned giants, supporting policy rollout and digital transformation.
- Shock Absorption: With wide sectoral spread and regional diversity, mid-sized enterprises offer strong resilience against macroeconomic uncertainties.

3. Why This Book Focuses on Globalizing Mid-Sized Medical & AI Firms?

- Many mid-sized Chinese companies face a "valuation ceiling" (~RMB 2–5B) and struggle to scale globally due to capital, compliance, and recognition gaps.
- Healthcare + AI firms hold global appeal due to clear monetization paths (e.g., license-outs), high-tech defensibility, and alignment with ESG trends.
- The author's long-standing mission is to help mid-sized Chinese innovators go global, especially through strategic capital architecture and legal alignment with U.S. and HK markets.
- This book therefore provides an integrated toolkit: Tokenized finance + PIPE mechanisms + ESG disclosures + Bilingual legal templates, starting from the medtech/AI use case and scalable across sectors.

Where is the next trillion-dollar blue ocean market?

China currently has more than 500 mid-sized innovative biopharma enterprises, each with a valuation of around RMB 2 billion, that are experiencing growth stagnation. These companies are caught in a structural mismatch—strong technological potential but insufficient capital access. They urgently need a systematic capital empowerment mechanism and a global growth pathway to overcome financing bottlenecks, unlock valuation potential, and achieve international scale-up.

Whoever can provide a structured growth solution for these enterprises will be positioned to unlock a trillion-level emerging capital market opportunity.

In comparison, leading U.S. investment banks like Goldman Sachs and Morgan Stanley have long managed multi-trillion-dollar assets, based on their ability to deeply structure mid-market enterprises and integrate global capital resources. If China's financial sector can seize this strategic window to build a new type of platform investment bank or empowered FA model supporting the globalization of mid-sized enterprises, it could give rise to the next generation of trillion-dollar international capital engines.

1. How many domestic healthcare and digital health companies are currently valued around RMB 2 billion?

Estimation framework:

- Based on 2024 data from China's primary market and pre-IPO companies
- Focused on biopharma, medtech, AI health, and clean energy sectors

Category	Estimated No. (≈ RMB 2B valuation)	Representative Companies
Innovative drug companies (pre-IPO)	~300	Duxi Biotech, Boan Biotech (early)
AI healthcare companies (post-Series A)	~100	Yitu Healthcare, Shukun Technology
Digital health platforms	~80	Weimai, DXY, Zhongyun Health

Category	Estimated No. (≈ RMB 2B valuation)	Representative Companies
Unlisted domestic firms with overseas BD capabilities	~50	Genetron Health, Codex

Total: ~500–600 companies currently sit within the RMB 2 billion valuation tier, but lack the structural tools and partners needed to cross the threshold toward RMB 10+ billion scale.

2. How to solve the financing challenge of old share transfers?

Old share transfers (i.e., secondary sales by existing shareholders) often face structural obstacles:

Key Challenges:

Pain Point	Description
No new capital injected	Merely a shareholder change; not beneficial to company growth
New investors sensitive to pricing	Skeptical about early exits—concerned about fundamentals
High valuation expectations from old shareholders	Reluctance to offer discounts slows down deals
Lack of exit mechanism	Particularly difficult in unlisted companies with illiquid equity

Strategic Solutions:

A. Combine with strategic partnerships: "Transfer + Enablement"

- Introduce strategic investors with industrial or international relevance (e.g., pharma or AI firms)
- Go beyond equity sale — create synergy-driven growth plans
- *Case: Huadong Medicine acquired old shares in Duxi Biotech and partnered on ADC development*

B. Use a Pre-IPO structure (NewCo + old share injection + new capital raise)

- *Example: ETAO International formed a NewCo to bundle old shares and attract new financing*
- Provides incoming investors a clear IPO-linked exit route

C. Leverage offshore platforms and USD capital

- Transfer old shares into offshore SPVs; raise capital via USD funds
- Offshore investors often more tolerant of valuation and offer flexible exits (e.g., HK/NASDAQ listings)

D. Legal and tax structuring

- Structure old share exits as deferred payments or performance-based earn-outs
- Transfer partial control in exchange for liquidity and value capture

3. How to scale from RMB 2 billion to RMB 10+ billion valuation?

Companies at the RMB 2 billion stage often succeed in a single product line or regional niche. To reach RMB 10+ billion scale, systematic growth models are essential. Options include:

1. Business model replication + scaling

- Package proven products/services/BD experience into a replicable platform
- Form regional joint ventures or licensing models
- *Example: Meinian Health scaled rapidly through "replicate + acquire"*

2. Dual engine: Products + Capital

- Expand product pipeline (especially in innovative drugs and AI health)
- Use M&A, BD deals, and license-ins to integrate new technologies
- Reprice valuation via Pre-IPO financing and bolt-on acquisitions

3. Enhance brand equity and pricing power

- Expand from B2B to B2C or government collaboration (e.g., NMPA, NHSA)
- Build clinical evidence and health economics to justify higher premiums

4. Use a NewCo structure for value re-rating

- Consolidate AI capabilities, global access, and external data into a platform
- Use NewCo to connect with international investors or pursue HK/NASDAQ listing arbitrage

4. Summary: Reshaping Business Logic is the Key

Strategic Objective	Corresponding Solution
Break financing bottlenecks	Old share transfer + strategic partnership + NewCo structure
Achieve scale-up to RMB 10B	BD deals + external M&A + model replication
Unlock value through capital	Pre-IPO fundraising + valuation re-rating
Build ecosystem momentum	Integrate AI + health data to form a closed-loop ecosystem

This chapter lays the foundation for identifying China's next breakout capital segment and frames the tools and structures needed for mid-sized innovative enterprises to transform from regional tech players into global capitalized platforms.

Chapter 4: Global Capital Market Landscape and Tri-Market Arbitrage Pathways

How vast is the world's treasure trove, And where will the next gold mine glow?

Global Capital Markets Overview and Rankings

I. Global Capital Markets Overview

Equity Market

By the end of 2023, the total market capitalization of publicly listed companies worldwide was approximately USD 111–115 trillion.

Fixed Income / Bond Market

As of 2023, the outstanding global long-term fixed income securities totaled about USD 140.7 trillion. The bond market is about 1.2–1.3 times the size of the equity market. If bank loans and other credit instruments are included, the total credit market is roughly three times the size of the stock market.

Derivatives & FX Markets

The foreign exchange derivatives market (OTC portion) reached approximately USD 118 trillion. Credit derivatives, structured products, and equity-linked notes are also experiencing rapid growth.

II. Top 10 Major Capital Markets

This includes a combined overview of the world's top 10 stock exchanges (by market cap) and top 10 banks (by total assets):

A. Top 10 Stock Exchanges (by Market Cap)

Rank	Exchange Name	Country	Market Cap (USD bn)
1	New York Stock Exchange (NYSE)	United States	25,241
2	Nasdaq	United States	20,577

3	Shanghai Stock Exchange (SSE)	China	6,263
4	Euronext	Multi-national (France, etc.)	6,263
5	Tokyo Stock Exchange (TSE)	Japan	5,752
6	National Stock Exchange of India (NSE)	India	5,130
7	Shenzhen Stock Exchange (SZSE)	China	4,382
8	Hong Kong Stock Exchange (HKEX)	Hong Kong (China)	4,104
9	London Stock Exchange (LSE)	United Kingdom	3,423
10	Tadawul (Saudi Exchange)	Saudi Arabia	3,055

B. Top 10 Banks (by Total Assets)

Rank	Bank Name	Country	Total Assets (USD bn)
1	Industrial and Commercial Bank of China (ICBC)	China	6,303.4
2	Agricultural Bank of China (ABoC)	China	5,623.1
3	China Construction Bank (CCB)	China	5,400.3
4	Bank of China (BoC)	China	4,578.3
5	JPMorgan Chase	United States	4,002.8
6	Bank of America (BoA)	United States	3,349.4
7	HSBC	UK / International	2,919.8
8	BNP Paribas	France	2,867.4

9	Mitsubishi UFJ Financial Group (MUFG)	Japan	2,816.8
10	Crédit Agricole	France	2,736.9

III. Total Size of Global Capital Markets

Market Type	Approx. Size (USD trillion)
Equity Market	USD 111–115 trillion
Bonds / Long-term Fixed Income	USD 140.7 trillion
FX Derivatives Market	USD 118 trillion
Credit Market (including loans)	USD 330 trillion

Where are the world's biggest companies, and how do we find the next target?

Top 10 Companies by Market Cap (Mid-2025)

Rank	Company	Market Cap (USD tn)	Stock Market
1	NVIDIA	4.20	Nasdaq (NVDA)
2	Microsoft	3.79	Nasdaq (MSFT)
3	Apple	3.15	Nasdaq (AAPL)
4	Amazon	2.40	Nasdaq (AMZN)
5	Alphabet (Google)	2.25	Nasdaq (GOOG/GOOGL)
6	Meta Platforms (Facebook)	1.77	Nasdaq (META)
7	Saudi Aramco	1.60	Tadawul (2222.SR)
8	Broadcom	1.33	Nasdaq (AVGO)
9	TSMC (Taiwan Semiconductor)	1.25	Taiwan OTC (TSM)

Rank	Company	Market Cap (USD tn)	Stock Market
10	Tesla	1.06	Nasdaq (TSLA)

Summary Highlights

- Technology giants dominate the list, taking 6 of the top 10 spots.
- NVIDIA leads with a market cap over USD 4 trillion
- Microsoft (~3.79 tn) and Apple (~3.15 tn) follow closely
- Amazon, Alphabet, Meta, Broadcom, TSMC, and Tesla all exceed USD 1 trillion
- Saudi Aramco remains the top non-tech company with ~1.6 tn market cap and trades on the Saudi Tadawul

From Illinois to Wuxi: Ge Li and WuXi AppTec's Journey to Global Capitalization

In the 1990s, in the heart of Illinois, USA, a young Chinese student arrived with little more than a suitcase and a dream. His name was Ge Li, and he stepped into a research lab at the University of Chicago Medical School—not yet aware that he would go on to become a pioneer in China's pharmaceutical outsourcing industry and a trailblazer in global capital strategy.

At that time, the U.S. was entering a golden age of biotech. Pharmaceutical giants were flourishing, technological innovation was accelerating, and the capital markets were dynamic and highly efficient. Ge Li spent his days shuttling between the lab and the library, but his curiosity extended far beyond data and experiments—he was deeply fascinated by the organizational structures, industrial division of labor, and capital mechanisms behind the American research ecosystem.

Later, he joined a large Contract Research Organization (CRO) in New York, where he had a pivotal realization: drug development could be outsourced, drastically improving efficiency and enabling global collaboration in innovation. That experience planted the seed of a new business model in his mind.

Step One: Returning to China — Bringing American Efficiency Back Home

In 2000, armed with years of insight and experience from the U.S., Ge Li made a bold move: he returned to China to found WuXi AppTec in Wuxi, with the vision of making China the "world's new drug laboratory."

But he wasn't simply replicating the American model. Instead, he chose to deconstruct and rebuild:

- In the U.S., CRO services were standardized but expensive;
- In China, labor was cheaper, but systems were fragmented and unregulated.

Ge Li set out to create a hybrid platform—one that combined international compliance standards with China's executional efficiency. This fusion reflected the essence of what he had learned in the U.S. over a decade:
Global vision + Local execution + Structural integration = A new business paradigm.

Step Two: Building a Global Capital Highway — From Company to Platform

At the beginning of his entrepreneurial journey, many advised Ge Li to chase quick profits in China's domestic market. But he remained firmly committed to long-termism. From day one, he structured WuXi AppTec as a "global capital company," not a local cash machine.

He understood that capital is not about one-off fundraising—it is a systemic design.

- He planned early for U.S. listings by setting up subsidiaries and preparing for a Nasdaq strategy;
- He understood investor psychology in the Hong Kong market and structured the company as a red-chip;
- Most importantly, he spent eight years preparing the financial and compliance groundwork to return to China's A-share market via a reverse merger.

Each move reflected the foresight of an entrepreneur who truly grasped the logic of global capital ecosystems.

Step Three: From Personal Journey to Corporate Strategy — Tri-Market Listing Made Inevitable

Ge Li understood that for a Chinese industrial company to truly "go global," it wasn't enough to export products—it had to become a participant in the global capital ecosystem.

This was the foundation for WuXi AppTec's ultimate success in achieving a tri-market listing on the Shanghai Stock Exchange (SSE), the Hong Kong Stock Exchange (HKEX), and Nasdaq.

This was not just about raising funds—it was a strategic deployment of capital structure:

- In the U.S., the company gained tech-centric valuations and global visibility;
- In Hong Kong, it connected with international capital and Asian liquidity;
- In Shanghai, it won the trust of regulators and reaped the rewards of policy support.

All of this traces back to a core lesson Ge Li once absorbed in the U.S.:

"Capital is the language for allocating global resources—those who understand it, hold global influence."

Epilogue: A Company's Horizon Is Defined by Its Founder's Mental Latitude

WuXi AppTec's tri-market listing is not just a financial story—it's a story of vision and cognition.

Ge Li's U.S. education, global mindset, and long-termist principles have infused his company with the ability to grow across borders and beyond regulatory boundaries.

From a small lab in Illinois to a pharmaceutical giant on the shores of Lake Tai in Wuxi, his journey proves one thing:

A person's global experience can shape a company's global destiny

The Story Beyond Ge Li: A New Era of Smart Capital Strategy

Ge Li's journey offers more than just a personal success story—it delivers a profound insight for a new generation of entrepreneurs with global ambitions:
A true visionary does not only integrate into the **global product chain**, but also builds bridges across the **global capital chain**.

The tri-market listing strategy he implemented stands as a key pillar in the **Smart Capital Formula**—a strategy that transforms the structural disparities of global capital markets into leverage for enterprise growth.

Now, we take this exploration one step further by systematically decoding a hybrid capital strategy that blends CeFi (Centralized Finance) with DeFi (Decentralized Finance):
The **Tri-Market IPO + STO Arbitrage Pathway**.

Tri-Market IPO + STO Arbitrage Strategy: A Hybrid Capital Market Architecture

A. Tri-Market IPO: Coordinated Access to Global Capital Hubs

By listing simultaneously or sequentially on three major global exchanges—Nasdaq, Hong Kong Stock Exchange (HKEX), and Shanghai Stock Exchange (SSE)/STAR Market—enterprises can attract investors operating in the world's three dominant sovereign currency systems: USD, HKD, and RMB.
This approach allows for layered investor access and multi-currency fundraising across regulatory jurisdictions.

For mid-sized enterprises with Chinese or overseas Chinese roots, tri-market listing is not just a financing tactic, but a deliberate global capital allocation strategy:

- In the U.S., listing on the world's largest exchanges—NYSE or Nasdaq—connects the company to tech-oriented funds and the valuation power of Wall Street;

- In Hong Kong, issuing H-shares on HKEX taps into Asian liquidity and international family offices;
- In mainland China, listing on SSE, STAR Market, or SZSE unlocks long-term capital from strategic RMB investors and benefits from policy endorsements.

Economic Advantages:

- **Diverse capital sources**: USD institutional funds, Hong Kong/Macao investors, Chinese state-backed funds;
- **Valuation arbitrage**: For instance, AI companies may receive higher valuations on Nasdaq, while biotech firms may be better positioned on HKEX;
- **Multi-currency financing**: Enables efficient asset allocation and currency hedging;
- **Regulatory diversification**: Spreads compliance risks and enhances resilience during policy shifts.

Capital Insight:

This reflects a real-world application of **Cross-Market Portfolio Theory**—leveraging geographical and institutional diversity to stabilize fundraising volatility, diversify valuation benchmarks, and optimize investor composition. It builds a **resilient capital architecture** that strengthens a firm's structural immunity to external shocks.

B. STO: The Innovative Gateway of Decentralized Finance

If tri-market IPOs represent the **regulated paths** of centralized finance (CeFi), then **STO (Security Token Offering)** represents a new frontier of **capital innovation in the decentralized finance (DeFi)** ecosystem.

By issuing digital tokens on blockchain networks, companies can directly connect with global retail investors, developers, and Web3 communities—particularly suited for projects with strong network effects, community governance, and data-driven value creation.

▶ Economic Advantages:

- **Bypassing traditional financial intermediaries**: No need for VCs, underwriters, or brokers;
- **Global direct retail participation**: Anyone with internet access and a digital wallet can invest instantly;

- **Embedded governance mechanisms**: Tokens act as instruments for decentralized community-driven growth;
- **High agility**: Ideal for early-stage technology projects, novel asset classes, and tokenized public goods.

Capital Insight:

STO represents a hallmark of **permissionless financial innovation**, laying the groundwork for tokenized business models and enabling capital markets that are **decentralized, programmable, and globally inclusive**.

Convergent Thinking: CeFi + DeFi = Stability + Innovation

The integration of **Tri-Market IPO** and **STO** encapsulates the core philosophy of the Smart Capital strategy:

It is not about choosing sides between competing systems—**but about building bridges between them**.

Tri-Market Listing = IPO + STO = CeFi + DeFi = Regulatory Credibility + Structural Innovation

Through this hybrid capital pathway design, mid-sized enterprises are no longer constrained by local financing bottlenecks. Instead, they gain the ability to:

- **Self-price**,
- **Self-mobilize liquidity**, and
- **Self-design exit mechanisms**
  within the global capital ecosystem.

This is not merely an evolution in financial engineering—it is a manifestation of **institutional imagination** for a new era of corporate sovereignty.

Chapter 5: The New Capital Language: Synergy of RWA, Tokens, and NewCo Structures

This chapter explores the fundamentals of tokens, including definitions, classifications, market size, development trends, and their relationships with digital assets and stablecoins.

I. What Is a Token?

A "Token" is a blockchain-based, programmable digital certificate that represents rights, assets, or value. It is the core vehicle for enabling asset digitization and the internet of value.

Key Features:

- Decentralized issuance (based on Ethereum, Solana, BNB, etc.)
- Controlled by smart contracts (programmable logic, issuance supply)
- Divisible, transferable, and traceable
- Can represent real-world assets (equity, debt, commodities) or virtual rights (points, governance)

II. Functional Classification of Tokens

Type	Description	Example Projects
Payment Token	Used for currency and value exchange	Bitcoin (BTC), Litecoin (LTC)
Utility Token	Access to services or platforms	Ethereum (ETH), Chainlink (LINK)
Security Token	Represents equity/debt, subject to securities laws	tZERO, INX, RealT
Governance Token	Grants rights to vote in protocol/platform decisions	UNI, AAVE
Stablecoin	Pegged to fiat currencies to maintain stability	USDT, USDC, DAI
RWA Token	Digitized form of real-world assets (RWA)	PAXG, RealT (real estate)

III. Number of Tokens and Market Size (As of July 2025)

- Over 30,000 token projects listed (DeFi, GameFi, NFT, DAO, RWA)
- Total digital asset market capitalization: $2.5–3.0 trillion
  - Bitcoin ~45%
  - Ethereum ~18%
  - Stablecoins: ~$140B (USDT $110B, USDC $33B, others)

IV. Development Trends: From Speculation to Compliance + Assetization

Trend	Description
Regulatory Integration	EU MiCA, SEC, HK SFC are launching token compliance frameworks
Rise of RWA Tokens	Real estate, bonds, art, invoices becoming tokenized on-chain
Token + ESG / Token + IPO	ESG metrics embedded into tokens; token financing integrated with IPO pathways
AI + Tokenization	Tokens as units for data, compute, or content value in AI platforms

V. Token vs. Digital Asset vs. Stablecoin

Term	**Definition**	**Relation to Token**
Digital Asset	Any asset that can be used/stored/traded in digital form	Token is a digital asset type on blockchain
Stablecoin	Token pegged to fiat currency, used for settlement/trading	Stablecoins are a specialized form of token
Tokenized Asset	On-chain representation of real assets	Token is the carrier of tokenized assets

Example Use Case: Token-Enabled Capital Structure in Biotech

- Tokenize NewCo equity as RWA Token
- Attract PIPE investment from global funds using USDC
- Use token to record shareholder rights, enable secondary trading
- Embed ESG indicators into token (e.g., carbon footprint disclosure)
- Achieve 'Token + ESG + IPO' integration

Token Layers:

- RWA-A: Equity + license revenue rights
- RWA-B: License-out dividend token
- RWA-C: Sponsor incentive token (FA/team)

Liquidity Structure:

- 12-month lock-up during private placement
- Buyback/swap window after T+6 months
- IPO swap ratio example: 1 token = 1.5 shares
- On-chain KYC and compliant issuance via INX/Securitize

ESG-Driven Token Capital Structure: Examples by Type

1. ESG-Focused Token Projects

- Green Token (XGT) / GreenX (Greenpro Capital): ESG-anchored RWA token on Nasdaq GreenX platform.
- Tokenized Carbon Credits: CarbonHood, Blubird enable fractional trading and tracking of carbon credits.

2. Asset Management / Fund Tokenization + ESG

- Securitize + BlackRock BUIDL: On-chain compliant fund with sustainable project investments.
- Redbelly Network: Tokenizing private equity and carbon credits with full KYC/AML compliance.

3. Token + IPO Integration

- Allbirds SPO: ESG-enhanced IPO structure (still traditional equity-based).
- Rheo Energy Finance: Green Energy Token (GET) via CeDeFi + IPO roadmap.
- Quadrant Biosciences: Tokenized equity case reflecting pre-IPO digital equity issuance.

Industry Trends & Impact

Trend	**Impact**
Tokenized Carbon Credits	On-chain ESG transparency and fractional trading
RWA + ESG Platforms	Tokenizing energy, carbon, and rental assets compliantly
SPO / Token IPO Hybrid	Attracts ESG investors and innovates public offering models

Summary:

- ESG Token Leaders: Green Token, CarbonHood, Redbelly
- Compliant Fund Tokenization: Securitize + BlackRock
- Token + IPO Exploration: Allbirds, Rheo, Quadrant

Token capital structures are evolving beyond payment and speculation to support real asset financing, ESG transparency, and IPO integration.

Token Valuation and Compliance Models

Three Valuation Approaches for Tokens – DCF, Comparables, Cost-Based

Token Valuation and Compliance Model (Supporting RWA Token Financing)

Below is an additional module focused on token valuation and compliance model design. It aims to strengthen transparency, regulatory alignment, and investor confidence within the RWA tokenization framework under the "Strategic Plan for Enterprise Advancement into Global Capital Markets." This module helps USD LPs, PIPE funds, and token investors understand how token prices are formed and their legal compliance foundations.

I. Design Background and Strategic Purpose

To meet the expectations of international institutional investors, digital asset platforms, and regulators regarding transparency, valuation logic, and legal structuring of token investments, a systematic token issuance valuation mechanism + compliance model must be established. This creates a trust bridge equivalent to traditional finance.

Application Scenarios:
- RWA Tokens representing real-world assets, such as license-out proceeds, NewCo equity, and exit options;
- Suitable for PIPE + Token dual-track financing;
- Supports digital financing stage before HK/US IPOs (between T+6 to T+12 months).

II. Token Valuation Model Design (Three Combined Approaches)

1. Cost-Based Floor Pricing
Used to set the minimum issuance price for tokens to avoid valuation disruption caused by underpricing.

Examples:
- Capital costs: Clinical trial expenses, registration/BD costs, AI platform support fees, etc.
- Historical financing price: Last round legacy equity or Pre-A valuation as reference.
- Option value premium: If the token includes swap rights or revenue entitlements, add 0.5–1.0x as a negotiated premium.

Purpose: To legally justify a pricing floor (e.g., minimum token price = 0.10 USDT).

2. Comparables-Based Valuation
Estimates a reasonable price range by benchmarking other token projects in terms of pricing, trading volume, and dilution rate.

Examples:
- Comparable: BioToken (ADC revenue token on a specific platform) priced between 0.25–0.60 USDT.
- Similar AI health assets: HealthChain, AIpharma Tokens, etc.

Purpose: To align market consensus with USD-based FAs and PIPE funds and avoid discounting that could harm legacy equity liquidity.

3. DCF-Supported Valuation (Based on Future Cash Flows)
Models the discounted cash flows of the underlying assets represented by the token.

Example:
Assume token represents future license-out revenue rights (e.g., upfront payment + sales royalties).

DCF Input Parameters:
- Peak sales revenue: e.g., $500 million
- Revenue share ratio: 7%–10%
- Discount period: 10 years; Discount rate: 15%–20%
- Token holders are entitled to 80% of total distributed cash flow

The calculated net present value of future returns per token then serves as the upper anchor for token valuation.

Token Circulation, Buyback, and Exit Mechanism Design

1. Token Issuance and Compliance Structure Model

Module	Content	Compliance Path
Token Carrier	ERC-3643 standard, compliant transferable security token	Supports compliant KYC/AML mechanisms
Legal Structure	BVI Fund → SPV holds equity → Token mirrors rights	Supports Reg D/Reg S compliant issuance
Investor Suitability	LPs, PIPE funds, family offices, qualified individuals	Open to Qualified/Accredited Investors only
Financing Mechanism	Set issuance window, lock-up period, and target annual return	Structured similar to convertible debt or yield notes
Token Management	Integrate with on-chain governance: lock-up voting rights, audit reports on-chain	Enhances regulatory compliance and liquidity control

2. Token Trading and Liquidity Design Mechanism

Path	Description	Risk Control Focus
Token OTC Transfers	Peer-to-peer transfer among KYC-approved investors	Whitelist limitation to prevent illicit trades
Secondary Market Trading (Delayed Listing)	Listing on permissioned platforms (e.g., INX, ADDX)	Control listing time and volatility range
Buyback Mechanism	ETAO or NewCo repurchases token at 1.5–2.0x pricing	Aligns with PIPE exit windows and liquidity options

3. Token Valuation Output Recommendations

Report Type	Use Case
Token Offering Memorandum	Detailed tokenomics, dividend rights, and valuation model
Token Valuation Deck (PPT)	Investor roadshows for PIPE funds and family offices

Legal Framework Whitepaper (Lite)	For compliance disclosure and token platform integration
KYC Policy & Issuance Restriction Memo	Ensure compliance with Reg D/Reg S standards

Conclusion

This token valuation and compliance model, based on traditional DCF and comparables methodologies, integrates Web3 token compliance standards and qualified investor mechanisms to establish a transparent, auditable, and logically priced RWA-based digital capital pathway. It enhances asset liquidity, safeguards market discipline, and builds a globally recognizable 'Token-structured PIPE' financing model.

NewCo Architecture and Value Amplification Pathways

Strategic Financing and Valuation Enhancement Plan for "Hong Kong ChenChen + ETAO"

I. Project Overview

"Joint Development & Legacy Equity Optimization Plan for Hong Kong ChenChen and ETAO International"

- Hong Kong ChenChen Biopharma ("ChenChen"): An innovative biopharmaceutical company based in Jiangsu, China, specializing in ADC (Antibody-Drug Conjugates) development. Its latest funding round valued the company at RMB 2.0 billion pre-money, with RMB 300 million invested by HKEX-listed Tibet Pharmaceuticals, bringing the post-money valuation to RMB 2.3 billion.
- ETAO International (NASDAQ: ETAO): A U.S.-listed healthcare technology company focused on AI healthcare, telemedicine, and chronic disease platforms. It offers international capital access and tech integration capabilities, targeting a multi-billion-dollar valuation.

Strategic Objective:
Enable ChenChen to break through its valuation ceiling by achieving strategic synergies and high-premium legacy equity transactions, leveraging ETAO's platform to drive secondary value creation and capital liquidity.

II. Strategic Design Framework

Module	Primary Goal	Implementation Mechanism
Legacy Equity Transfer	Enable partial exit for legacy shareholders	Via strategic investor acquisition or injection into NewCo
NewCo Structure	Bundle assets and uplift valuation	Establish new offshore holding entity (BVI/Cayman)
HK Market Integration	Lay groundwork for future IPO	Introduce HK-listed companies as strategic investors or listing platform

III. Core Structure and Transaction Steps

Step 1: Establish NewCo Platform

- Incorporate NewCo (Cayman or BVI), initiated by ETAO, which acts as majority shareholder or key strategic partner.
- ChenChen injects part of its legacy equity into NewCo to consolidate value and strategic assets.
- NewCo raises USD capital, potentially through ETAO's affiliated vehicle WSHP Capital.

Advantage: NewCo holds legacy shares, benefiting from USD-based valuation premiums; legacy shareholders can exit partially or participate in long-term value appreciation.

Step 2: Sign Strategic Cooperation Agreement

- ETAO and ChenChen sign a Strategic Cooperation Agreement, covering:
    - AI platform integration
    - Access to international clinical resources
    - Overseas regulatory strategy
    - Capital raising support
- ChenChen agrees to prioritize future licensing, global development partnerships, and financing through the NewCo/ETAO platform.

Step 3: Legacy Equity Transfer Mechanism Design

Content	**Description**
Target Amount	RMB 1.38 billion (~USD 200 million), based on 60% transfer of RMB 2.3 billion post-money valuation
Investor Composition	Strategic investors + HNW USD-based funds (introduced via ETAO)
Distribution Structure	Transfer proceeds distributed proportionally to original shareholders; part retained in NewCo for incubation or BD use
FA Fee	ETAO, acting as exclusive financial advisor, charges 7% success fee, payable in cash or NewCo shares

Step 4: HK Market Integration Plan

- ETAO assists ChenChen in designing an HK IPO route or M&A strategy within 12–18 months (including backdoor or reverse mergers).
- Introduce HK-listed strategic investors into NewCo (e.g., Tibet Pharmaceuticals or industry peers), providing dual-track exit assurance.
- Explore cooperation with main board-listed companies like United Medical, China Medical System (CMS) via strategic partnerships, equity participation, or licensing deals.

HK integration enhances investor appeal and provides clear exit visibility for new capital entrants.

IV. Revenue Model and Valuation Growth Roadmap

Timeline	Key Milestone	Valuation Target
T+0	Legacy equity transfer + Strategic Agreement	Maintain RMB 2.3B
T+6 Months	AI-enabled pipeline, license-out partnerships	RMB 3.0B+
T+12 Months	Prepares for HK/US listing	RMB 5.0B
T+24 Months	M&A expansion, global registration via ETAO	RMB 10.0B+ platform vision

V. Execution Priorities and Risk Controls

Execution Recommendations

- Expedite NewCo setup and complete preliminary share injection and structure (led by ETAO)
- Finalize the Strategic Agreement outlining rights, obligations, fees, and exit terms
- Select 1–2 synergistic HK-listed companies for strategic partnership or joint platform plans
- Engage a cross-border FA team with overseas capital market experience (e.g., Growing Pains Solution)

Risk Control Recommendations

- Conduct legal due diligence and third-party valuation verification for legacy share injection into NewCo
- Include milestone-based clauses and exit mechanisms (e.g., earn-out provisions) in

the strategic agreement

- Design investor disclosure protocols and transfer mechanisms to mitigate potential liquidity risks

VI. Appendix: Comparable Transaction Cases

Case	Content	Insight
Kelun Pharma – Merck	ADC asset license-out deal	License transactions can double valuations
Huadong Medicine – BMS	Joint development + equity partnership	Strategic equity + pipeline synergy raises market cap
WuXi AppTec – GHO Fund	Legacy equity sale + management restructuring	Legacy equity monetization with long-term growth incentives

VII. Conclusion

This plan leverages:

- ETAO's international capital access
- The valuation re-rating mechanism of the NewCo structure
- Mature HK/US exit pathways

to transform ChenChen's liquidity bottleneck into a scalable value creation opportunity. It not only solves the company's capital constraint but also delivers a replicable cross-border growth model for mid-sized Chinese innovators seeking global expansion.

Chapter 6: Why Smart Capital Is the Ultimate Valuation Amplifier for Mid-market Firms

The Stanford Insight: From Philosophy to Capital Strategy

During a visit to Stanford University's School of Engineering, I came across a sentence written on a wall that left a lasting impression:

"A good business model is nothing more than a solution to a critical industry pain point."

This statement cuts straight to the heart of entrepreneurial thinking. For entrepreneurs, the first responsibility is to identify the problem; the second is to solve it. At its core, the value of business and innovation arises from the intersection of problem recognition and solution delivery.

This reminded me of Karl Marx's famous words in the *Theses on Feuerbach*:

"The philosophers have only interpreted the world, in various ways; the point, however, is to change it."

Many view this as a declaration of action-oriented philosophy. Yet I only partially agree.

In my view, understanding the world is more fundamental than changing it. Why?

"A thousand-mile levee can be destroyed by an ant hole."

Yes, ants can change the world—but they don't understand it. When ants hollow out a levee, they may not realize that once it collapses, their own home will be washed away.

If they understood that "when the nest is overturned, no egg is left intact," they might stop before total destruction. If they grasped the fragility of systems and the interdependence of their own survival, perhaps they would choose a wiser, more sustainable way to live.

This is the essence of Confucian *zhongyong* (the Doctrine of the Mean):

"Live and let live" — to act with balance, to enable mutual survival and shared prosperity.

Thus, while changing the world is important, understanding it is even more crucial.

Only through deep insight into how systems function—their logic, boundaries, and ripple effects—can change avoid becoming destruction. Only then can action avoid unintentionally harming its originator.

The same is true in business: only by understanding structural contradictions and the evolutionary trajectory of an industry can one design business models that transcend cycles and define new eras—instead of becoming the next bubble or chaos.

This is the core mission of *Smart Capital*: to help companies reconfigure their capital structure and upgrade their strategic position, grounded in structural insight.

Seven Structural Bottlenecks Blocking Mid-Sized Enterprises From Global Capital Markets

For many Chinese mid-sized enterprises, the journey to becoming a global capitalized platform is not merely about scaling operations or raising more funds. It is about crossing seven systemic industry barriers that often function as invisible ceilings on growth and valuation.

These bottlenecks are not isolated challenges. They are interlinked structural constraints that prevent capital inflow, valuation uplift, and global exit potential. In the following sections, we explore each of these in detail, offering actionable, fundable, and exit-ready strategies.

1. Misaligned Capital Structure: No USD Access, No Global Vision

Common symptoms: Domestic funding is overly localized, relying on RMB debt or short-term equity. It is shortsighted, unstable, and inadequate to support global expansion or long-term R&D.

Strategic solutions:

- Set up a global financing platform (NewCo) in Cayman, BVI, or Singapore for offshore fundraising and asset consolidation.
- Introduce international investors via PIPEs, convertible notes, Reg D/Reg S placements.
- Build a dual-currency structure where the parent raises USD offshore, while the subsidiary operates in RMB domestically.

2. Rigid Shareholding Structure: Old Shareholders, No Exit Path

Common symptoms: Early shareholders (often family or industrial investors) have no clear exit, while new investors resist entering due to valuation concerns and governance friction.

Strategic solutions:

- Replace legacy equity via asset injection into a NewCo structure.
- Use Pre-IPO exit funds or buyout commitments from PE firms to offer old shareholders a guaranteed exit.
- Design "Old-Co to New-Co" blended structures, where legacy investors retain upside through partial rollover.

3. Non-Compliant Financial Systems: Lacking Visibility and Trust

Common symptoms: Financial reports do not meet US GAAP or IFRS. There is no SOX-compliant internal control. Tax structures are outdated.

Strategic solutions:

- Engage top-tier global audit firms to upgrade financial reporting.
- Implement SOX-compliant systems (internal controls, compliance officers, disclosure protocols).
- Reconstruct tax frameworks to avoid double taxation and enhance post-tax profit quality.

4. Unclear Asset Valuation & Weak Narrative

Common symptoms: Businesses are scattered and lack a clear growth engine or value anchor recognized by capital markets.

Strategic solutions:

- Spin out high-potential business units (AI, biotech, SaaS) into a clean NewCo structure.
- Use license-out, SPVs, or asset bundling to create well-defined financial models and valuation benchmarks.
- Bring in industry advisors to co-develop compelling, investor-oriented narratives: Tech Breakthrough + Market Demand + Capital Exit Path.

5. Weak Cross-Border M&A Integration Capability

Common symptoms: Domestic teams lack experience in cross-border deal execution, post-merger integration, and regulatory compliance.

Strategic solutions:

- Build a multidisciplinary M&A team with international legal, tax, audit, and cultural expertise.
- Set observation periods and incentive mechanisms to smooth post-deal integration.
- Plan exit strategies alongside acquisition (IPO, license-out, secondary sales).

6. Weak Brand & International BD Channels

Common symptoms: Weak global recognition, low client trust, and broken international business development pipelines.

Strategic solutions:

- Use reverse mergers or strategic partnerships with listed companies to amplify credibility.
- Build brand visibility through participation in global forums (JP Morgan Healthcare, BIO International).
- Recruit experienced international BD talent to drive outbound licensing and global sales.

7. Founders' Mindset Bottleneck: From Owner to Operator

Common symptoms: Founders over-centralize decisions, mistrust capital, and lack corporate governance awareness.

Strategic solutions:

- Establish an international board with clear separation of CEO, COO, and board functions.
- Introduce a professional executive team. Founders may become Chairman focusing on strategy and ecosystem.
- Empower founders with executive education (Mini-MBA, IPO coaching) to shift from "owner mindset" to "capital platform steward."

Conclusion: Redesigning Capital Structure Is Redefining the Growth Path

Overcoming these seven structural challenges is not just about accessing capital—it's about redesigning the company's growth engine.

A capital roadmap that combines structural clarity, narrative credibility, and exit feasibility is the core engine for mid-sized enterprises to leap over valuation ceilings and enter the global capital stage.

AI × Healthcare: The Primary Track for the Next Capital–Industry Resonance Cycle

In an era where technology and healthcare are deeply converging, "AI × Healthcare" is emerging as a strategically critical and capital-intensive track. This trend is driven by internal structural forces such as China's demographic changes, the U.S. capital market's long-standing preference for healthcare, and AI's natural fit with data-rich environments.

1. China's Aging Population Drives Structural Healthcare Demand

China is rapidly entering a stage of deep demographic aging. According to the National Bureau of Statistics, by 2035, more than 400 million people will be over 60 years old—exceeding 30% of the total population. This surge will create massive demand for chronic disease management, elderly care, and long-term rehabilitation.

At the same time, the Chinese healthcare system faces structural bottlenecks: unequal distribution of medical resources, physician shortages, and low diagnostic efficiency. AI-powered health technologies offer a critical solution—driven by standardization, scalability, and data intelligence—to help rebalance supply and demand.

AI can replicate portions of physician capabilities across perception, cognition, and decision-making, solving supply bottlenecks and becoming a core driver of cost-efficiency in China's healthcare reform.

2. U.S. Capital Markets Favor the Healthcare Sector

Over the past decade, the two most favored sectors on the Nasdaq have consistently been TMT (Technology, Media, Telecom) and Healthcare. Within healthcare, digital health, precision medicine, AI diagnostics, and SaaS-based chronic care platforms have received high valuations and long-term capital attention.

This preference is underpinned by several structural advantages:

- Policy moat: Public insurance and regulatory systems ensure predictable cash flows;
- High valuation models: Healthcare companies are often priced based on long-term projected revenues and lifetime patient value, expanding upside potential;
- Defensive attributes: Healthcare performs well during economic downturns;

- Clear exit pathways: U.S. markets offer well-developed IPO and M&A mechanisms, particularly attractive for Chinese firms pursuing dual listings in Hong Kong and the U.S.

3. AI's "Data-Native" Nature Is a Natural Fit for Healthcare

Healthcare is fundamentally a data-intensive, decision-critical, and risk-sensitive knowledge industry. From medical imaging and genomics to EHR analytics, diagnostics, and drug discovery, AI has multiple natural entry points.

In China—home to one of the world's largest and most diverse healthcare datasets—AI has unparalleled opportunities to train models and refine algorithms. The data volume, complexity, and variety make it a global leader in raw material for machine learning.

Moreover, with the rise of generative AI (such as ChatGPT), we are now seeing breakthroughs in multi-turn consultations, health Q&A, and personalized treatment recommendations. AI is evolving from a backend tool into an active health decision-making partner, accelerating its integration into real-world care delivery.

Conclusion: AI × Healthcare Is Not Just an Industry Integration—It's a Systemic Solution

AI × Healthcare is not merely the sum of "technology + healthcare"—it represents a threefold convergence of industrial upgrading, demographic urgency, and capital market structure.

For China's mid-sized enterprises, this is more than a technological transformation—it's a strategic opportunity to connect with global capital markets and position themselves as cross-border healthcare platforms.

New Frontiers in Digital Health, RWA Tokenization, and Global Capital Alignment

This chapter aims to extend the strategic foresight of the book through thematic analysis, focusing on three major emerging trends: (1) AI + healthcare, (2) RWA tokenization, and (3) coordinated funding through Hong Kong and Middle Eastern sovereign funds, alongside China's pro-globalization policies. The goal is to strengthen a three-dimensional pathway of "Technology + Capital + Policy."

I. The Future of Digital Health RWAs: AI × Health × Token

Digital Health RWA: The Convergence of AI, Healthcare, and Tokenization

RWA (Real World Asset) tokenization is expanding from traditional sectors like real estate and art into healthcare, with strong potential in the following areas:

- Tokenization of healthcare data rights (e.g., imaging, chronic disease management)
- Token mapping of license-out revenues and projected dividends
- Assetization of transferable revenue from AI models (e.g., diagnostics, synthetic biology)

Recommended Structure:

- Use a NewCo to hold licensing agreements or revenue-sharing rights
- Issue tokens via Cayman or BVI entities, compliant with Reg D/Reg S through platforms like INX or Securitize
- Tokens represent "future yield + investment exit pathway"

Reference Cases:

- Akili Interactive (U.S. digital therapeutics + RWA experiment)
- AiMi Health (AI diagnostics + tokenized structure design)

II. Hong Kong + Middle East Funds: A New Cross-Border Funding Axis

HK + Gulf Sovereign Funds: A New Cross-Border Funding Axis

A new collaborative landscape is emerging involving G42 (Abu Dhabi AI platform), Mubadala (sovereign wealth fund), and Hong Kong intermediaries (HKEX, Bank of China International), forming a structure to channel RMB assets abroad.

Emerging Trends:

- "Abu Dhabi tech + China data + Hong Kong token gateway"
- Issuer based in Hong Kong; SPV in Abu Dhabi (tax-free, compliant), with token issuance to guide primary funding
- Preferred sectors: healthcare, synthetic biology, renewable energy

Strategic Recommendations:

- Establish multilateral LP structures: China industrial funds + HK brokerages + Middle Eastern FOs/FAs
- Launch dual-currency token models (USD + AED/HKD)

Example Explorations:

- G42's investments in BioMap and XtalPi
- Mubadala's healthcare channels with Tencent and Fosun Pharma

III. How Chinese Policy Encourages Biopharma Globalization

Policy Landscape: How China Encourages Biopharma to Go Global

Recent Policy Signals:

- The 14th Five-Year Plan for the Pharmaceutical Industry encourages innovative drug companies to "go global" and pursue international license transactions
- China's NMPA supports "overseas clinical + domestic submission" dual-track registration
- MOFCOM promotes M&A facilitation and IP asset cross-border pricing mechanisms

Supportive Measures:

- Endorsement of NewCo structures to attract foreign capital (especially RMB reinvestment)
- Local governments launching "Outbound Biotech Special Funds"
- Pilot programs expanding tax optimization and FX settlement for cross-border executive compensation

Recommended Tactics:

- Leverage policy windows to set up a dual equity + token structure in Hong Kong in advance
- Connect with national TCM export platforms and cross-border tech parks for ecosystem resources

【Summary】

This chapter proposes "AI-driven healthcare + RWA-based assets + tokenization" as the new capital logic for mid-sized enterprises going global. It further highlights the emergence of a "Gulf Capital + Hong Kong Mechanism + Chinese Assets" golden triangle for cross-border funding. Enterprises are encouraged to upgrade their technology, governance, and compliance structures to align with global capital standards.

From Ecosystem Loops to Structural Clarity: Practical Strategies to Overcome Seven Capital Barriers

In the AI × Healthcare domain, building a data-driven closed loop and generating ecosystem momentum has become one of the most compelling capital strategies today. Success requires not only technological and scenario integration, but also a corporate architecture that can communicate fluently with international capital markets, support cross-border collaboration, and demonstrate a structural logic that is **clear to articulate, feasible to finance, and practical to exit**.

Capital markets never lack stories—what they lack are **verifiable pathways and credible exit mechanisms**. For mid-sized enterprises aiming to move from "regional innovator" to "global capitalized platform," solving seven key structural obstacles is a prerequisite.

In the following section, we break down these seven common capital bottlenecks specific to the healthcare and pharmaceutical sectors using a "Problem – Insight – Solution" framework, with actionable strategies designed to be **fundable, operable, and exit-oriented**.

1. Misaligned Capital Structure: Localized Funding Cannot Support Global Ambitions

Real-world example: A mid-sized AI diagnostic company holds a world-class algorithm but remains constrained by RMB-denominated debt financing, resulting in short funding cycles, high capital costs, and limited ability to invest in global expansion or R&D.

Strategic Solutions:

1. **Establish an offshore financing vehicle (NewCo)**
   Choose Cayman, BVI, or Singapore as the registration base to receive USD capital and consolidate international assets.

2. **Attract international investors**
   Utilize PIPEs, convertible notes, and Reg D/Reg S private placements to bring in long-term global capital.

3. **Build a dual-currency structure (RMB–USD)**
   Parent company raises USD offshore; subsidiaries operate in RMB domestically—achieving both currency risk mitigation and funding diversification.

2. Complicated Shareholding Structure: Legacy Shareholders Block New Capital

Typical challenge: Early shareholders—often family or industrial capital—hold significant stakes but lack a clear exit path. New investors hesitate due to governance rigidity and valuation conflicts.

Structure Optimization Strategies:

1. **Legacy equity transfer + NewCo asset restructuring**
   Existing shareholders inject core assets into NewCo in exchange for equity, completing a governance-aligned transition.

2. **Pre-IPO exit fund mechanism**
   Partner with investment banks or PE firms to set up guaranteed exit structures ("buyback + upside") for legacy shareholders.

3. **Design "Old-to-New" shareholding blend**
   Allow partial exits for legacy shareholders while retaining a strategic equity stake in the new platform, aligned with future IPO growth.

3. Outdated Financial & Compliance Systems: Not IPO-Ready

Common issue: Financial reports do not comply with US GAAP or IFRS. Lack of audit transparency and SOX-compliant internal controls creates a hard barrier for IPOs or international M&A.

Solutions:

1. **Engage a Big Four or U.S.-qualified audit firm**
   Establish investor trust through standardized international audit procedures.

2. **Build SOX-compliant internal governance**
   Implement internal control reports, compliance officer structures, and mandatory disclosure systems—essential for U.S. listings.

3. **Restructure tax and reporting architecture**
   Separate domestic and international accounts, reduce double taxation risks, and improve after-tax earnings quality.

4. Ambiguous Asset Valuation: No Clear Narrative, No Market Confidence

Investor perspective: Businesses are scattered, lack a compelling focus, and offer no "valuation anchor" or "growth engine" that resonates with public markets.

Clarity-building Measures:

1. **Spin out the most promising business unit into a NewCo**
   Focus on AI, biotech, or SaaS—verticals that command high multiples and international capital interest.

2. **Use license-out, SPV carve-outs, and asset bundling**
   Structure each asset package with clear revenue models, growth pathways, and comparable valuation benchmarks.

3. **Engage industry experts to co-develop investor-facing narratives**
   Combine "tech breakthrough + market necessity + capital pathway" into an integrated and persuasive equity story.

5. Weak Cross-Border M&A Integration Capabilities

Case in point: A Chinese firm acquires a U.S. digital pathology company but fails to integrate due to culture clash, incompatible audit standards, and a lack of post-deal planning.

Remedies:

1. **Assemble a cross-border integration team**
   Include financial advisors, lawyers, auditors, and tax consultants familiar with both U.S. and Chinese regulatory frameworks.

2. **Set up an integration observation period and incentive system**
   Retain original teams post-M&A, implement phased KPIs and equity-linked rewards to ensure smooth collaboration.

3. **Plan the capital exit at the time of acquisition**
   Define downstream options like IPO, license-out deals, or secondary share sales—presenting a capital-marketable M&A story.

6. Weak Global Brand & Go-to-Market Strategy

Common symptom: Strong technical team, good product—but no brand recognition abroad, broken BD pipelines, and poor conversion in license negotiations.

Breakthrough Tactics:

1. **Use reverse mergers or strategic partnerships to boost credibility**
   Collaborate with U.S. or Hong Kong-listed companies to "borrow a license" for faster market entry and investor confidence.

2. **Global brand-building through flagship events**
   Co-brand at top-tier conferences like JP Morgan Healthcare and BIO International to gain exposure and credibility.

3. **Recruit international BD executives**
   Hire BD directors with U.S./EU pharma networks to drive outbound licensing, partnerships, and global sales.

7. Founders' Mindset Gap: From "Owner Logic" to "Capital Logic"

Leadership dilemma: Founders centralize decision-making, mistrust capital, and lack governance understanding—leading to weak management bench and investor disengagement.

Upgrading Leadership Architecture:

1. **Establish an international board with clear governance**
   Separate CEO/COO roles from board functions to enhance institutional maturity and accountability.

2. **Introduce a professional executive team**
   Founders may transition to Chairman role, focusing on vision and ecosystem building while COOs and CFOs execute operational strategy.

3. **Enable mindset shift through education**
   Offer Mini-MBA programs or IPO coaching to help founders evolve from "private enterprise owner" to "global capital platform steward."

Conclusion: Redesigning Capital Structure = Redefining Growth Strategy

Solving these seven structural barriers is not just a means to raise funds or go public—it is a fundamental **transformation of the enterprise's growth architecture**.

A capital strategy that combines **structural clarity, strategic narrative, and a viable exit plan** will become the core engine for mid-sized companies to break through valuation ceilings and enter the global capital arena with confidence.

Part II: RWA Structuring & Valuation Mechanism

Explains how future income rights, licenses, and AI models can be transformed into tradable RWA tokens. Demonstrates how valuation anchoring and asset tokenization enable financing and listing strategies, with practical case studies in healthcare and AI sectors.

Chapter 7: What is RWA? Future Income Rights, Licensing, and AI Model Valuation Approaches

Real World Assets (RWA) refer to tangible or intangible off-chain assets that are tokenized or otherwise structured to interact with digital financial ecosystems. These assets serve as a critical bridge between traditional finance (TradFi) and decentralized finance (DeFi), enabling broader access to capital, liquidity, and financial innovation. For mid-market enterprises—particularly in sectors like healthcare and artificial intelligence—RWA structuring offers a compelling framework for unlocking undervalued or underutilized assets.

1. Future Income Rights as Core Components of RWA

Future income rights are contractual claims to a company's anticipated revenues. These may include income from IP licensing, service agreements, product royalties, or milestone-based payments from R&D partnerships. Such rights can be securitized and tokenized, offering flexibility in financing. For example, a biotech firm developing a late-stage oncology drug might tokenize its expected licensing revenue from a global pharmaceutical partner, enabling it to raise capital even before commercialization.

2. Licensing as a Valuation Anchor

Licensing agreements—particularly in biotech, pharma, and AI software—serve as strong valuation anchors. A license signed with a prominent market player (e.g., Big Pharma or a major tech platform) validates the enterprise's core technology and represents a quantifiable asset for capital markets. These licenses, especially those delineated by territory, application, or user base, can be valued using historical deal data (such as from BioCentury or Evaluate Pharma) and discounted cash flow (DCF) models.

3. Valuation of AI Models as Emerging Intangible Assets

Valuing AI models introduces a new paradigm in asset recognition. Unlike physical products, AI algorithms are dynamic, data-driven, and highly scalable. Key factors in valuation include: size and quality of training data, generalizability, proprietary methodologies, regulatory approvals (such as FDA 510(k) for diagnostic AI), and commercialization progress. When structured as part of a service model or embedded in a licensing framework, an AI model becomes a monetizable RWA.

4. Structuring Investable RWA Vehicles

To transform these asset components into investable structures, companies often adopt a multi-layered legal and financial strategy. This may involve setting up a NewCo to hold IP and future revenue rights, issuing tokens or SPV equity backed by those rights, and embedding clear valuation, reporting, and audit mechanisms. The NewCo structure provides risk segregation, cross-border investment accessibility, and legal flexibility (especially in Cayman Islands or BVI jurisdictions). When paired with stablecoins, this structure enhances both pricing transparency and liquidity.

5. Strategic Implications

RWA is more than a trending term—it is a strategic tool that enables mid-market enterprises to quantify, structure, and unlock the value of their intangible assets. By converting future income rights, licenses, and AI models into structured and tradable financial instruments, companies can improve valuation transparency, raise global capital, and lay a foundation for IPOs or token-based exits.

Chapter 8: Structuring Transferable RWAs in Healthcare and AI Industries

1. Project Background and Strategic Objectives

Hundreds of mid-sized Chinese innovative enterprises with market valuations around RMB 2 billion hold high-quality assets but are undervalued. Traditional equity financing channels fail to meet international investors' demands for liquidity, asset verification, and exit mechanisms. By introducing an RWA tokenization structure and AI-driven data verification system, a digital financing and asset circulation platform targeting international capital markets can be built.

2. Structural Overview

Module	Description	Function
NewCo Structure	Establish NewCo in BVI/Cayman to hold assets and authorized rights	Support overseas financing and asset integration
RWA Token Structure	Tokenize equity/license rights/future income in NewCo into digital tokens or SPV shares	Create tradable digital equity assets
AI Data Verification	Generate AI-powered reports for clinical data, R&D progress, and partnership milestones	Enhance asset transparency and valuation anchors
On-Chain Compliance	Use Ethereum/L2 blockchain for token registration, integrated with KYC compliance	Enable partial liquidity and on-chain investor management
Digital Financing	Raise USD LP funds via token private placements or SPV funds	Offer low-barrier, high-liquidity investment entry
Multiple Exit Mechanisms	Token buyback + share swap + HK/US IPO exit options	Meet diverse LP exit preferences

3. Implementation Steps

Step 1: Asset Verification and Wrapping

- Value license-out assets, future cash flows (upfront/milestones), and AI medical data with predictive models
- Cooperate with Big Four/FA firms to produce AI-driven asset verification reports and future income modeling
- Create SPV or token structure (e.g., ERC-3643 compliant token) to represent equity rights

Step 2: RWA Token Structure Design (Digital Asset Issuance)

Suggested Structure Levels:
- RWA-A (60%): Core equity token – packaged equity/license revenue
- RWA-B (30%): Dividend token – fund-like token for distributions
- RWA-C (10%): Management incentive token – for GP/FA

All tokens should be implemented with smart contracts to enable traceability, verification, and transfer restrictions.

Step 3: Compliant Token Issuance and USD Fundraising

- Fund structure: Offshore SPV (BVI fund structure) mapped to token
- Issuance platforms: Securitize, Tokeny, INX, etc.
- Fundraising via Reg D/Reg S for international LPs
- Settlement in USDC/USDT with KYC-linked LP accounts

Step 4: Liquidity and Exit Path Design

Path	Description	Investor Fit
Equity Buyback	Token repurchased by NewCo/SPV at premium	PIPE/FA
IPO Share Swap	Tokens converted into HK/US shares upon NewCo listing	LPs/Institutions
Secondary Transfer	OTC transfer of token units via institutional platforms	HNW Individuals
Ongoing Dividends	Token dividends triggered by license-out or upfront payments	Yield-oriented Investors

4. Legal and Technical Compliance Recommendations

Project	Recommended Partners
Token Compliance Issuance Platform	Securitize / Tokeny / ADDX

Legal Framework Design	Ogier / Loeb Smith (Cayman) + Akin Gump (USA)
KYC/AML Services	Chainalysis / Onfido / Sumsub
Smart Contract Audit	Certik / Quantstamp

5. Value Innovation from Tokenization

Dimension	**Innovative Value**
Investors	Digitized equity, enhanced liquidity, flexible exit options
Project Owners	Improved valuation, greater transparency, international capital attraction
Partners	Standardized valuation and ownership model for AI-driven healthcare assets
Regulatory Compliance	Dual SPV + Token structure linking traditional legal systems with digital markets

Recommended Perspective:

Tokenization is not a 'token-for-token' speculative model, but a new capital channel anchored in AI-driven data verification, real-world asset (RWA) backing, and governed by USD-denominated fund compliance and international securities law.

It builds a novel digital capital framework for mid-sized innovative enterprises to connect global investors, enhance liquidity, and unlock valuation leverage.

Chapter 9: Operationalizing RWA Listings: Case Study on AI Diagnostics + Global BD

In the field of AI healthcare and digital health, structuring Real World Assets (RWA) for overseas fundraising and public listings has become a critical strategy for mid-sized innovative companies to overcome valuation bottlenecks and access cross-border capital. This section takes InferVision as a representative case to analyze how it combines AI-assisted diagnostic technology with international business development (BD) to implement a practical RWA-based IPO model.

Founded in 2015, InferVision specializes in AI-based medical imaging analysis, with core products including lung nodule detection and intelligent chest CT analysis systems, widely adopted by top-tier hospitals and regional imaging centers in China. Since 2018, the company has actively expanded overseas, initiating pilot collaborations with healthcare groups in Europe, Japan, and the Middle East. Its technology has obtained CE certification and FDA exempt status in several countries, laying a solid foundation for international commercialization.

In terms of financing structure, InferVision adopted a classic RWA model involving asset bundling, offshore SPV formation, and future licensing revenue securitization. Its domestic operating entity (OpCo) retains R&D and local operations, while a Cayman-based NewCo was established to hold global IP and international business rights. NewCo signed licensing agreements with hospitals abroad, securing rights to 3–5 years of future overseas income. These rights were then used as the basis to issue convertible bonds or tokens, attracting overseas investors for Pre-IPO financing.

This structure offers several key advantages:

- first, the licensing agreements provide predictable cash flows that support asset valuation;
- second, the NewCo enables legal risk isolation and tax optimization;
- third, overseas licensing agreements qualify as identifiable, forecastable, and redeemable RWAs, meeting the expectations of international investors for asset security and liquidity.

Notably, in 2021, Shukun Technology completed a $100 million Pre-IPO financing round led by Goldman Sachs Asia and Fidelity International, with a valuation exceeding $800 million. The key lay in leveraging an RWA model that integrated its AI imaging models, overseas licensing agreements, and future income rights into an investable asset bundle.

This structure achieved legal clarity and audit readiness through an offshore entity, laying the groundwork for a future IPO on the Hong Kong Stock Exchange or NASDAQ.

Unfortunately, Shukun encountered setbacks: during the Pre-IPO structuring, it failed to conduct a thorough equity restructuring, resulting in unclear rights for legacy shareholders and a lack of priority protection for new USD investors. This led to shareholder conflicts, and with IPO windows delayed, investors eventually demanded to withdraw, causing the company's valuation to be slashed in half. (see Chapter 31: Strategic Pitfalls in Globalization: Failure Case Studies)

Despite this outcome, the "RWA + AI + BD" structured approach presents a replicable capital pathway model for AI healthcare companies. By combining product globalization, licensing agreements, and future income tokenization, it transforms intangible tech assets into financeable and tradable structured rights. As global capital markets increasingly emphasize monetization pathways for deep tech, such structures are becoming critical engines for cross-border value creation in the healthcare technology sector.

Chapter 10: Data Ownership, Regulatory Tolerance, and RWA Pricing Practices

With the development of artificial intelligence and digital assets, data has become an increasingly critical production factor in capital markets. Especially in data-intensive sectors like healthcare, finance, and industrial internet, the ability to establish ownership and value for data assets directly determines whether they can be included in the RWA (Real World Assets) framework for financing and trading purposes.

1. The Necessity and Practice of Data Ownership

Data ownership refers to the legal or technical clarification of rights related to data ownership, usage, and monetization. In China, the Data Security Law and the Personal Information Protection Law have laid the groundwork for a governance logic of 'who collects, who is responsible; who uses, who complies.' For enterprises, however, data ownership needs to be implemented through practical steps, including:
1) Building a stable, continuous, and legally sourced data asset package;
2) Utilizing blockchain or trusted computing platforms for original data registration, timestamping, and access tracking;
3) Establishing clear authorization, licensing, and revenue-sharing mechanisms through contracts or user agreements;
4) Engaging third-party assessment agencies to provide independent data valuation and audit reports.

For example, an AI diagnostic company collaborated with top-tier hospitals to build a medical imaging database, using it to train high-quality lung nodule detection models. In terms of ownership, the company signed joint development agreements with hospitals to define rights and commercial profit-sharing, and used blockchain to timestamp and register all training data. This enabled the company to package its AI models and data foundation into a verifiable RWA asset eligible for valuation and financing.

2. Regulatory Tolerance and Legal Acceptance of RWA Structures

The core of RWA lies in asset authenticity and clear ownership. However, for RWAs built on data, algorithms, and service income, regulatory acceptance varies across jurisdictions:
- In Singapore and Switzerland, regulators are relatively open: as long as assets are identifiable and generate predictable cash flows, they can be accepted in private placements;
- In Hong Kong, the SFC has not yet published clear rules for data tokens but supports 'asset-backed RWA' tied to real-world sectors like healthcare and education;

- In the United States, the SEC emphasizes the four elements of an investment contract, including expected profit and third-party efforts, and reviews data or AI-based RWAs case-by-case.

Therefore, enterprises structuring data-based RWAs should assess local regulatory baselines, legal disclosure requirements, and risk control mechanisms. Recommended strategies include setting up a NewCo, custodizing data assets, signing compliance agreements, and seeking legal exemptions under Reg D or Reg S for compliant securitization and cross-border financing.

3. RWA Valuation Practices and Anchoring Methods

The valuation of data-driven RWAs is primarily based on future income rights and comparable market benchmarks. Common methods include:

1) Discounted cash flow (DCF) modeling based on licensing revenue;
2) Referencing historical deal valuations for similar assets (e.g., AI model transactions);
3) Technical scoring frameworks based on model accuracy, reusability, and IP barriers;
4) Third-party audit and valuation reports to support transparency and investor confidence.

In summary, data ownership, regulatory tolerance, and practical valuation form the three key pillars for structuring data-based RWAs. Only when these elements work in concert—with clear standards, legality, and disclosure—can mid-market tech firms truly capitalize on their data assets and pursue transparent, investable, and exit-ready digital finance pathways.

Chapter 11: Token Offering Memorandum Template

This chapter provides a standardized Token Offering Memorandum (OM) template, designed for use during the private placement stage of a token offering to disclose key project components, risk clauses, exit arrangements, and legal structures to qualified investors (LPs). The template is structured in bilingual format (Chinese-English) to support international compliance and legal review.

I. Project Overview

Project Name: ________

Issuer Entity: ________ (e.g., Cayman Fund, BVI Company, etc.)

Token Name: ________

Token Type: [Utility / Governance / Revenue-Backed / Hybrid]

Project Vision: Concise summary of how the token is designed in connection with real-world industry applications (e.g., AI + Healthcare + ESG)

Target Raise: $________ million USD

Round Type: [PIPE / Pre-A / Strategic Round]

II. Token Design and Tokenomics

Total Supply: ________

Initial Price: $________/Token

Token Allocation Plan:

Category	Proportion	Vesting Schedule
PIPE Investors	xx%	12-month lockup + linear release
Team	xx%	1-year lockup, 36-month vesting
Advisors	xx%	6-month lockup
Ecosystem Incentives	xx%	DAO-governed release

Category	Proportion	Vesting Schedule
Strategic Reserve	xx%	Non-circulating, board-supervised

Key Economic Mechanisms:

Dividend Features: Yes / No / Optional (see Token Exit Memo)

Governance Rights (Voting): Yes / No

Equity Conversion Rights: e.g., 1 Token = 0.1 Share under specific conditions

Buyback Mechanism: e.g., Up to 5% per quarter

III. Use of Proceeds & Team Background

Use of Funds:

Technology & Product Development: _%

Legal & Compliance / Audit: _%

Market Expansion & BD: _%

Team Incentive Pool (TGE Budget): _%

Strategic Reserve & Liquidity: _%

Founding Team:

[Name], CEO – Former [Company] executive, in charge of strategy and global expansion

[Name], CTO – Cross-disciplinary background in blockchain and AI, core technical leader

[Name], CFO – Experienced in public company finance and PIPE fund structuring

Legal & Compliance Team:

Cayman Counsel: Ogier / Maples

U.S. Reg D Legal Advisor: Loeb Smith / DLA Piper

Compliance Platforms: INX / Securitize / Tokeny

Auditor: PwC / EY

IV. Risks and Exit Rights

Risk Disclosures:

Market Risk (price volatility, high uncertainty)

Legal/Regulatory Risk (differences in token classification, evolving global policies)

Project Execution Risk (clinical failure, BD termination, etc.)

Liquidity Risk (limited circulation, exchange access issues)

Exit Options: (See Token Exit Rights Memo for full details)

PIPE Buyback Mechanism (e.g., max 5% repurchase per quarter)

Equity Conversion Rights (triggered by M&A, IPO, etc.)

Secondary Market Liquidity (restricted to whitelisted wallets)

V. Legal Disclaimers

This token offering is conducted under Reg D (for U.S. investors) and Reg S (for non-U.S. investors)

This token is not a registered security with the U.S. Securities and Exchange Commission (SEC)

Investors must be accredited and provide a signed AI Certificate

All fund transfers must pass KYC/AML procedures and be monitored via a regulated custodian

The issuer reserves final interpretative authority and may amend offering terms in response to regulatory developments

VI. Appendices

Appendix A: KYC/AML Policy Summary (with compliance platform screenshots)

Appendix B: Draft Form D (for SEC filing)

Appendix C: Executive Whitepaper (technical logic + use cases + architecture diagram)

Appendix D: Token Exit Memo (Bilingual)

Appendix E: Subscription Agreement + AI Certificate (Blank Templates)

Note: This template is designed for dual-language presentation in Word format. It is suitable for disclosure during token private placements and is recommended to be reviewed by legal counsel before external distribution.

Part III: Stablecoin & Digital Capital Infrastructure

Analyzes the role of stablecoins as capital bridges in global LP networks. Compares regulatory frameworks across major jurisdictions and evaluates their feasibility in RWA pricing, financing, and liquidity—empowering digital capital flow and investor connection.

Chapter 12: Stablecoins as Capital Bridges in Global LP Networks

The Role of Stablecoins in the Global Capital Chain: LP Connector

With the rise of digital finance, stablecoins are playing an increasingly strategic role in global capital allocation and liquidity optimization. Acting as a "bridge" between real-world assets and digital financial markets, stablecoins serve as key enablers in connecting limited partners (LPs), facilitating cross-border fund flows, and pricing RWAs (Real World Assets).

I. The Nature and Advantages of Stablecoins

Stablecoins are crypto assets pegged to fiat currencies such as the US dollar, Hong Kong dollar, or euro. They are designed to maintain price stability while offering the transactional efficiency of digital currencies. Common types include:

- Fiat-collateralized stablecoins (e.g., USDT, USDC): Issued by centralized institutions backed by fiat reserves.
- Crypto-collateralized stablecoins (e.g., DAI): Backed by excess cryptocurrency collateral held on-chain.
- Algorithmic stablecoins (e.g., FRAX): Maintain their peg through supply and demand mechanisms and algorithmic adjustments.

Within the RWA framework, stablecoins offer several core advantages:

- Fast settlement and cross-border payments, especially effective in emerging markets or regions with capital controls;
- Enable on-chain clearing infrastructure, allowing RWAs to be mirrored and transacted in real-time on-chain;
- Act as valuation anchors, mitigating distortion caused by volatility in tokenized assets;
- Improve transparency and controllability of LP capital inflows, supporting regulatory acceptance.

II. Stablecoins as LP Connectors: Practical Use Cases

In traditional private equity or venture capital structures, LPs typically commit capital using fiat currency. However, in digital capital pathways, stablecoins provide a more flexible, efficient, and compliant method for LP funding. Typical use cases include:

- LPs invest in NewCo or SPVs using stablecoins (e.g., USDC), achieving real-time T+0 settlement;
- Fund managers can deploy received stablecoins directly into on-chain assets (e.g., DeFi pools or RWA-backed smart contracts);
- Investment records can be logged via smart contracts, facilitating audit trails and cross-border tax disclosure;
- Upon LP exit or project monetization, stablecoins allow efficient repatriation or fiat conversion.

For example, an Asia-based AI healthcare project brought in a U.S. family office as an LP. The LP invested $2 million via USDC, and a Cayman-based NewCo issued convertible tokenized debt in return. The received funds were partially deployed to train AI models, with the remainder used as RWA-collateralized assets for secondary financing. This structure balanced liquidity, auditability, and cross-border compliance, establishing a classic "Stablecoin + RWA + LP" model.

III. Regulatory Trends and Policy Evolution for Stablecoins

Despite their efficiency, the legal and regulatory framework for stablecoins remains in flux globally. Key policy trends include:

The U.S. Treasury and SEC now require stablecoin issuers to undergo compliance audits and adopt AML frameworks (e.g., MiCA in the EU);

The Hong Kong Monetary Authority is piloting "regulated stablecoins" tied to the Hong Kong dollar;

Singapore's MAS recognizes stablecoins as "digital settlement currencies", but requires full custodial audits and redemption mechanisms;

Mainland China does not permit issuance of stablecoins, but supports the use of e-CNY (digital RMB) in cross-border pilot programs.

Therefore, when designing a "Stablecoin + RWA" structure, issuers should prioritize highly regulated and transparent stablecoins (such as USDC) and assess their legal acceptability in the jurisdictions of target LPs. It is advisable to route capital through neutral NewCo jurisdictions (e.g., Cayman Islands or Abu Dhabi) and use multi-chain compliance solutions (e.g., Circle, Fireblocks) for cross-chain clearing and custody.

Conclusion

As an "LP connector" in the global capital chain, stablecoins not only solve long-standing issues in cross-border LP contributions—such as exchange delays, regulatory friction, and settlement lag—but also provide essential financial infrastructure for mid-market enterprises to access global LP capital. In the future, as regulatory standards converge and tokenized assets gain broader legitimacy, stablecoins will become even more central to the architecture of digital capital structuring.

Chapter 13: Comparing Digital Asset Regulatory Frameworks in US, EU, China, HK, Singapore and UAE

This chapter summarizes the global regulatory landscape for Bitcoin, digital currencies, stablecoins, and tokens (as of July 2025), across key jurisdictions including the U.S., EU, China, Hong Kong, Singapore, and UAE.

Global Legal Landscape Comparison: Bitcoin, Stablecoins, Tokens, CBDCs

Jurisdiction	**Bitcoin**	**Stablecoin**	**Token**	**CBDC**	**Regulatory Trend**
USA	Legal; treated as commodity (CFTC)	Under SEC/NYDFS supervision; strict rules	Security tokens under SEC; case-by-case enforcement	Fed developing digital dollar (FedNow)	Strong compliance, strict disclosure
EU	Legal under MiCA	MiCA applies, license required	MiCA classifies utility/security tokens	ECB digital euro pilot	Most systematic global framework (MiCA)
China	Prohibited for trade/mining, holding allowed	Treated as digital financial asset, cross-border restricted	Not open, sandbox trials	e-CNY fully deployed	Risk prevention focus
Hong Kong	Legal with SFC-licensed exchanges	2023 regulatory framework in progress (1:1 peg, license)	Security tokens under SFC pilot RWA programs	Evaluating e-HKD	Third path for virtual assets, innovation encouraged
Singapore	Legal with MAS license, AML focus	Allowed with license, disclosure on reserves	Tokenized bonds, equities, carbon credits	Project Ubin (wholesale CBDC)	Tech-friendly + prudent supervision

UAE	Legal under Dubai VARA regime	Allowed, dual federal and local regulation	Launched token securities market (ADGM)	CBDC cross-border pilot underway	Emerging digital asset hub of Middle East

Detailed Comparison Across 6 Regulatory Dimensions

Dimension	USA	EU	China	HK	Singapore	UAE
Asset Classification	Commodity / Security	MiCA categories	Illegal for trading	Security/Utility tokens	Utility token-based	Multi-class depending on regulator
Market Access	Requires SEC/CFTC approval	Licensing regime	Trading banned	SFC license + whitelist	MAS registration + AML	VARA + ADGM dual licenses
Stablecoin Reg.	SEC + NYDFS; Tether unregulated	Full reserve + disclosure	Restricted cross-border use	Drafting full regulatory system	High license bar, liquidity controls	Accepted but regulated
KYC/AML	Strict (FATF)	Banking-level	High scrutiny	Financial-grade KYC	Mandatory full compliance	FATF-compliant
Token Regulation	Securities must register	MiCA allows broad categories	Not yet legalized	STO pilot regime underway	Support for bond/carbon tokenization	Promotes digital securities, carbon tokens
CBDC Development	FedNow pilot + R&D	ECB-led pilot	e-CNY broadly implemented	Technical review ongoing	Exploring wholesale model	Cross-border CBDC platform in progress

Three Global Regulatory Trends

1. ESG + RWA tokenization in sandbox pilots (HK, SG, UAE)
2. Stablecoins shifting to compliance and full reserve disclosure (esp. US, EU, HK)
3. Token securities classified under securities law (SEC, SFC, MAS all require disclosure/audit)

Legal Structuring Workstreams

- Base Infrastructure: Cayman Fund + BVI SPV + Token Issuer Vehicle
- Legal Advisors: Ogier / Walkers (offshore); Akin Gump / Loeb & Loeb (U.S.)
- Compliance Considerations:
  - Token ≠ security vs. Token as digital securities under Reg D / Reg S
- Recommended Path:
  - RWA rights mapping + compliant token standard (e.g., ERC-3643)
  - Private placement to accredited investors only

Recommended Reading & Analysis

- Full text + analysis of EU MiCA Regulation
- HK SFC Virtual Asset Platform Guidelines (2023)
- SEC v. Ripple case and token classification implications
- MAS white paper on tokenized bonds and carbon credits
- UAE VARA regulatory framework handbook

Chapter 14: Feasibility of Stablecoins as RWA Pricing and Liquidity Intermediaries

As the tokenization of real-world assets (RWA) accelerates, the integration of stablecoins into digital financial infrastructure is emerging as a key driver of pricing efficiency and market liquidity. This chapter examines the feasibility of using stablecoins as valuation anchors and transaction intermediaries in the RWA ecosystem, focusing on regulatory trends, market applications, and technical infrastructure.

1. The Role of Stablecoins in the RWA Framework

Stablecoins are blockchain-based digital tokens pegged to fiat currencies such as USD, EUR, or HKD. With minimal volatility and interoperability across decentralized applications, stablecoins are increasingly used as value anchors in volatile crypto environments. In the context of RWA, stablecoins play two strategic roles:

Pricing references for RWA-backed tokens;

Liquidity mediums for transaction settlement, cross-border fund flows, and DeFi-integrated credit models.

When combined with the issuance of RWA tokens—such as tokenized invoices, fractionalized real estate shares, or future income rights—stablecoins enable real-time price discovery using a stable unit of account. This allows investors to evaluate asset value based on predictable returns rather than speculative demand. Additionally, stablecoins support automated settlement workflows, yield distribution, and on-chain valuation snapshots.

2. Market Adoption and Use Cases

Several protocols and platforms have adopted stablecoins in RWA implementations. Examples include:

Centrifuge, which uses DAI as a settlement asset for tokenized real-world invoices;

Maple Finance and Goldfinch, which use USDC in undercollateralized lending models for SMEs and fintech borrowers;

In hybrid DeFi-TradFi structures, stablecoins increasingly serve as bridges between off-chain yields and on-chain execution.

Real estate tokenization platforms like RealT (US) and Tangible (EU) price property tokens in USDC or EUR-backed stablecoins, supporting fractional ownership, rental income distribution, and instant buybacks. In tokenized trade finance, stablecoins serve as the common medium for LP contributions, interest accrual, and credit delegation—evidencing their growing maturity in real-world capital markets.

3. Regulatory and Infrastructure Considerations

Despite their utility, stablecoin adoption in RWA pricing and settlement must align with evolving regulatory frameworks:

The EU (under MiCA), Singapore, Hong Kong, and the UAE have released regulatory guidance emphasizing reserve transparency, auditability, and on-chain controls;

USDC and EUROC, issued by Circle, are commonly cited as compliant stablecoin models under these regimes.

From a technical perspective, stablecoin infrastructure—such as smart contracts, oracles, custodial protocols, and compliance middleware—must ensure price accuracy and redemption guarantees. Institutional-grade stablecoins are typically embedded in firewalled RWA platforms with KYC, AML, and reporting mechanisms, making them acceptable to LPs and regulated investors. Furthermore, Layer 2 integrations (e.g., Arbitrum, Optimism) provide low-cost, high-speed settlement rails for RWA transactions.

4. Limitations and Risk Factors

Despite their potential, stablecoins face several risks in RWA pricing applications:

Counterparty risk associated with centralized issuers (e.g., concerns about USDT reserves);

Regulatory fragmentation across jurisdictions;

Instability of algorithmic stablecoins in volatile markets (e.g., the TerraUST collapse);

Smart contract vulnerabilities in custodial systems.

Risk mitigation strategies include using regulated issuers, independent reserve attestation, insurance mechanisms, and redundant settlement protocols.

5. Strategic Implications for Capital Markets

If properly structured, stablecoins can lower barriers for institutional access to RWA markets, improving valuation transparency and capital efficiency. Benefits include:

Real-time NAV (Net Asset Value) calculations;

Interoperable investment instruments across platforms;

Seamless global onboarding of investors without reliance on traditional banks.

Their programmability also enables features like automated interest payments, tax withholding, and DAO-integrated governance.

Conclusion

Stablecoins are no longer just tools for crypto trading—they are evolving into core infrastructure for next-generation capital markets. As real-world assets become tokenized, stablecoins provide the unit of account, settlement medium, and liquidity rail needed to make RWAs investable, tradeable, and auditable.

Their feasibility as pricing and liquidity intermediaries depends not only on technological architecture, but also on integration into a compliant, transparent, and scalable financial system.

Chapter 15: Designing Stablecoin Structures for Corporate Financing (USD/HKD/Crypto)

As more corporations explore blockchain-based financing solutions, stablecoins have emerged as a key tool for structuring capital flows. Whether used in pre-IPO fundraising, cross-border equity issuance, or tokenized revenue-sharing agreements, stablecoins offer a programmable, borderless, and cost-efficient alternative to traditional banking rails. This article explores how to design stablecoin-enabled corporate financing structures across three categories: USD-pegged (e.g., USDC), HKD-pegged, and crypto-native stablecoins.

1. Strategic Rationale for Using Stablecoins in Corporate Financing

Stablecoins combine the price stability of fiat currencies with the programmability and global accessibility of crypto assets. For corporates, this translates into:

Faster capital settlement and lower intermediary costs;

Smoother onboarding of international investors without currency conversion delays;

Real-time fund tracking and auditing via on-chain transaction records;

Compatibility with DeFi tools for treasury management, liquidity deployment, and yield distribution.

2. USD-Pegged Stablecoin Structures (e.g., USDC)

USDC, backed by fiat reserves and regulated in the U.S., is the most widely adopted stablecoin for corporate use. In a typical USDC-based financing structure:

Investors contribute capital in USDC to a smart contract or Special Purpose Vehicle (SPV);

The issuing company receives USDC, which can be partially converted into fiat or directly deployed into on-chain treasury strategies;

Smart contracts automate interest disbursements, token issuance, and embed conversion rights.

Case Study:
A U.S.-based biotech firm raised $3 million in a pre-IPO round via USDC using a Cayman Islands NewCo. Smart contracts issued tokenized convertible notes with equity conversion rights and milestone-based payment triggers.

Advantages:

Regulatory clarity and transparency (USDC complies with U.S. frameworks);

KYC integration with platforms like Circle and Fireblocks;

Institutional-grade custody options.

3. Opportunities with HKD-Pegged Stablecoins

As Hong Kong establishes itself as a regulatory hub for digital assets, the development and application of HKD-pegged stablecoins are gaining traction. Banks and fintechs are currently exploring models to:

Facilitate HKD-denominated fundraising and remittances for Greater Bay Area enterprises;

Act as settlement tokens for tokenized securities on HKEX or private markets;

Boost liquidity in HKD-based DeFi ecosystems.

Design Tip:
Corporates may use Hong Kong-based SPVs and integrate with regulated custodial platforms to support cross-chain swaps and asset clearing between HKD and USD stablecoins.

4. Crypto-Native Stablecoin Structures (e.g., DAI, LUSD)

Crypto-native stablecoins like DAI (collateralized by on-chain crypto assets) offer decentralized alternatives ideal for Web3-native companies or DAO-governed projects. Applicable use cases include:

Token issuance or initial liquidity bootstrapping;

Smart contract-escrowed revenue-sharing arrangements;

DeFi-native treasury deployment strategies.

Challenges:
High collateral volatility and regulatory uncertainty. Best practices include multisig governance, over-collateralization, and robust risk control mechanisms.

5. Legal, Tax, and Governance Considerations

When designing a stablecoin-based financing structure, companies must address:

Jurisdictional compliance: e.g., pairing Cayman/BVI NewCos with onshore legal advisors;

Securities classification: ensure tokens fall under safe harbor exemptions or file under Reg D;

Tax impact: plan for capital gains, token distributions, and stablecoin redemption taxation;

Governance: embed voting or redemption rights into smart contract-enabled token designs.

Additional Advice:
Set up KYC/AML processes and provide investor dashboards for transparency and credibility.

6. Strategic Recommendations

Use fiat-backed stablecoins (e.g., USDC, EUROC) for highly regulated markets;

Leverage HKD-pegged stablecoins for Hong Kong–China cross-border initiatives;

Reserve crypto-native stablecoins for DeFi-native use cases with experienced LPs;

Regardless of structure, incorporate auditability, legal wrappers, and investor-facing portals.

Conclusion

Stablecoins are evolving from payment instruments into core components of modern corporate finance. With thoughtful structuring—using USDC, HKD stablecoins, or crypto-native assets—companies can raise capital more quickly, with lower costs and greater flexibility. Future financing models will likely blend stablecoins with traditional instruments, enabling enterprises to optimize capital structures across jurisdictions, currencies, and digital networks.

Chapter 16: How Digital Capital Enhances Valuation Liquidity for Enterprises

I. Introduction: Valuation Bottlenecks and Capital Dilemmas

Amid globalization and technological transformation, many mid-sized enterprises with strong technologies and products often face valuation bottlenecks and financing obstacles under traditional capital pathways. These challenges are especially evident in the following aspects:

Severe dilution and lengthy cycles in equity financing;

Poor liquidity in secondary markets, with unclear exit paths;

Difficulty for investors to accurately assess future income or intangible asset value;

High complexity and cost of cross-border financing and regulatory compliance.

This has given rise to a new solution—Digital Capital—which is increasingly becoming a bridge between corporate valuation, liquidity, and access to global capital.

II. Definition and Components of Digital Capital

Digital capital refers to the use of technical mechanisms (such as blockchain, smart contracts, and RWA authentication) to convert corporate equity, revenue rights, usage rights, intellectual property, and other entitlements into digitized, tradable, programmable, and verifiable asset units, thereby enhancing financing capability, asset liquidity, and valuation transparency.

Module	Description	Value Enhancement
RWA Authentication	Convert tangible assets and revenue rights into on-chain assets (e.g., Tokens)	Enhances asset transparency and audit efficiency
Token Design	Tokenize future income, IP licensing, or platform usage rights	Establishes liquidity channels for previously illiquid rights
Smart Contract Embedding	Automate dividend, licensing, and buyback mechanisms	Reduces governance and enforcement costs

Module	Description	Value Enhancement
On-Chain Audit & Disclosure	Provide investors real-time visibility into key indicators and valuation drivers	Strengthens trust and cross-border visibility

III. How Digital Capital Enhances Enterprise Valuation

Transparency + Verifiability = Stronger Valuation Anchors
By authenticating key data—such as clinical progress, R&D milestones, and partnership agreements—on-chain, companies enable investors to more confidently forecast future cash flows and assess risk, resulting in higher valuation multiples.

Securitization and Modularization of Value
Enterprises can unlock hidden value by structuring licenses, platform usage rights, or IP into independent digital rights units—thus shifting valuation from a single-dimensional revenue/profit model to a multi-asset framework.

Access to Global Investors and DeFi Capital Pools
Tokenized capital formats (such as digital securities or RWA bonds) can be listed on blockchain-based platforms and global digital exchanges, tapping into a broader base of liquidity and price discovery mechanisms beyond traditional VC/PE channels.

IV. How Digital Capital Improves Liquidity

Function Module	Traditional Capital Pathway	Digital Capital Pathway
Exit Mechanism	IPO or M&A, typically 3–5 years	Secondary transfers via digital platforms for early liquidity
Investor Structure	Primarily regional VC/PE	Global investors including Web3 funds and on-chain family offices
Trading Instruments	Equity transfer or subscription agreements	Digital tokens and programmable asset certificates
Funding Rhythm	Round-based fundraising with potential gaps	Continuous financing enabled by "issuance + trading" structures

V. Conclusion: Digital Capital as the Key to Overcoming Capital Barriers

Digital capital is more than just a technological tool—it is a capital philosophy. It redefines valuation logic from being purely profit-based to being driven by future potential, uniqueness, and structural creativity. In the era of Web3 and global digital assets, those who master the language and architecture of digital capital early will lead in the international capital markets.

Legal Document Templates for Digital Capital Offerings

Lite White Paper Template (For Reg D Investors)

1. Executive Summary

This Lite White Paper provides a concise and legally compliant overview of the token offering, designed specifically for accredited investors under Regulation D of the U.S. Securities Act. It summarizes the project's mission, token economics, and investor rights without constituting a public offering.

2. Project Overview

- Project Name: [Insert Project Name]
- Legal Entity: [Insert Cayman or Delaware SPV]
- Business Focus: [e.g., Healthcare AI Platform / Decentralized Data Marketplace]
- Target Market: [e.g., U.S. institutional investors, global qualified LPs]
- Core Objectives: [Summarize the mission and technology focus]

3. Token Description and Economics

- Token Name: [Insert Token Name]
- Total Supply: [e.g., 1,000,000,000 Tokens]
- Token Type: [e.g., Utility / Governance / RWA-backed Token]
- Use of Token: [e.g., staking, voting, access rights, dividend rights]
- Vesting & Lock-up: [e.g., 12-month lock-up + 24-month linear release]
- Distribution: [Breakdown by team, investors, ecosystem, treasury, etc.]

4. Use of Proceeds

- R&D and Technology Development: [xx%]
- Market Expansion: [xx%]
- Legal & Compliance: [xx%]
- Team & Operations: [xx%]
- Treasury & Reserves: [xx%]

5. Legal and Regulatory Disclaimers

- This offering is made pursuant to Regulation D, Rule 506(c), of the U.S. Securities Act.
- Tokens are not registered with the SEC and are only offered to accredited investors.
- No secondary resale is permitted for U.S. persons within the restricted period.
- This document is for informational purposes only and does not constitute an offer to the public.

6. Risk Factors

• Regulatory Risk: Future changes in laws may affect token legality.
• Market Risk: Token price may be volatile.
• Technology Risk: Smart contract vulnerabilities or platform failure.
• Liquidity Risk: No guarantee of resale or secondary market.
• Governance Risk: Decisions may be subject to DAO or committee voting.

7. Contact & Additional Documents

• Contact: [Insert Email / Legal Entity Address]
• Additional documents available upon request:
  - Token Offering Memorandum
  - Subscription Agreement
  - Accredited Investor Certificate
  - Exit Rights Memorandum

Token Offering Memorandum

Token Offering Memorandum Template

1. Legal Notice and Offering Restrictions

This Token Offering Memorandum (the "Memorandum") is confidential and intended solely for accredited investors under Regulation D of the U.S. Securities Act of 1933, as amended. This offering is not registered with the SEC. The Tokens offered are speculative and involve a high degree of risk.

2. Project Summary

• Issuer: [Insert Issuer Name & Legal Entity Structure]
• Token Name: [Insert Token Name]
• Sector Focus: [e.g., AI-Powered Healthcare / Decentralized Finance / RWA Tokenization]
• Jurisdiction: [e.g., Cayman Islands / BVI / Delaware]

3. Token Economics and Allocation

• Total Supply: [e.g., 1,000,000,000 Tokens]
• Initial Offering Price: [e.g., $0.10/token]
• Allocation:
 - Private Placement Investors: xx%
 - Team and Advisors: xx%
 - Treasury/Reserves: xx%
 - Community Incentives: xx%
• Vesting Schedules:
 - Founders: [e.g., 12-month cliff, 36-month linear vesting]
 - Investors: [e.g., 6-month lock-up, 12-month vesting]

4. Valuation Methodology

The token valuation has been derived based on the following methodologies:
• Comparable Protocol Analysis (CPA): Benchmarked against similar projects with known tokenomics and market cap.
• Discounted Cash Flow (DCF): If applicable, projected cash flows discounted at [insert rate]%.
• NAV-Based Model: For asset-backed tokens, value is calculated as Net Asset Value of underlying assets / token supply.
• Sensitivity Analysis: Token price under multiple scenarios provided in Annex I.

5. Use of Proceeds

• Product Development: xx%
• Market Expansion: xx%
• Legal and Compliance: xx%

- Operations and Staffing: xx%
- Treasury Reserve: xx%

6. Liquidity and Transfer Restrictions

- Reg D Lock-up Period: 12 months from date of issuance
- Secondary Market: Tokens may only be traded on registered alternative trading systems (ATS) or whitelisted venues.
- Transfer: Permitted only among KYC/AML-approved wallets on the issuer-maintained whitelist.
- Optional Buyback Mechanism: Issuer may establish periodic buyback windows subject to board approval.

7. Governance and Investor Rights

- Voting Rights: [e.g., token-weighted voting on protocol proposals or limited governance]
- Reporting Obligations: Issuer to publish semi-annual financial reports and annual token economics updates.
- Exit Rights: Details described in the Token Exit Rights Memorandum.

8. Risk Disclosures

- Regulatory Uncertainty
- Market Volatility
- Smart Contract Vulnerabilities
- Illiquidity Risks
- Legal Classification Risks

9. Annexes

Annex I – Token Valuation Model and Assumptions
Annex II – Legal Entity Structure and Cap Table
Annex III – Technical Architecture of Token System
Annex IV – KYC/AML and Investor Qualification Procedures

Token Subscription Agreement

This Token Subscription Agreement (the "Agreement") is entered into as of [Date], by and between:

Issuer: [Issuer Name], a [Jurisdiction] company with its principal place of business at [Address] ("Company"); and

Subscriber: [Investor Name], a qualified accredited investor ("Subscriber").

1. Subscription The Subscriber hereby subscribes for [Number] of [Token Name] tokens ("Tokens") at a purchase price of $[Price] per Token for a total purchase amount of $[Total Amount] (the "Purchase Amount").

2. Payment The Subscriber agrees to remit the Purchase Amount to the Company's designated wallet or bank account pursuant to wire instructions provided separately.

3. Representations and Warranties of the Subscriber The Subscriber represents and warrants that: (a) They are an "accredited investor" as defined under Regulation D of the U.S. Securities Act; (b) They are acquiring the Tokens for their own account and not with a view to resale; (c) They have received and reviewed the Token Offering Memorandum and related documents; (d) They understand the Tokens are subject to restrictions on resale.

4. Lock-Up and Transfer Restrictions The Subscriber agrees not to sell, transfer, or otherwise dispose of any Tokens for a period of twelve (12) months from the date of issuance, except as permitted under Regulation D or applicable exemptions.

5. Tax Responsibility The Subscriber shall be solely responsible for any taxes arising from the purchase, ownership, or disposition of the Tokens.

6. Governing Law This Agreement shall be governed by and construed in accordance with the laws of the State of [Delaware/New York/Cayman Islands], without regard to its conflict of law principles.

7. Miscellaneous (a) This Agreement constitutes the entire agreement between the parties. (b) Any notices shall be delivered via electronic mail or registered mail. (c) This Agreement may be executed in counterparts and delivered electronically.

IN WITNESS WHEREOF, the parties have executed this Token Subscription Agreement as of the date first written above.

[Issuer Name] By: ______________________
Name:
Title:

[Subscriber Name] By: ______________________
Name:
Title:

Annex A – Wallet Address of Subscriber
[Insert Wallet Address Here]

Annex B – Accredited Investor Certificate
[To be submitted separately or appended]

Accredited Investor Certificate

This Accredited Investor Certificate (the "Certificate") is executed and delivered by the undersigned (the "Investor") in connection with the proposed purchase of digital tokens (the "Tokens") offered by [Issuer Name] (the "Issuer") pursuant to Regulation D of the U.S. Securities Act of 1933, as amended (the "Securities Act").

1. Investor Information

Full Name: ________________________

Address: ________________________

Phone: ________________________

Email: ________________________

Country of Residence: ________________________

2. Accredited Investor Status The undersigned certifies that he/she/it qualifies as an "Accredited Investor" under one or more of the following criteria:

☐ (a) An individual with income exceeding $200,000 (or $300,000 jointly with spouse) in each of the past two years and a reasonable expectation of the same income in the current year.

☐ (b) An individual with a net worth over $1,000,000 (excluding primary residence).

☐ (c) A trust with assets in excess of $5,000,000, not formed to acquire the Tokens, and directed by a sophisticated person.

☐ (d) An entity where all equity owners are accredited investors.

☐ (e) A corporation, partnership, LLC, or similar entity with total assets exceeding $5,000,000.

3. Supporting Documentation The Investor agrees to provide supporting documentation to verify accredited status, which may include:

Tax returns or W-2 forms

Bank or brokerage statements

Third-party verification letter (CPA, attorney, investment advisor)

4. Acknowledgements The Investor acknowledges and agrees that: (a) The Tokens are not registered with the SEC; (b) The Tokens may be subject to resale restrictions; (c) The

investment is speculative and involves risk; (d) The Issuer relies on this Certificate for compliance with securities laws.

5. Signature and Confirmation I hereby certify that the above information is true and correct and that I qualify as an Accredited Investor under applicable law.

Signature: ____________________
Name: ______________________
Date: ______________________

Optional – Notary or Third-Party Confirmation
(To be completed by CPA, attorney, or registered investment advisor if applicable)

I, the undersigned, confirm that I have taken reasonable steps to verify that the above-named individual/entity qualifies as an Accredited Investor under Regulation D.

Signature: ____________________
Name: ______________________
Title: ______________________
Firm: ______________________
Date: ______________________

Token Exit Rights Memorandum

This Token Exit Rights Memorandum (the "Memorandum") outlines the rights and mechanisms by which holders of [Token Name] tokens (the "Tokens") issued by [Issuer Name] (the "Issuer") may exit or monetize their positions, subject to applicable legal and regulatory limitations.

1. Buyback Rights The Issuer may, at its discretion or based on board approval, initiate token buybacks under the following terms:

Buyback Price: Determined based on NAV or a fixed formula [insert details]

Frequency: [e.g., Quarterly / Semi-annually]

Eligibility: Token holders must have completed KYC/AML and comply with lock-up restrictions

Buyback Limits: Subject to [e.g., 5% of circulating supply per period]

2. Unlocking and Vesting Tokens distributed to investors shall follow a predefined unlocking schedule:

Lock-up Period: [e.g., 6 or 12 months from issuance]

Vesting Terms: [e.g., Linear release over 24 months]

Acceleration: In case of M&A, IPO, or strategic liquidity event, tokens may be fully or partially accelerated

3. Equity Conversion Option (Swap Rights) Subject to approval and conditions:

Tokens may be convertible into equity in [Issuer or affiliated entity] at a predefined ratio

Conversion Triggers: [e.g., Qualified Financing, IPO, M&A]

Valuation Benchmark: Based on last priced round or fair market value approved by board

Documentation: Subscription Agreement and Equity Certificate to be executed upon conversion

4. Secondary Market Transfers

Tokens may be transferred via authorized venues/platforms post lock-up

All transfers must involve whitelisted wallets with completed compliance review

Issuer reserves the right to deny transfers that breach jurisdictional or regulatory rules

5. Termination of Exit Rights Exit rights may lapse if:

Tokens are held by an ineligible party (non-KYC/AML)

Fraud, misuse, or breach of Subscription Agreement occurs

Token project is dissolved or rendered non-operational (subject to notice)

6. Legal Disclaimers

Nothing in this Memorandum shall constitute a guarantee of liquidity

All mechanisms are subject to change with board and investor approval

This Memorandum should be read in conjunction with the Token Offering Memorandum and Subscription Agreement

Issued by: [Issuer Name]
Effective Date: [Insert Date]
Contact: [Insert Email or Legal Counsel Info]

Part IV: Tri-Market Listing & STO Strategies

Combines SPAC, U.S. IPO, HKEX listing, and STOs into an integrated strategy. Explores differing valuation models and arbitrage mechanisms across markets, offering a hybrid pathway that bridges traditional and decentralized finance for valuation uplift and diversified exits.

Chapter 17: Dual Listings: NASDAQ (SPAC/RTO), HKEX (18A)

I. U.S. Main Board Listing Process (Nasdaq / NYSE via IPO)

Regulatory Framework: SEC + SOX Compliance

Timeframe	Key Step	Description
T-12 mo	Strategic Planning & Advisor Engagement	Hire investment bank, U.S. counsel, Big Four auditor, IR, and CoSec; set up Cayman/VIE structure
T-10 mo	Financial Audit & Internal Control Setup	Complete 2–3 years of US GAAP audit; establish SOX 404 controls; form audit and ESG committees
T-6 mo	File Form S-1 / F-1	Submit IPO registration statement to SEC (S-1 for U.S. firms, F-1 for foreign issuers)
T-5 mo	SEC Comment Letter Rounds	Expect multiple rounds of comments; legal and audit teams assist in responses
T-3 mo	Test the Waters	Non-deal roadshow with institutional investors to gauge market appetite
T-2 mo	Roadshow & Pricing	Bookbuilding and price discovery via public roadshow
T	IPO Listing	Official listing on Nasdaq or NYSE; post-listing filings begin (10-K, 10-Q, 8-K)

Additional Compliance Notes (U.S.):

- Accounting Standard: US GAAP + PCAOB registered auditor
- SOX Internal Control: SOX 404 opinions required from management & external auditor
- Corporate Governance: Independent directors, audit/compensation/nomination committees required
- Form Types:
    - S-1: U.S. companies' IPO

- F-1: Foreign private issuers (e.g., Cayman structure)
- 20-F / 6-K: Annual/interim post-listing reports

Exchange Comparison (Nasdaq vs. NYSE)

Item	Nasdaq	NYSE
Min Market Cap	$50M (Market Value Standard)	$100M (IPO Standard)
Financial Criteria	Net profit / Cash flow / Revenue options	Similar multiple financial tests
Disclosure	10-K, 10-Q, 8-K compliance	Same

U.S. Listing Cost Reference:

- Underwriting Fee: 5%–7% of gross proceeds
- Legal + Audit + Filing Costs: $2M–$5M
- Ongoing IR / PR / Reporting: $500K+ annually

II. Hong Kong Main Board Listing Process (HKEX)

Regulatory Framework: Hong Kong Listing Rules

Timeframe	Key Step	Description
T-12 mo	Strategic Planning & Advisor Appointment	Select sponsor, auditor, lawyers, valuer, PR team; confirm listing path (Red-chip/H-share/full circulation)
T-10 mo	Financial & Internal Control Preparation	Complete 3 years of HKFRS/IFRS financials; strengthen ESG and governance framework
T-8 mo	Initial Due Diligence	Legal, financial, commercial, ESG due diligence; prep application materials
T-6 mo	Submit A1 Form to HKEX	File Form A1 + Application Proof (draft prospectus)
T-5 mo	HKEX RFI & Response	Respond to HKEX inquiries (1–3 months on avg)

T-3 mo	Listing Hearing	Approval by Listing Committee; issuance of PHIP (Post-Hearing Information Pack)
T-2 mo	Roadshow & Pricing	Investor engagement and bookbuilding
T	Official Listing	Shares begin trading on Main Board

Additional Compliance Notes (HK):

- Main Board Profit Test:
    - Most recent year profit ⩾ HKD 50M and prior two years combined ⩾ HKD 30M; or
    - Market Cap Test: ⩾ HKD 5B + revenue ⩾ HKD 500M; or
    - Biotech/Innovative Tech: Chapter 18A/18C exemptions apply
- Financials: 3 years of audited financials under HKFRS/IFRS
- Auditor: Must be HKEX-recognized accounting firm

Sponsor Regime:

- Sponsor signs off on A1 Form and conducts full DD
- Sponsorship period covers pre-listing to 6 months post-listing

HK Listing Cost Reference:

- Sponsor + Legal + Audit: HKD 20M–35M
- Exchange + SFC Fees: HKD 1M–5M (based on valuation)
- Total Cost Estimate: ~6%–10% of funds raised

NASDAQ IPO Compliance Checklist

Compliance Items	Timeline	Responsible Party
Establish Cayman Entity	T-18 Months	Company Legal Counsel
3-Year US GAAP Audit	T-12 Months	Big Four Audit Firm
Pre-IPO PIPE Financing Completed	T-6 Months	Investment Bank / FA

Form F-1 or S-1 Filing	T-5 Months	US Counsel + Underwriters
SEC Comment Letter Exchange	T-4 to T-2 Months	Company + Auditor + Legal Team
Roadshow	T-1 Month	Investment Bank / IR Team
IPO and Listing	T=0	SEC + NASDAQ

Comparison of U.S. and Hong Kong Capital Markets: Key Highlights

Category	Hong Kong Listing	U.S. Listing
Accounting Standards	HKFRS / IFRS	US GAAP (PCAOB-audited)
Disclosure Language	Chinese + English	English only
ESG Compliance	Early stage, gradually improving	Mature framework (SEC + ESG metrics)
Investor Base	Institutions + Retail (HK-based investors dominate)	Institutionally driven, with active tech-focused PE funds
Financing Instruments	IPO, Private Placement, Strategic Placement	IPO, PIPE, SPAC, Convertible Bonds
Valuation Logic	Profit-oriented, prefers PE multiples	Tech and growth-oriented, DCF model commonly used
Exit Mechanism	Long lock-up, inflexible board transfer mechanism	M&A, liquid secondary market, multiple exit options

Recommended Route – NASDAQ First, HKEX Spinoff Later

Strategic Recommendation:

Prioritize NASDAQ first, then pursue Hong Kong spinoff — a "top-down advantage" strategy.

Stage-by-Stage Roadmap

Stage	Strategic Action	Objective
T+0 ~ 24 months	Merge into **ETAO's NASDAQ-listed platform**	- Avoid high IPO thresholds via independent listing
• Raise funds via ETAO's existing listing status		
• Quickly re-rate valuation and gain global exposure		
T+24 ~ 36 months	Spin off into a **NewCo** entity	- Establish standalone valuation unit
• Prepare for HK IPO with greater pricing flexibility		
T+36 ~ 48 months	Go public on **HKEX Main Board or 18A** as a "mature subsidiary"	- Leverage top-down advantage in Hong Kong market
• Achieve dual liquidity and cross-border capital arbitrage		

Why is NASDAQ First, HKEX Later a Superior Strategy?

Top-down advantage = Entering a lower-dimensional market from a higher-standard market

- **Stricter Regulation → Global Trust Anchor**
  Achieving SEC compliance builds international credibility, which elevates perception and valuation in the HK market.
- **Support for Global BD**
  A NASDAQ identity facilitates licensing and co-commercialization discussions with Top 20 pharmas like Pfizer and BMS.
- **Capital Structure Flexibility**
  NASDAQ supports PIPE, RWA, SPAC, and digital token-based capital structures—tools that are **restricted** in HKEX.
- **Mature Spinoff Mechanisms**
  NASDAQ allows internal reorganization and spinoffs, giving a **clear path** to future HK listings.
- **Reduced Trial-and-Error Cost**
  Initial development within the ETAO ecosystem reduces **compliance, financial, and regulatory burdens** of early independent IPO attempts.

Recommended Path (Inspired by WuXi AppTec's "Dual-Capital Platform Strategy")

Stage 1: Merge into ETAO's NASDAQ Listing Platform

Integrate with ETAO to gain quick access to the U.S. capital market, utilize existing listing credentials to raise USD capital, achieve international compliance, and anchor global valuation.

Stage 2: Execute PIPE Financing & Global Branding

Complete PIPE financing, license-out deals, and strategic partnerships on the NASDAQ platform. Enhance AI capabilities, BD engagement, and build global investor confidence.

Stage 3: Build NewCo for Valuation Uplift & Business Focus

Within 2 years, carve out key pipelines/assets into a focused NewCo structure backed by ETAO's M&A and capital capabilities. Establish standalone valuation, confirm AI data ownership, and implement an RWA (real-world asset) structure.

Stage 4: Return to HKEX Main Board or Mainland A-Share Market

As an "internationally validated mature subsidiary," list independently on HKEX Main Board (or A-share market), forming a **dual-platform capital structure** akin to WuXi AppTec—blending **global pricing power with local liquidity.**

Strategic Logic Summary

"Start with global regulatory rigor and capital innovation; follow with a top-down approach to domestic markets."

This forms the most scalable and globally penetrative growth strategy for China's mid-sized innovative enterprises.

Chapter 18: STO + RWA: A New Multiplier for Valuation Uplift

As the tokenization of real-world assets (RWA) gains traction across capital markets, a new financing model is emerging at the intersection of decentralized fundraising and asset-backed security:Security Token Coin Offerings (STO) powered by RWA structures. Unlike early-stage STOs that relied solely on whitepapers and speculative utility tokens, the next generation of STOs is increasingly tied to verifiable off-chain assets, including intellectual property, data rights, licensing agreements, and future revenue. This fusion creates a more credible, asset-anchored token model that can serve as a valuation multiplier for startups and mid-market companies.

1. Redefining STOs Through Asset-Backed Logic

Traditional STOs were largely speculative and often decoupled from real-world business operations. The introduction of RWA-backed STOs brings enhanced credibility and valuation anchoring by tying token issuance to measurable assets or income streams. This approach mirrors asset-backed securities (ABS) but operates on-chain, with programmable features and cross-border investor access.

For example, a biotech company can issue tokens representing future royalty income or licensing fees. Token holders benefit from revenue participation while the issuer accesses working capital without equity dilution.

2. Structuring STOs with RWA Components

An effective STO + RWA structure involves several core elements:
- Underlying Assets: These may include future licensing revenue, clinical data rights, AI algorithms, or equipment leases;
- Legal Vehicle: Typically a Cayman or BVI NewCo that owns the RWA and interfaces with token holders;
- Smart Contracts: Code that governs token issuance, revenue-sharing, redemption, or conversion rights;
- Compliance Layer: Mechanisms for KYC, AML, and regulatory disclosure (e.g., Reg D / Reg S exemptions).

This hybrid structure bridges the strengths of DeFi (liquidity, decentralization, composability) and TradFi (valuation clarity, compliance, credibility), offering a more scalable path to early-stage funding, especially for mid-sized firms with valuable but illiquid assets.

3. Benefits of STO + RWA Models

- Enhanced Valuation Anchoring: Tokens backed by future cash flows or IP provide a tangible foundation for investor valuation;
- Global Fundraising Reach: Access to a broader base of retail and institutional crypto investors without geographic limitations;
- Improved Liquidity: Token listings on compliant exchanges or DeFi platforms allow for secondary trading and price discovery;

- Programmable Distribution: Revenue-sharing, staking, or milestone rewards can be automated through smart contracts.

Case Study: A deep tech firm developing AI medical diagnostics structured an STO based on tokenized data licensing rights. Investors purchased RWA-backed tokens representing a share in future data license revenue. Proceeds were used for R&D and regulatory trials. The STO reached $10M from global participants, and the tokens were later integrated into a DeFi staking model offering yield.

This approach led to:
- 3x higher valuation than traditional pre-IPO rounds;
- Early liquidity for token holders;
- Greater international investor engagement.

4. Key Challenges and Risk Mitigation

Despite its potential, STO + RWA structures face several challenges:
- Regulatory Arbitrage: Jurisdictional inconsistencies may raise questions around token classification and investor protection;
- Asset Valuation Complexity: RWA like future IP income or milestone payments may be hard to model reliably;
- Exchange Listing Risk: Secondary market integration depends on compliance and liquidity partners.

Mitigation strategies include:
- Choosing compliant jurisdictions (e.g., Cayman, Abu Dhabi);
- Embedding third-party valuation and audit layers;
- Structuring optionality into tokens (e.g., buyback, convertibility, governance rights).

5. Strategic Fit for Mid-Market Enterprises

For mid-sized innovation-driven firms—especially in biotech, AI, and clean tech—STO + RWA models offer a way to monetize intangible assets while preserving equity cap tables. These firms often face long R&D cycles, limited banking support, and valuation compression in local markets. An RWA-backed STO enables them to:
- Access capital without equity dilution;
- Tap into decentralized liquidity pools;
- Build communities of early adopters, data providers, and token advocates.

Conclusion

STO + RWA represents a next-generation financing paradigm that merges real asset validation with the flexibility of tokenized capital formation. By bridging Web3 tools with traditional asset securitization models, it provides a compelling multiplier effect for valuation uplift, investor access, and business scalability. As regulation matures and token standards evolve, this model is poised to become a cornerstone of future corporate finance strategies.

Chapter 19 : Valuation Model Differences and Arbitrage Mechanisms Across Three Markets

Comparative Analysis: U.S. (NASDAQ) vs. Hong Kong (HKEX Main Board/18A)

In the global capital market layout, **NASDAQ (U.S.)** and **HKEX (Hong Kong)** represent two distinct paradigms in terms of valuation logic, regulatory systems, and investor structures. For technology or biotech companies seeking globalization, understanding these **structural differences** and designing arbitrage pathways accordingly is crucial to achieving valuation breakthroughs and capital liquidity.

I. Comparative Valuation Logic of Three Markets (U.S., Hong Kong, Middle East)

Dimension	U.S. (NASDAQ)	Hong Kong (HKEX Main Board/18A)	Middle East (Tadawul/ADX)
Valuation Level	High, driven by global tech and growth-oriented logic (e.g., OpenAI, Moderna)	Relatively conservative, focused on profitability and traditional financial metrics; biotech often discounted	Early-stage valuations can be high, often driven by government strategy and national funds
Pricing Logic	DCF and forward-looking growth; supports pre-revenue tech firms	Cash flow and EBITDA-based; financial multiples are dominant	Focus on local industry alignment and strategic partnerships
Investor Base	Global tech/AI/biotech funds, hedge funds, sovereign wealth funds	Mix of local institutions and retail investors, with fluctuating activity	Government funds and family offices dominate; international capital is growing
Valuation Leverage	AI, SaaS, Cloud, BioAI themes yield high multiples	Healthcare and hard-tech firms often trade at 20–40% discount	Less mature pricing models, but strategic and policy-driven premiums are common

II. Arbitrage Pathways and Structural Design Strategy

Firms can build arbitrage channels through **"Tri-market Strategy + Multi-layered Structures"**:

1. **Anchor High Valuation via U.S. Listing (SPAC or RTO)**
   - Use U.S. listing to establish global brand and valuation benchmark;
   - Secure core institutional investors pre-listing via PIPE deals;
   - Build international-level compliance, audit, and governance systems to boost investor confidence.
2. **Unlock Liquidity via Hong Kong or Middle East Secondary Listings**
   - List a subsidiary or platform NewCo in HKEX 18A to unlock secondary liquidity;
   - Alternatively, pursue strategic placement via Tadawul with government fund support;
   - Simultaneously design license-out and BD models to convert brand power into revenue.
3. **Recommended Structure Design**
   - Set up BVI/Cayman-based NewCo for asset reorganization and IP licensing;
   - Adopt RWA and tokenization structures to bridge digital liquidity in offshore markets;
   - Utilize Convertible Notes, SAFE, and SPVs to accommodate diverse investor preferences.

III. U.S. vs. Hong Kong Capital Pathway: Detailed Comparative Table

Dimension	U.S. (NASDAQ) Path	Hong Kong (HKEX Main Board/18A) Path
Valuation Level	Higher: global logic, tech + growth premium	Moderate: profit and financial metric-driven; tech often discounted
Financing Capability	PIPE, Reg D, and public offerings are flexible; ample USD capital	Unstable financing windows; lower trading activity
Investor Base	Global funds (many specialized in AI, biotech, etc.)	More localized, retail + institutional mix
Tech/AI Friendliness	High: ChatGPT, BioAI, SaaS get premium valuations	Low: HK lacks mature tech valuation system
Regulatory Standards	Strict: SOX compliance, SEC disclosure, high audit standards	More flexible, but easier to be marginalized
IPO Threshold	High: revenue, governance, compliance all strictly enforced	Lower threshold, especially with 18A biotech exemption
Policy Environment	Supportive of China ADR return + SPAC M&A policies continue	Limited by HKEX review speed and conservative pricing for innovation
Capital Structure Innovation	Diverse: PIPE, Convertible Note, SPAC, RWA, etc.	Traditional structures dominate, limited innovation space
Brand Globalization	Strong: supports global BD and license-out credibility	Limited impact; mostly recognized in Asia-Pacific

Chapter 20: Recommended Pathway - SPAC + HK Spinoff + STO Hybrid Strategy

In today's increasingly competitive global capital markets and rapidly evolving regulatory landscape, designing a capital strategy that simultaneously enhances valuation, improves liquidity, and ensures regulatory feasibility has become a core challenge for entrepreneurs and financial advisors. This article proposes a multi-layered, integrated capital pathway—SPAC listing + Hong Kong spin-off + STO token financing—tailored specifically for technology-driven companies, particularly those in the healthcare, artificial intelligence, and clean energy sectors. This model is replicable, executable, and globally attractive for mid-sized enterprises.

1. Step One: Anchor Valuation through a SPAC on Nasdaq

SPACs (Special Purpose Acquisition Companies) have become a critical route for mid-market companies to access the U.S. capital markets. Key advantages include:

Faster listing process with controllable timelines;

Negotiated valuation, avoiding IPO price uncertainty;

Combined with PIPE financing to secure anchor investors pre-listing;

Strong fundraising capabilities to support future integration and expansion.

For companies with revenue models, initial international traction, or robust R&D pipelines, merging with a SPAC and listing on Nasdaq can not only anchor a DCF-based tech-oriented valuation, but also establish strong market credibility for subsequent capital operations.

2. Step Two: Spin Off Business or Assets in Hong Kong

After completing the SPAC listing, companies can spin off business units with independent revenue streams or regional strategic value for listing on the Hong Kong Stock Exchange.

Benefits of the HK spin-off include:

Access to dedicated fundraising and valuation via Chapter 18A or Main Board listings;

Strengthened local recognition and relationships with Hong Kong regulators and institutions;

Cash flow and asset realization for the parent company;

Enhanced regional synergy across Greater Bay Area and Southeast Asia.

Recommended structure: Use a Cayman parent company, set up an SPV in Hong Kong to manage the spin-off entity, and collaborate with a licensed sponsor and audit team to pursue a compliant fast-track listing.

3. Step Three: Unlock Tokenized Liquidity and Community Value via STO

After building institutional capital exposure in the U.S. and Hong Kong markets, companies can further leverage Security Token Coin Offerings (STO) to unlock digital asset liquidity and cultivate community participation.

Suggested STO structuring principles:

Tokens should be backed by future income rights—e.g., AI model service fees, diagnostic platform revenue, or carbon credits;

Apply RWA tokenization structures for valuation and rights certification, referencing DeFi or CeFi frameworks;

Design smart contract models supporting staking, governance, and redemption;

Issue tokens in compliant jurisdictions such as Abu Dhabi, Cayman Islands, or Hong Kong regulatory sandboxes.

Key benefits include:

Opens access to alternative capital sources such as Web3 communities, crypto funds, and overseas retail investors;

Amplifies valuation by turning on-chain data into financial assets;

Enhances user engagement and global brand recognition;

Lays the foundation for long-term token economics and platform-based business models.

4. Integrated Structure and Capital Execution Timeline

SPAC → HK Spin-off → STO is not a purely sequential process, but rather a "nested and phased" deployment to maximize synergy.

Suggested timeline:

T0–T6 months: Complete SPAC merger; announce PIPE financing and strategic roadmap;

T6–T18 months: Initiate HK spin-off process, supported by industry partnerships to secure valuation milestones;

T12+ months: Launch STO whitepaper and RWA token model construction;

Post-T18 months: List tokens, activate staking mechanisms, and introduce DAO-based community governance.

The integrated strategy delivers:

Multi-valuation model synergy (DCF + PE + Token);

Multi-currency capital orchestration (USD + HKD + stablecoins);

Multi-channel investor engagement (institutions + retail + communities);

Multi-exit flexibility (M&A, buybacks, platform-based liquidity).

Conclusion

The SPAC + HK Spin-Off + STO model is more than just a sum of its fundraising parts—it represents a breakthrough in capital structuring logic. It enables companies to anchor and amplify valuation, integrate centralized and decentralized capital markets, and balance transactional efficiency with long-term governance.

For mid-market companies with core technologies and global ambitions, this is a capital pathway that is executable, iterative, and scalable—an ideal roadmap for next-stage growth in the era of digital finance.

Part V: Corporate Structuring for Value Uplift

Explains how the synergy between OpCo and NewCo enables asset unbundling, revaluation, legacy shareholder exits, and Pre-IPO structuring. Enhances governance, risk control, and transparency through flexible corporate architecture.

Chapter 21: NewCo Equity Transfer and Valuation Process Table

NewCo Equity Transfer and Valuation Process Table

1. Target Asset Valuation (30 days)
2. Legacy Equity Rights Transfer into NewCo (MOU Signed)
3. Valuation Report via FA (15 days)
4. PIPE/Buyer Due Diligence (30–45 days)
5. Equity Transfer Agreement Signed + Capital Transfer (10 days)
6. Valuation Reference: DCF / Comparables / BD Transactions

What is NewCo?

NewCo stands for **New Company** — a newly formed legal entity used for a specific strategic, financial, or operational purpose. In international capital operations and biotech transactions, NewCo is often a **special-purpose vehicle (SPV)** used to:

Typical Functions of NewCo:

1. **Asset Packaging**
   Transfer of intellectual property, pipeline assets, licenses, or specific regional rights (e.g., "global rights excluding China") into a clean, auditable structure.
2. **Cross-Border Fundraising**
   NewCo is often incorporated in jurisdictions like **Cayman**, **BVI**, or **Delaware**, making it eligible for PIPE financing, private equity, or tokenization (RWA structure).
3. **License-out or Joint Venture Platform**
   Used as the contractual counterparty for out-licensing transactions with Big Pharma or setting up joint ventures for co-development.
4. **M&A Exit Readiness**
   Enables clean, fast exits through share sales of NewCo without entangling legacy assets or domestic regulatory hurdles.
5. **Governance Separation**
   Allows global partners and investors to hold equity in a foreign-facing unit without affecting the cap table of the original Chinese or domestic entity.

What is BD (Business Development)?

In biotech and medtech, **BD** refers to all activities related to **external growth**, including partnerships, licensing, co-development, acquisitions, and global expansion. It is distinct from organic R&D.

Common BD Activities:

1. **License-Out**
   Out-licensing clinical-stage or marketed products to a global or regional partner (e.g., Pfizer, BMS, or Merck) for non-China rights. Includes upfront payments, milestones, and royalties.
2. **Co-Development Alliances**
   Partnering with overseas biotech or CROs to jointly develop a product, often sharing costs and rights.
3. **Cross-Border M&A / JV**
   Acquiring, merging, or forming a JV with international companies to access IP, pipelines, markets, or regulatory paths.
4. **BD-Driven Valuation Anchoring**
   In many Hong Kong- or U.S.-listed companies, BD transactions serve as **valuation anchors** — creating objective market pricing ahead of PIPE or IPO rounds.

How NewCo and BD Work Together Strategically:

Strategic Objective	**Operational Path**	**Case Reference**
Global License-Out	Inject product rights into NewCo and promote international BD transactions	RemeGen, BeiGene
Cross-border Financing + Valuation Anchor	Use NewCo as a PIPE financing platform to attract USD funds	Ascentage Pharma
Reduce Compliance Risks	Set up an offshore NewCo to bypass VIE restrictions	WeDoctor, Venus Medtech
M&A Exit Path	Use NewCo as an independent acquisition target	Kelun Pharma's ADC platform
Token Structure Experiment	Inject RWA assets into NewCo and issue Tokens	Digital health platform exploration

Operational Notes (Implementation Tips):

- **NewCo is not a shell company**, but a **strategic design tool** that must be implemented in coordination with financial modeling, legal structuring, asset agreements, and the pacing of business development (BD) activities.
- **BD (Business Development)** is not merely part of the sales or marketing function; rather, it serves as a **bridge connecting R&D, capital, and global markets**, and thus requires **cross-disciplinary integration capabilities**.
- **Capital + BD synergy** is currently the mainstream path for **market capitalization growth** among innovative pharmaceutical companies listed on the **Hong Kong and U.S. stock markets**.

Chapter 22: Using NewCo to Revalue Assets and Enable Strategic Exits

Valuation Assessment of Hong Kong ChenChen's NewCo

To assess a fair valuation range for the authorized global rights assets transferred to **Hong Kong ChenChen's NewCo**, we adopt a systematic approach using **three valuation methods**:
(1) Sum-of-the-Parts Analysis,
(2) Comparable Company Method, and
(3) DCF-based Logical Estimation,
providing strong valuation support for investors and M&A negotiations.

I. Key Assumptions

Item	Details
Previous Valuation	Jiangsu ChenChen: Pre-money valuation of **RMB 2.0 billion** (China rights); post-money valuation of **RMB 2.3 billion**, with RMB 300 million investment from HKEX-listed Tibet Pharmaceuticals.
NewCo Rights	Global (ex-China) rights to **Zorletinib** and pipeline assets (e.g., CD7 CAR-T / ML-NK platforms).
License Scope	Exclusive license including development, registration, business development, and commercialization.
Development Stage	Zorletinib is already approved in China, supported by international Phase III data. Some cell therapy programs are in IND or Phase I–II. U.S. development has not yet started. NewCo will assume all overseas clinical development and commercialization responsibilities.
ETAO's Future Role	ETAO may merge with NewCo in the future. Valuation must account for strategic synergies, future returns, and investor appeal.

II. Valuation Pathway 1: Benchmarking Based on Domestic Market Valuation (Baseline Approach)

Assumptions:

- China rights valued at RMB 2.3 billion.
- Overseas markets (esp. U.S.) have significantly larger patient bases, higher pricing, and stronger payor systems.
- U.S. peak sales could be 2–3x that of China.
- Need to factor in international regulatory costs, longer timelines, and risk adjustments.

Estimated Value Ratios:

Region	Market Size / Pricing	Rights Complexity	Estimated Value vs. China
U.S.	High pricing, larger sales	High risk, longer time	**1.0 – 1.5x**
EU / Japan / Emerging Markets	Medium	Medium	**0.5 – 0.8x**

Inference:
Global (ex-China) rights may reasonably be worth **1.5 – 2.2x** the China valuation.

→ Based on the RMB 2.3 billion China valuation, the **NewCo valuation range** is:

RMB 3.45 – 5.06 billion (approx. **USD 480 – 700 million**)

III. Valuation Pathway 2: Overseas Comparables (CompCo Method)

Comparable Case	Asset Background	Valuation / Deal Size	Takeaway
ArriVent	Licensed global (ex-China) rights to furmonertinib from Allist	IPO valuation of USD 220M; raised USD 175M	Valid peer benchmark
Telavant	Licensed U.S. rights to Pfizer's RVT-3101 for 1 year	Acquired by Roche for USD 7.1B	Illustrates arbitrage potential

Comparable Case	Asset Background	Valuation / Deal Size	Takeaway
Cerevel	Joint venture between Pfizer & Bain Capital	Acquired by AbbVie for USD 8.7B	Its product may hold similar potential

Conclusion:

- Its product has already been approved in China with solid safety and differentiated clinical profile.
- Addresses unmet need in U.S. (e.g., brain metastasis in NSCLC).
- Compared to ArriVent, Its product is more clinically advanced and could command a **valuation premium**.

Recommended Valuation Range (based on ArriVent benchmark with premium adjustment):

USD 300 – 450 million (approx. **RMB 2.16 – 3.24 billion**)

IV. Valuation Pathway 3: Simplified DCF Simulation

Assumptions:

- overseas peak annual sales = **2× China** = **RMB 4B/year (~USD 550M)**
- Net profit margin: **20%**
- 10-year revenue horizon, 20% discount rate, no terminal value, license period = 20 years

Calculation:

- DCF Value = Annual Profit × Discounted Multiplier = 550M × 20% × 8 = **USD 88M/year × 8 = USD 440M**

→ Aligns with other methods and supports a **central valuation range of USD 350–500 million**

V. Consolidated Valuation Recommendation

Item	Recommended Valuation	Remarks
NewCo Valuation Range	**USD 350 – 500 million** (RMB 2.45 – 3.5 billion)	Balanced between reasonableness and market appeal
Suggested Investment Entry Price	Based on **USD 380 million valuation**, 60% stake = **USD 228 million** (~RMB 1.65 billion)	Can serve as negotiation anchor
If using equity swap with listed company	Recommend setting a valuation anchor condition to avoid over- or under-valuation	

VI. Additional Strategic Suggestions (from ETAO's Perspective)

ETAO may consider the following structures:

- **Phased investment** with **put/call options** for risk control and flexibility
- **Dual valuation anchors**: short-term valuation target + long-term M&A synergy premium
- Post-IPO, ETAO can acquire NewCo via **SPV merger**, enhancing the valuation narrative of the listed entity

Chapter 23: Synergizing OpCo and NewCo for Valuation Alignment

USD LP Return Logic and Multi-path Exit Framework

I. IRR Return Model (Internal Rate of Return)

Scenario Setup (based on valuation growth of Hong Kong ChenChen's NewCo):

- Initial Investment: $20M (equivalent to 30% equity in NewCo)
- Initial Valuation: $66.7M (based on $380M pre-money valuation)
- Exit Time Horizon: 24 months (T+24)
- Exit Valuation Assumptions:
    - Conservative Case: valuation grows to $100M
    - Base Case: valuation grows to $150M
    - Optimistic Case: valuation grows to $200M

IRR Calculation:

Exit Valuation	Investment Multiple	IRR (Annualized CAGR)
$100M	1.5x	22.5%
$150M	2.25x	47.6%
$200M	3.0x	65.8%

Note: The IRR model assumes no interim dividends and a 2-year exit horizon, which aligns with typical return expectations for PIPE funds and family offices.

II. Dividend Distribution Mechanism (Waterfall Structure)

Purpose:
To enhance the appeal of the structure for institutional USD LPs, a dividend-sharing mechanism can be introduced, especially for cash-flow generating assets (e.g., licensing deals with upfront payments).

Recommended Distribution Waterfall (based on SPV fund structure):

1. Return of Capital
    - All dividends and exit proceeds are first allocated to fully repay LPs' initial capital.

2. Preferred Return (Year 1)
    - LPs receive an 8% annualized preferred return (non-cumulative) before GP sharing.
3. Carried Interest
    - Once preferred return is met, 80/20 profit split applies (LP 80%, GP 20%).
4. Structural Options
    - Can include lookback provisions or catch-up clauses to incentivize the GP while preserving LP priority.

Note: This structure is suitable for USD-denominated SPV funds or internal NewCo profit-sharing models—especially relevant to family offices and partnership-based funds.

III. Exit Mechanisms and Scenario Design

The model provides three exit routes, each aligned with a different investor profile:

Exit Path	Description	Best Fit Investors
1. IPO (HK/US)	NewCo independently lists or spins off via ETAO within 24 months	PIPE funds, Pre-IPO funds
2. Trade Sale	License-out or full M&A transaction with strategic buyers (e.g., Pfizer, BMS) within 12–18 months	Strategic investors, PE funds
3. Secondary Sale	Transfer of LP equity to next-round USD fund / FA / SPAC structure	HNW investors seeking flexible short-term exits

Configurable Exit Instruments:

- Buy-Back Option: ETAO or sponsor may repurchase LP shares at a predefined multiple at T+12 or T+24.
- Share Swap Clause: If NewCo is acquired by ETAO, LPs can convert NewCo shares into ETAO stock at a 1:1.5 ratio.
- IPO Lock-Up Terms: Negotiable lock-up periods for PIPE funds (e.g., unlock at T+6 or T+12 months post-listing).

Conclusion

This NewCo financing structure is custom-built for USD LPs, combining:

- A compelling IRR-based growth model
- A structured capital return and dividend mechanism
- A three-path exit framework

This design maximizes institutional investor interests across capital appreciation, downside protection, and exit liquidity.

By integrating with ETAO's U.S. listing platform and its robust business development (BD) capabilities, the structure provides global USD capital with a strategic conduit connecting China's tech innovation with international capital markets.

NewCo Collaboration Agreement

Standardized NewCo Structure Cooperation Agreement
Applicable to scenarios involving Chinese asset injection, offshore financing, and platform co-construction.

Key Components:

- Asset injection pathway and valuation logic
- NewCo jurisdiction (BVI/Cayman) and legal representative arrangement
- Optional token issuance and buyback terms
- Shareholder rights and governance structure design
- Exit rights aligned with PIPE investors
- Annex: Standard Template of NewCo Strategic Collaboration Draft Agreement

Strategic Cooperation Framework Agreement
("This Agreement") is entered into on [Date of Signing] at [Location] by and between the following Parties:

Party A: ETAO International Co., Ltd.
Registered Address: Cayman Islands
Legal Representative/Authorized Signatory: Wilson Liu

Party B: ABB Biopharma HK Limited
Registered Address: [To be filled in]
Legal Representative/Authorized Signatory: [To be filled in]

(Collectively referred to as the "Parties", individually a "Party")

Article 1: Background and Purpose

Whereas Party B is the holding company of Jiangsu Chencheng Biopharma Co., Ltd. ("Jiangsu Chencheng"), and holds the global rights to the first third-generation TKI innovative drug approved for certain genes mutation causing brain metastases with significant international commercial potential;
Party A intends to assist Party B in establishing a U.S.-based joint venture company named AiMi Health Inc. ("NewCo") to advance regulatory filings, clinical development, business

development (BD) partnerships, and commercialization efforts globally, with a focus on the U.S. market.

Article 2: Collaboration Model and NewCo Formation

1. Company Formation
   The Parties agree to jointly assist in forming NewCo (AiMi Health Inc.), which shall serve as the designated overseas licensing and commercialization entity for Party B's specified products. The company will be registered in the United States with an initial registered capital of [to be filled in] USD.

2. Equity Structure
   The initial proposed equity structure (subject to future amendment by mutual agreement) is as follows:

- Investors (USD Funds / Third-Party VCs): 51%
- Party B (Asset / Pipeline Licensor): 20%
- NewCo Management Team (including Party A's designated personnel): 29%

3. License Arrangement
   Party B agrees to exclusively license or transfer the rights to develop, register, promote, and commercialize its product(s) and related pipeline assets in all global markets outside of China to NewCo. Licensing details shall be defined in a separate supplemental agreement.

Article 3: Responsibilities and Obligations of the Parties

3.1 Party A Responsibilities:

1. Assist Party B in the establishment of NewCo and the compliance framework;
2. Introduce and secure offshore USD capital for NewCo's seed and Series A rounds;
3. Assist in building an international management team for NewCo and lead clinical, BD, strategic partnerships, and IPO planning in the U.S.;
4. When appropriate, Party A will facilitate ETAO International's acquisition of NewCo after successful Nasdaq listing, thereby integrating global rights and maximizing valuation and synergies.

3.2 Party B Responsibilities:

1. Provide core technical documents, clinical data, and global development

background of the target product(s);

2. Complete licensing and technical integration of the pipeline to NewCo;
3. Collaborate with Party A and NewCo on global partnerships, registration, and clinical development;
4. Assist in recommending and participating in management team formation and supporting NewCo's ongoing operations.

Article 4: Investors and Financing Terms

1. Party A or its investment partners will lead NewCo's seed round financing, with a total target of [to be filled in] USD;
2. Investors will receive proportional equity in NewCo, with rights including co-investment rights, pre-emptive rights, and future M&A proceeds allocation rights;
3. NewCo's financing agreements will explicitly outline mechanisms for converting Party B's licensed technology rights into shareholder value and medium- to long-term returns.

Article 5: M&A Expectations and Exit Mechanism

1. Party A intends to initiate acquisition of NewCo after ETAO International successfully lists on Nasdaq and reaches a predetermined valuation threshold;
2. The acquisition may take the form of cash buyout, equity swap merger, or acquisition via a special purpose vehicle (SPV);
3. If not acquired, NewCo may pursue IPO, be acquired by a multinational corporation (MNC), or enter into strategic exits, with exit proceeds distributed among Party B and investors based on their shareholding.

Article 6: Confidentiality

Both Parties shall keep the contents of this Agreement and all related cooperation confidential. Disclosure to any third party is prohibited without the other Party's written consent, unless required by law or necessary for fulfilling the objectives of this Agreement.

Article 7: Governing Law and Dispute Resolution

1. This Agreement shall be governed by the laws of the State of New York, USA;
2. Any disputes arising from this Agreement shall first be resolved through friendly consultation. Failing which, the dispute may be submitted to the New York

International Arbitration Center (NYIAC) for arbitration, whose ruling shall be final and binding.

Article 8: Miscellaneous

1. This Agreement serves as a framework of intent; detailed license agreements, investment agreements, and M&A agreements shall be signed separately.
2. This Agreement becomes effective upon execution and seal by both Parties and shall remain valid for 12 months, unless otherwise agreed in writing.
3. This Agreement may be executed via email and shall carry the same legal effect as the original.

Party A: ETAO International Co., Ltd.
Signature: ________________
Date: ________________

Party B: ABB Biopharma HK Limited
Signature: ________________
Date: ________________

Chapter 24: Legacy Shareholder Exit Mechanisms and Pre-IPO Structuring

Real-World Case Analysis

I. Challenges and Key Considerations in Legacy Equity Transfer Financing for Hong Kong ChenChen

Dimension	Details
Nature of Financing	Involves transfer of legacy equity; no new issuance, no capital into company accounts, and investors do not receive new equity rights.
Large Transaction Size	The target transfer amount is RMB 1.38 billion (approx. USD 200 million), which is significantly larger than typical growth-stage biotech rounds.
High Investor Threshold	Requires investors who can accept majority control (60%) and are capable of asset integration and supporting BD or IPO exits.
Specialized Assets	Involves innovative drugs and an ADC pipeline; investors must have experience in drug development, international expansion, or major M&A.
Lack of Immediate Exit Channel	No ready access to U.S. or HK capital markets; return on investment depends on future BD deals, HK IPO, or acquisition.
Limited Valuation Anchoring	Pre-money valuation of RMB 2B and post-money of RMB 2.3B are based on the last round, with no international BD term sheet or external validation yet.
Information Asymmetry	As the company has not engaged in large-scale external fundraising, transparency is low; due diligence and trust-building will take time.
Regulatory Risk	Involves VIE structure or PRC equity transfer; requires expert design of compliant cross-border transaction structure.

II. Advantages After Signing Strategic Cooperation with ETAO International

Advantage Dimension	Specific Impact
Backed by International Capital Platform	ETAO is a **NASDAQ-listed company**, with mature Pre-IPO and PIPE fundraising channels, enabling direct access to U.S. dollar capital for ChenChen.
Establishment of NewCo	Joint establishment of a U.S.-based NewCo to hold **global rights (excluding China)** of Zorletinib and raise capital, resolving the difficulty of directly trading legacy equity.
Well-Designed Exit Mechanism	ETAO has NASDAQ relisting experience and can offer returns through **M&A, HK IPO, or global BD deals**.
Extensive BD Experience	ETAO has deep understanding of multinational pharma BD practices and can facilitate deals with top pharma (e.g., **Pfizer, BMS, Merck**), targeting large upfront licensing transactions.
Optimized Transaction Structure	Flexible configurations using **equity + assets + exit rights**, e.g., introducing VC as lead in NewCo, granting ETAO priority M&A rights.
Enhanced Confidence and Credibility	Strategic cooperation agreement is well-structured (with FA clauses, valuation lock-in, and acquisition rights), which increases investor confidence and project credibility.
Project Integration Under ETAO	ChenChen can be positioned as part of ETAO's **pipeline/ecosystem**, enhancing overall group valuation and incorporated into **Pre-IPO narrative** to attract PIPE funds.

Summary Recommendations

Topic	Recommendation
Legacy Equity Financing Challenge	High difficulty; requires sector-specialized investors, innovative structuring, and strong platform support.
Breakthrough Post-Partnership	Leverage ETAO platform and NewCo structure to **convert legacy equity into international rights authorization + capital injection**, bypassing liquidity and pricing challenges of direct equity sales.
Strategic Direction	Structure financing via **asset authorization or injection into NewCo**; ETAO retains M&A rights, investors gain clear equity and exit visibility.
Shift in Investment Logic	Transition investor mindset from **"legacy equity sale" to "growth equity in a new platform"**, significantly improving market acceptance.

Elevator Pitch Summary

After entering strategic cooperation with ETAO International, Hong Kong ChenChen successfully transforms the complex legacy equity transfer challenge into an integrated solution of:

"Global Rights Licensing + Offshore Capital Platform + Structured Exit Pathways,"

fully leveraging ETAO's value as an international capital enabler—offering a highly executable strategy with strong implementation potential.

PIPE Financing and Secondary Shareholder Exit Design

I. The Role of PIPE Financing in the Globalization of Mid-Sized Enterprises

PIPE (Private Investment in Public Equity) refers to private placements of shares by a publicly listed company to specific qualified investors. With its flexible structure, high efficiency, and fast execution, PIPE is commonly used for public companies to supplement liquidity or finance mergers and acquisitions.

For growth-stage enterprises with access to international capital markets (such as ETAO), PIPE serves as an effective bridging tool that connects U.S. dollar institutional capital with strategic project assets. It is particularly suitable for integration with NewCo structures, asset acquisitions, and legacy equity exit plans, ultimately enhancing valuation and financing feasibility.

II. Key Elements of PIPE Structure Design

Element	Description
Investor Selection	Targeted toward family offices, USD private equity funds, PIPE-specialized institutions, or strategic investors with mid- to long-term holding interest.
Pricing Mechanism	Typically offered at a discount (10–30%) or with valuation-based performance clauses (e.g., linked to T+6M or T+12M share price), providing investors with expected returns.
Attached Rights Design	May include price protection clauses, anti-dilution provisions, warrants, or convertible bonds (CBs).
Lock-Up and Exit Routes	Generally locked for 6–12 months. Exit options include open-market sales, company buybacks, or payout via future M&A.
Integration with NewCo	PIPE proceeds may be directed into the NewCo platform and used for product globalization, BD up-front payments, or Pre-IPO bridge funding.

III. Risks and Design Logic of Legacy Equity Exit

For companies like "Hong Kong ChenChen" that have established valuation but limited liquidity, legacy equity transfer is often challenging due to:

- Lack of USD-based valuation platform, making it difficult to price legacy shares reasonably;
- No acceptable exit mechanism for investors, reducing deal appeal;
- Structural design deficiencies, resulting in intense negotiations between investors and legacy shareholders.

ETAO can resolve this through a structure combining PIPE + NewCo + Legacy Share Authorization, creating a new pathway for shareholder exit.

IV. Integrated Structure: PIPE Financing + Legacy Share Exit

Step 1: Anchor NewCo Valuation

- Inject a portion of legacy shares into NewCo and authorize corresponding global rights;
- Use NewCo valuation as the pricing basis for PIPE financing, anchoring a USD-based valuation for legacy shares.

Step 2: PIPE Capital Injection into NewCo

- Bring in strategic or institutional PIPE investors at a discount or structured entry price;
- Funds raised are used for licensing transactions, international trials, or acquisition preparation.

Step 3: Phased Exit for Legacy Shareholders

- A portion of PIPE proceeds can be allocated for legacy shareholder payouts or share buybacks;
- Set a timeline and exit roadmap, such as ETAO acquiring NewCo and offering share premiums.

Step 4: Exit Pathways and Investor Return Design

- Investor exits may include NewCo's future listing in Hong Kong or the U.S., reverse merger into ETAO, or monetization via licensing deals;
- Performance-based earn-out clauses can be embedded (e.g., if valuation targets are not met, compensatory mechanisms are triggered).

V. Summary: A Practical PIPE + Legacy Equity Solution

PIPE financing should not be seen as a standalone transaction, but rather as part of an integrated strategy for value amplification, liquidity resolution, and global capital alignment.

Through:

- A well-anchored NewCo valuation,
- A structured and phased legacy equity exit plan,
- And strategic deployment of PIPE proceeds,

Enterprises can significantly boost transaction efficiency, build investor confidence, and unlock higher valuations.

This structure not only provides liquidity for existing shareholders, but also brings in strategic funding, accelerates globalization, and opens IPO or M&A pathways—serving as a powerful capital accelerator for mid-sized innovative enterprises seeking global scale.

Term Sheet (Non-binding)

This template is suitable for preliminary investment proposals during PIPE, strategic rounds, or license-out deals. A bilingual format is recommended to cover:

- Investment amount and valuation range
- Type of equity and shareholding percentage
- Priority rights (anti-dilution, liquidation, information)
- Exit strategies (IPO, buyback, M&A)
- Exclusivity, confidentiality, and due diligence clauses

Attachment: Standard Bilingual Word Template – Term Sheet (Non-Binding)

1. Transaction Overview

Establishment of AiMi Health Inc. in the United States ("NewCo") and introduction of ETAO International as a strategic investor to support the registration, development, and commercialization of its existing products and other pipelines in all markets excluding China.

2. Parties

- **Licensor / Shareholder:** Jiangsu ABB Biopharma Co., Ltd.
- **Investor:** ETAO International Co., Ltd.
- **Target Company (NewCo):** AiMi Health Inc. (a newly incorporated U.S. entity)

3. Basic Information of NewCo

Item	Description
Place of Incorporation	Delaware, U.S. (or another jurisdiction as mutually agreed)
Legal Representative	To be jointly appointed by both parties
Initial Business	Exclusive global rights (excluding China) to develop, register, and commercialize Its product and other candidates

Item	Description
Technology Source	Exclusively licensed from Jiangsu Alpha Biopharma

4. License Scope

Jiangsu ABB Biopharma shall grant NewCo the **exclusive global rights (excluding China)** to its existing products and its related pipeline, including but not limited to:

- Clinical development
- Regulatory filings
- Commercialization rights (marketing and sales)
- Strategic partnerships or sublicensing

Licensee shall hold full exclusive global rights (ex-China) including development, registration, commercialization, and sublicensing rights.

5. Proposed Valuation & Capital Structure

Item	Content
Pre-Money Valuation	USD 380 million (approx. RMB 2.7 billion)
ETAO Investment Amount	USD 228 million
Shareholding	60% equity (in common or convertible preferred shares)
Investment Method	Cash in two tranches (see Section 6)
Use of Funds	Clinical trials, FDA registration, team building, BD, etc.

6. Funding Plan

Tranche I (Closing I):

- Amount: Approx. USD 100 million
- Conditions: Share transfer completion, initial team setup, IP handover

Tranche II (Closing II):

- Amount: Approx. USD 128 million
- Conditions: Achieving milestones such as FDA Pre-IND Meeting or Phase I clinical trial initiation

7. Corporate Governance

Item	**Arrangement**
Board Composition	5 members: ETAO (3), Alpha (1), Independent Director (1)
Key Management	CEO nominated by ETAO; CTO/CMO jointly appointed
Shareholders' Rights Agreement	ETAO entitled to information rights, preemptive rights, M&A priority, and tag-along rights
Profit Distribution	According to shareholding ratio unless otherwise agreed

8. Exit Strategy

- ETAO shall have the right to acquire 100% of NewCo after its successful Nasdaq listing via cash or equity swap
- M&A valuation to be anchored on projected market value after completion of Phase I/II trials or based on a negotiated premium mechanism
- In case of third-party M&A or IPO, ETAO is entitled to **tag-along** and **right of first refusal**

9. Due Diligence

- ETAO will conduct a 30-day financial, legal, and technical due diligence
- Alpha shall provide a full registration dossier, clinical data, patent list, and internal audit reports

10. Exclusivity

- For 90 days from the signing of this Term Sheet, Alpha agrees not to engage in similar negotiations or transactions with third parties concerning ex-China rights of Its product

11. Confidentiality

- This Term Sheet and related cooperation details are strictly confidential and shall not be disclosed to any third party unless required by law or for internal compliance review

12. Governing Law

- This Term Sheet shall be governed by the laws of the State of New York, U.S.
- All disputes shall be submitted to arbitration by the **New York International Arbitration Center (NYIAC)**, and its decision shall be final and binding

13. Miscellaneous

- This Term Sheet is non-binding; however, Sections on **Exclusivity**, **Confidentiality**, and **Governing Law** are legally binding
- Both parties shall work toward executing formal **Share Purchase Agreement (SPA)** and **License Agreement** within 45 days of signing this Term Sheet

Party A: ETAO International Co., Ltd.

Signature: ________________

Date: ________________

Party B: Jiangsu ABB Biopharma Co., Ltd.

Signature: ________________

Date: ________________

Chapter 25: Real-World Application of Smart Capital Formula

Case 1: "The Desert Rose Turnaround" — A True Case Based on the Smart Capital Formula

Act I: The Crisis

Early 2024, winter in Shenzhen was unusually damp and cold. Outside the glass façade of Desert Rose Biotech's headquarters, heavy clouds loomed over the tech park. The company had just completed a 200 million RMB funding round, and the office had been filled with anticipation for the launch of its new drug.

But a sudden industry news alert shattered it all— a competitor had released clinical data for a product strikingly similar to Desert Rose's core asset and claimed to have already submitted applications to U.S. and European regulators. The market reaction was swift and brutal: the company's equity valuation was slashed from 2 billion RMB to under 1 billion, and the SPAC listing partner, who had already signed a letter of intent, withdrew that very night.

The cash flow sheet looked like a face drained of all color— R&D funds could only sustain four more months. In a project meeting, the head of R&D cautiously asked, "Should we halt Phase III trials to save cash?" CEO Lin Hai didn't answer, his eyes fixed on a thick contract on the table— the SPAC merger agreement, now nothing more than scrap paper.

Worse yet, several core team members began updating their LinkedIn profiles, and word had already reached potential investors. Lin understood that this wasn't just a funding crisis; it was the collapse of the company's entire trust framework.

Act II: The Structural Reversal

Lin dialed a number he hadn't called in years— MK, a capital advisor with three decades of Wall Street battle scars. When MK arrived in Shenzhen, he carried an old leather case, not filled with contracts, but with decades of capital structuring experience.

After hearing Lin's story, MK didn't rush to talk about funding. Instead, he wrote a formula on the whiteboard:

Smart Capital = RWA × Stablecoin × (Tri-Market Listing: IPO + STO) × (OpCo + NewCo)

"Lin," he said, "you're not short of money— you're short of a structure that can generate its own lifeblood and attract global valuation attention."

He proposed carving out the international patents, overseas regulatory rights, and clinical data for the drug into a **NewCo** registered in Hong Kong. This would not only isolate risk but also allow overseas investors to invest directly into a clearly defined asset package— a true "capital bulletproof vest."

Next, the future licensing income and data usage rights would be packaged as **RWA (Real World Assets)** and tokenized on compliant platforms in the Middle East and Singapore, backed by stablecoins, enabling global LPs to participate via digital capital.

Finally came MK's "Tri-Market Path": NewCo would list on HKEX under the 18A mechanism, OpCo (the parent) would merge with a SPAC for a NASDAQ listing, and the Middle Eastern market would serve as a third valuation and liquidity window, creating an arbitrage corridor.

In just three months, the meeting room whiteboard had transformed from flashing "CASH ALERT" in red to complex diagrams, arrows, and valuation models. For the first time, Lin felt he wasn't waiting for a rescue— he was building his own runway for capital escape and ascent.

Act III: The Outcome

One year later, NewCo successfully listed on HKEX under the 18A mechanism, with its market cap rebounding past its previous high to 3 billion RMB— 1.5 times its pre-crisis level.

The parent company OpCo completed its SPAC merger in the U.S., tapping into NASDAQ's tech valuation system. Meanwhile, the RWA-backed stablecoin issuance drew in long-term Middle Eastern capital, not only stabilizing cash flow but also prompting global investment banks to publish research reports that for the first time described "structural innovation" as a key investment highlight.

On listing day, Lin stood at the HKEX gong, gripping the same pen that had sat on his desk since the crisis began. He told his team: "We didn't wait for the market to save us— we built a market ourselves through structure."

In the crowd, the head of R&D, the general counsel, and the CFO exchanged looks, each recalling the winter when that formula appeared on the whiteboard— not as a mere set of numbers, but as the very key that carried the company from the edge of the cliff into the spotlight.

Case Analysis

Formula Match:
Smart Capital = RWA × Stablecoin × (Tri-Market Listing: IPO + STO) × (OpCo + NewCo)

Formula Element	Case Application	Function & Impact
RWA (Real World Assets)	Packaged future licensing income and data usage rights	Anchored international investor interest and valuation baseline
Stablecoin	Issued tokens backed by RWA in Middle East & Singapore	Enabled cross-border liquidity and faster capital inflow
Tri-Market Listing	HKEX 18A + NASDAQ SPAC + Middle East pricing platform	Amplified valuation and created arbitrage opportunities
OpCo + NewCo	Parent retained domestic ops, NewCo held international assets	Risk isolation + asset revaluation

Summary:

- **Structural Role:** Transformed the company from a funding crisis into a multi-market capital player.
- **Strategic Highlight:** Proactively created market conditions instead of passively waiting.
- **Replicability:** Suited for mid-sized enterprises with high technical barriers but valuation constrained by a single market.

Case 2 : Hong Kong Morning Biopharma Ltd.: Global Expansion Plan Based on the Smart Capital Formula

Core Formula: Smart Capital = Digital Asset RWA × Stablecoin × Tri-Market Listing × (Operating Company + NewCo)

1. Project Overview and Vision

Hong Kong Morning Biopharma Ltd. is an innovative biopharmaceutical company focused on antibody-based therapies and cell immunotherapy. It is committed to addressing significant unmet needs in oncology. The company is headquartered in Shanghai, China, with a GMP-certified modern manufacturing facility in Suzhou. It also has R&D or partnership operations in Hong Kong, Beijing, and the United States, with operational capabilities spanning China and the U.S. and a global deployment outlook.

2. Product Pipeline Highlights

- Core Product: A third-generation TKI specifically targeting brain metastases in NSCLC patients, approved in China in 2025 after successful Phase III trials. It demonstrates strong CNS penetration and non-efflux characteristics, with a projected annual peak sales revenue exceeding RMB 2 billion.
- Cell Therapy Platform: The company has developed an in-house off-the-shelf CAR-T and memory NK cell platform. Its pipelines cover T-ALL, AML, solid tumors, and autoimmune diseases. Some products have already reached international Phase II clinical trials.

3. Core Competitive Advantages

- Drug Design & Translational Capability: Targeting brain metastasis indications, the company has built a complete vertical platform from R&D and regulatory filing to CMC, GMP manufacturing, and commercialization.
- International Collaboration & BD Capacity: It maintains strategic partnerships with leading global academic and industrial institutions (e.g., Wugen, USA), and is capable of executing outbound licensing deals and obtaining multi-jurisdictional market access.
- Experienced Team: Core executives hail from top-tier global pharmaceutical firms with over 20 years of average industry experience, combining strong execution with deep strategic insight.

4. Development Plan

- 2025: Core product launched in China; cell therapy product enters Phase II trials; NewCo structure is established.
- 2026: RTO listing on NASDAQ and application for Hong Kong 18A listing; first international license deal launched; token financing and PIPE structure initiated.
- 2027: A-share listing or strategic M&A exit in China to achieve profitability.

5. Valuation Positioning

- Benchmark companies include Ailis (SH:688578), BeiGene, and RemeGen, with a target market valuation exceeding USD 1 billion.
- The company possesses a unique, differentiated drug product and holds a first-mover advantage in targeting specific gene mutations for brain metastasis, as well as in the scalable global cell therapy space.

6. Why Morning Biopharma's Core Product Qualifies as Legal and Compliant RWA

Real World Assets (RWA) refer to assets that generate predictable cash flows, are legally owned, and can be assigned value through transparent mechanisms. In the blockchain and digital capital space, RWAs are typically used to:
- Anchor the intrinsic value of Token offerings
- Enable hybrid issuance alongside securities products (e.g., funds, bonds, license income rights)
- Provide a tangible and verifiable foundation for investor trust and compliance

Why the core product qualifies as an RWA:
- Cash Flow Potential: The lead product has completed Phase III clinical trials and received market approval in China with stable revenues, and has license-out potential in Southeast Asia and the Middle East. Projected cash flow can be estimated using DCF models.
- Clear Ownership: The product's full IP and regulatory approvals are held by Morning Biopharma, with license rights transferable to a NewCo (e.g., Cayman SPV) to support Token issuance.
- High Transferability: License rights are contractual cash flow assets and can be lawfully assigned to the Token issuer via legal agreements.
- Auditability: All agreements, forecasts, and registrations can be reviewed and confirmed by major accounting firms (e.g., EY, PwC) to support valuation under U.S. Reg D requirements.

7. RWA Identification and Asset Structuring

- Identified RWA Assets:
  - ADC pipeline (ADC-102, ADC-203) with IND completed
  - Clinical data package in collaboration with a top CRO
  - License-out deal under negotiation in the EU (estimated value: $25M)
- Asset Transfer:
  - Assets will be transferred or licensed to a newly established Cayman NewCo
  - Legal contracts will confirm income rights, data ownership, and license assignment
- Valuation Anchors:
  - DCF-based forecasted license cash flow ≥ $150M
  - Valuation references from comparable companies (e.g., RemeGen, Lepu Biotech)

8. Stablecoin Settlement and LP Onboarding

- Funding Currencies:
  - Accepts USDC, USDT, and HKD stablecoins for PIPE round, settled in USD equivalent
- Investor Onboarding:
  - U.S. institutional investors through Reg D 506(c)
  - Overseas family offices through Reg S
- Compliance Process:
  - Identity and wallet screening via Onfido / Chainalysis
  - Whitelisting mechanisms to control Token holder eligibility

9. Tri-Market Listing Path and Arbitrage Mechanism

The "**Triple Listing IPO + STO**" strategy is a core component of the Smart Capital pathway, designed to optimize global capital access and valuation efficiency. By leveraging the complementary strengths of capital markets in the **United States (Nasdaq)**, **Hong Kong (HKEX 18A)**, and **China (A-shares/STAR Market)**, this model harmonizes diverse investor preferences, valuation frameworks, and regulatory advantages. It is further enhanced by an **STO (Initial Coin Offering)** module, which adds a digital capital layer, forming a highly liquid and forward-looking fundraising ecosystem.

1. First Listing: RTO on Nasdaq (Q1 2026)

A reverse takeover (RTO) will be executed through the NewCo structure and SPAC merger with the listed U.S. company **ETAO International Group**.

Key benefits: faster timeline, higher pricing, and improved valuation multiples due to strong tech attributes (comparable to **XtalPi**, **I-Mab**).

2. Second Listing: Hong Kong (Q3 2026)

Either the parent company (ChenChen Pharma) or its NewCo subsidiary will apply for an 18A listing on the HKEX.

Expected fundraising size: approximately **HKD 800 million**.

3. Third Listing: China A-shares, Abu Dhabi, or Singapore (Q3 2027)

Potential third IPO will be pursued on the **Shanghai STAR Market**, **Abu Dhabi ADX**, or **Singapore Catalist** depending on strategic alignment.

The Token component will also be eligible for trading in MENA markets, potentially incorporating future **license income dividend rights**.

4. STO Issuance Module Design

Based on the NewCo structure, a token will be issued to build a digital financing channel integrated with PIPE financing and Web3 governance principles.

Compliance Framework: Reg D Rule 506(c) + Reg S + Cayman legal opinions

Investor Segmentation: U.S. institutional investors, Middle Eastern LPs, and Asian family offices

Rights Structure: License revenue rights + buyback clause + equity conversion mechanism

Strategic Benefits:

Enables global liquidity participation

Strengthens valuation anchors

Serves as a USD stablecoin inflow vehicle

By combining the **Triple IPO + STO** structure, **ChenChen Pharma** achieves not only vertical integration across global capital markets but also builds a bridge between traditional finance and tokenized digital capital—offering a repeatable capital strategy and structural model for mid-sized enterprises expanding internationally.

10. NewCo Structure and Token Model Design

- NewCo Setup: Cayman registered
  - Holds: license contracts, AI algorithm IP, and token smart contracts
- Token Economics:
  - Total supply: 100 million tokens
  - PIPE allocation: 15%
  - Unlock schedule: 12-month lock, quarterly buyback, equity swap post-IPO
- Token Rights:
  - Pro-rata license revenue dividends
  - Convertible equity rights upon IPO
  - Governance participation (e.g., Snapshot voting)

11. PIPE Financing Structure and Investor Terms

- Target Raise: $30M (Seed Round)
- Token Price: $1.00 (includes 10% bonus)
- Exit Options:
  - Quarterly PIPE buyback window of 5%
  - 1:1.25 token-to-equity swap ratio post-IPO
  - Secondary trading via Securitize platform
- Legal Documents:
  - Offering Memo, Subscription Agreement, Exit Memo, ESG Disclosures

12. ESG Disclosure and IFRS Compatibility

- ESG reporting aligned with IFRS S1/S2 standards
- Disclosures include:
  - Carbon emissions

• Data governance
• Board oversight
• Clinical ethics review mechanisms
- On-chain Synchronization:
• ESG data uploaded to blockchain via IPFS for transparency

13. U.S.-China LP Communication Q&A

Category	English Question	Suggested Answer (English)
Legal Structure	Is the token Reg D compliant?	Structured under a Cayman SPV with Reg D private placement and KYC whitelist system.
Token Valuation	What justifies the token price?	Anchored by License DCF modeling, peer company benchmarks, and AI-based valuation.
Exit Mechanism	What's my exit if IPO fails?	Exit options include token buyback, secondary market trading, and equity swap via M&A.
Risk Management	How do you address regulatory risk?	A multi-jurisdictional legal structure designed by legal teams in the U.S., Hong Kong, and MENA.

14. Team and Advisory Network

- Core Team: Alumni of Fosun Pharma, BeiGene, and MIT AI Lab
- Legal Advisors: Ogier (Cayman), Loeb Smith (U.S. SEC), DeHeng (Hong Kong)
- FA Support: Securitize Capital, Wall Street Huangpu Center

15. Timeline and Execution Roadmap

meline	Milestone
Q4 2025	Establishment of NewCo + Launch of PIPE fundraising
Q1 2026	RTO listing on NASDAQ (U.S.) via SPAC merger
Q3 2026	Filing for HKEX Main Board listing + Completion of Token issuance
Q3 2026	Signing of first international License-out transaction
Q3 2027	IPO on China A-Shares or equivalent Innovation Board

Closing Statement

This business plan is developed by the Hong Kong Morning Biopharma team based on the 'Smart Capital Pathway' framework. We welcome strategic global investors, cross-border funds, and regulatory-compliant advisors to jointly establish a new paradigm for global biotech expansion.

Part VI: Case Studies of Mid-sized Biopharma Enterprises

This section offers a comparative and strategic deep dive into five representative case studies of mid-sized biopharma enterprises that have successfully pursued global capital pathways. These cases—BeiGene, RemeGen, WeDoctor, WuXi AppTec, and Ascentage Pharma—demonstrate diverse but replicable models of international expansion through tools such as dual listings (NASDAQ + HKEX), ADC license-out transactions, tokenized financing experiments, and dual-capital platform structures.

This section provides both replicable frameworks and valuation-enhancing strategies for mid-sized firms seeking to overcome bottlenecks in old share exits, overseas BD licensing, and global visibility.

Chapter 26 : BeiGene- A Model for Dual Listing on NASDAQ and HKEX

I. Company Background and Early-Stage Challenges

1.1 Company Background: From Local Chinese Startup to Global Pioneer in Innovative Oncology Drugs

BeiGene Ltd., founded in 2010 and headquartered in Beijing, with a global operations center in Cambridge, Massachusetts, is one of China's earliest biotech companies focused on the research and development of innovative oncology drugs. The company was co-founded by Dr. Xiaodong Zhang, Dr. Xiaobin Wu, and a team of internationally experienced pharmaceutical scientists. From the outset, BeiGene adopted a science-driven, globally oriented approach grounded in international regulatory standards, aiming to build a globally synchronized drug R&D system with Chinese innovation at its core.

Unlike traditional generic drug companies or those reliant on license-in models, BeiGene chose a fundamentally different path from the beginning—high R&D investment, globally concurrent clinical development, and full in-house innovation. This strategic positioning helped the company stand out among its domestic peers and gradually build a globally competitive pipeline, including:

- BTK inhibitor (Zanubrutinib),
- PD-1 monoclonal antibody (Tislelizumab),
- PARP inhibitor (Pamiparib).

In under 15 years, BeiGene has transformed from a startup biotech firm into a global biopharmaceutical powerhouse:

- Over 5,000 R&D personnel across China, the United States, Europe, and Australia;
- A clinical pipeline of more than 40 investigational programs, including several in Phase III or commercial stages;
- In-house GMP manufacturing facilities, capable of producing both clinical and large-scale commercial drug batches;
- Strategic partnerships with leading pharmaceutical companies like Novartis, Amgen, and Bristol Myers Squibb (BMS), facilitating global licensing deals and asset transactions.

Notably, BeiGene became a dual-listed company by going public on NASDAQ in 2016 and completing a secondary listing on the Hong Kong Stock Exchange in 2018, leveraging both capital markets to secure multiple rounds of high-quality funding. This dual listing laid a strong foundation for the company's subsequent global expansion.

1.2 Early-Stage Challenges: Three Major "Mountains" Testing Its Global Vision

Despite its clear strategic vision, BeiGene faced three major and unprecedented challenges during its formative years:

(1) The Financial Pressure of Intensive R&D Investment

As a biotech company committed to "heavy R&D," BeiGene made early decisions to invest aggressively in target discovery, preclinical validation, and multi-country clinical trials. A single program, such as the BTK inhibitor, required tens of millions of dollars just to move from target identification to early clinical stages—let alone the ongoing costs of multinational Phase III trials and regulatory submissions.

Without revenue to support operations, the company faced a triple dilemma in a cold funding environment: how to raise continuous financing, avoid excessive dilution, and retain control. In the early 2010s, China's venture capital ecosystem for biotech was still nascent, and dollar-based funds lacked confidence in R&D-driven Chinese firms. BeiGene had to work simultaneously across China and the U.S. to win trust from institutional investors on both sides.

(2) Challenges in Overseas Clinical Pathways and Regulatory Recognition

Although rooted in China, BeiGene opted early on for global multi-center clinical trials, particularly aligned with U.S. FDA standards. This required the company to build clinical teams in the U.S., engage CROs experienced in IND submissions, and navigate hurdles such as language barriers, time zone differences, ethical board standards, and varying submission cycles.

More critically, the company lacked a commercial infrastructure in overseas markets and had limited experience with foreign regulatory cultures and compliance protocols. Designing global clinical trial pathways and aligning data to international standards posed a high threshold. For example, Zanubrutinib's trials had to benchmark against Ibrutinib—an already approved international competitor—necessitating compelling head-to-head study designs to meet global expectations.

(3) Earning Trust and Value Recognition in International Capital Markets

Before 2015, Chinese biotech companies had yet to establish credibility in global capital markets. BeiGene had to convince international investors of its scientific originality, globally capable team, and sustainable pipeline. However, the prevailing skepticism around the "China R&D, U.S. approval" model—particularly concerning regulatory discrepancies, data integrity, and corporate governance—created hurdles.

To address these concerns, BeiGene had to implement transparent corporate governance, appoint internationally renowned independent board members, and establish disclosure systems in compliance with both SEC and HKEX standards. The company also brought in top-tier investment banks, law firms, and auditors to assist with its IPO process. These efforts gradually built a trust moat around BeiGene in the eyes of global capital markets.

2. Strategic Path and Global Capital Deployment

BeiGene's global strategy demonstrates a high degree of systematic planning and phased execution:

- In 2016, it completed its IPO on NASDAQ, raising $158 million, initiating its U.S.-centered international capital strategy and expanding global visibility.
- In 2018, it completed a secondary listing on the Hong Kong Stock Exchange (HKEX) under the Chapter 18A mechanism, raising approximately $900 million and gaining access to Asia-Pacific capital.
- The company also entered a series of BD (business development) licensing agreements with global pharmaceutical giants such as Novartis and Amgen, granting development and commercialization rights for its products across different regions—enabling a dual-engine model of monetization and strategic partnerships.

3. Key Success Factors and Lessons Learned

Success Factors:

- BeiGene developed a rare "dual regulatory + dual registration" capability, enabling parallel engagement with both the U.S. FDA and China's NMPA, which significantly accelerated its global regulatory approval timelines.
- It effectively integrated fundraising and BD licensing, establishing a virtuous capital cycle of "fundraising → licensing → reinvestment," enhancing capital efficiency and pipeline depth.

Lessons Learned:

- Complying simultaneously with both U.S. and Chinese regulatory frameworks increased compliance costs and governance burdens.

- The U.S. market's stringent requirements for disclosure and corporate governance created significant pressure, requiring early-stage Chinese firms to rapidly mature their organizational capacity.

4. Alignment with This Manual's Strategic Framework

BeiGene's capital strategy fully validates several of the key strategic principles outlined in this manual:

- It confirms the recommendation of "listing on NASDAQ first, followed by HKEX spinoff," demonstrating how establishing international credibility first can lead to valuation uplift and capital efficiency gains upon returning to regional markets.
- By integrating BD licensing with capital structuring, BeiGene created a replicable dual-engine model of "fundraising + licensing," offering a practical reference for mid-sized companies seeking internationalization.
- As a leading example of a mid-sized innovative drug company expanding globally, BeiGene exemplifies the "modular value elevation system" proposed in this manual and aligns closely with the "One Core, Two Wings" capital architecture framework.

Chapter 27 : RemeGen - A Pathway Model for ADC License-out Strategy

I. Company Background and Development Challenges

RemeGen Co., Ltd. (Stock Code: 688331.SH / 09995.HK), established in 2008, is one of the few innovative biopharmaceutical companies in China that centers its pipeline around Antibody-Drug Conjugates (ADCs). Headquartered in Yantai, China, RemeGen focuses on areas with significant unmet medical needs, including oncology, autoimmune diseases, and ophthalmology. Its core product, RC48 (Disitamab Vedotin, brand name: Aideixi®), targets HER2-positive cancers and is the first domestically developed and approved ADC drug in China.

1.1 Technological Barriers and Differentiated Advantages

ADCs, which combine monoclonal antibodies with cytotoxic small-molecule drugs, represent a new generation of precision therapy with extremely high development complexity. Since its inception, RemeGen has built a fully integrated ADC development platform covering antibody screening, linker design, and conjugation technology, all protected by proprietary intellectual property. RC48 was developed on this platform and features a proprietary linker and payload system. It has shown significant clinical efficacy even in patients with low to moderate HER2 expression, highlighting its differentiated competitive edge.

1.2 Three Major Challenges in Early-Stage Development

Despite its technological strengths, RemeGen faced three critical challenges during its early development phase:

- **High Capital Intensity and Funding Dependency:** ADC development requires long cycles and significant capital. Preclinical development alone can cost hundreds of millions of RMB, and even more funding is needed for clinical trials. For an early-stage biotech company, limited access to sustainable financing can severely slow down R&D progress.
- **Uncertainty in Global Commercialization Pathways:** To enter global markets, Chinese innovative drugs must be approved by major regulators such as the U.S. FDA and the European EMA. Differences in regulatory standards, as well as the lack of established global marketing and distribution networks, pose significant barriers to international expansion.
- **Lack of Global Credibility and Recognition:** As a high-barrier, high-risk field, ADC

development requires strong validation from global markets and international investors. Chinese biotech startups often face a "trust gap" due to low global brand recognition and insufficient publication of clinical data in internationally recognized journals.

1.3 Strategic Choice: License-Out as a Breakthrough Model

In response to these challenges, RemeGen adopted a globalization strategy distinct from the traditional "self-commercialization" model. By licensing out its core product RC48 to international pharmaceutical companies, RemeGen secured upfront payments, milestone-based compensation, and sales-based royalties. This license-out model allowed the company to share risks, access capital early, and accelerate its global expansion.

The license-out strategy not only eased cash flow pressure but also leveraged international partners' capabilities in clinical development and regulatory approval, thereby accelerating the commercialization process and enabling "leveraged globalization" for its innovative therapies.

2. Strategic Roadmap: Capital Integration and Global Validation

RemeGen's international capital strategy unfolded in three major phases:

• In 2020, the company successfully listed on the main board of the Hong Kong Stock Exchange through the 18A mechanism, raising approximately USD 500 million. It was one of the largest biotech IPOs in Hong Kong that year, achieving both financing goals and international brand recognition.

• In 2021, RemeGen signed a global (excluding China) license-out agreement with U.S.-based Seagen for RC48, receiving an upfront payment of USD 200 million. This deal not only brought substantial cash inflow but, more importantly, validated the global commercial value of RC48 and served as a valuation anchor.

• Prior to the IPO, RemeGen introduced PIPE financing funds as pre-IPO investors, helping establish its valuation framework and enabling a premium-priced offering that balanced financing needs with dilution control.

3. Key Success Factors and Lessons Learned

Success Factors:

• The license-out deal was not just a fundraising mechanism, but a critical 'international valuation anchor' that addressed information asymmetry and enhanced confidence among domestic and global investors.

• Given the high technical and capital thresholds for ADC development, RemeGen's early endorsement by international institutional investors helped build trust and facilitated its capital breakthrough.

Lessons Learned:

• While license-out deals can deliver short-term capital and international visibility, they may temporarily hinder domestic commercialization efforts. Balancing global BD and local execution is essential.

4. Alignment with Strategic Framework in This Playbook

RemeGen's pathway strongly supports multiple key strategic assertions in this manual:

• It showcases the effectiveness of the 'License-out + PIPE + HKEX 18A' three-pronged strategy, forming a standardized path from product validation to valuation uplift.

• The deal with Seagen validates the assertion that 'BD transactions are the nuclear weapon of valuation management'—allowing companies to exchange licenses for valuation anchors, cash flow, and international credibility, especially suitable for high-risk assets like ADCs.

• The introduction of PIPE financing optimized IPO pricing and helped offset market volatility—offering a key funding path for clinical-stage, pre-commercial companies.

5. Future Outlook and Replicable Lessons

• As RemeGen expands globally, it may explore further strategies such as joint post-licensing governance, renegotiation of development milestones, and cross-border M&A to deepen international collaborations.

• For other mid-sized biotech firms, the 'RemeGen model' offers a practical roadmap:

① Develop globally recognized products;

② Secure license-out deals as valuation anchors;

③ Introduce strategic PIPE capital;

④ Execute a high-valuation IPO and achieve capital elevation.

• For governments, FA teams, and biotech industrial parks, the RemeGen case presents a model for constructing hybrid financing structures that combine equity, licensing, and institutional endorsements into a cohesive global fundraising solution.

Chapter 28 : WeDoctor- Exploring Tokenized Financing in Digital Health

1. Company Background and Development Challenges

WeDoctor is one of China's earliest pioneers in using digital technologies to transform healthcare services. In its early stages, the company focused on developing "Internet Hospital" services, becoming one of the first to integrate the entire online healthcare process—from appointment booking, remote consultations, and e-prescriptions to payments and pharmaceutical delivery—thereby reshaping the traditional healthcare delivery model. Over time, WeDoctor expanded its offerings by integrating medical insurance payment systems, chronic disease management, family doctor services, health insurance, and a centralized data platform, building a full-service digital healthcare ecosystem spanning pre-diagnosis, diagnosis, and post-treatment. To date, the platform has served over 100 million users and connected with more than 2,700 hospitals and 300,000 doctors, making it one of the dominant "super gateways" in China's digital health sector.

1.1 First-Mover Advantage in Data and Technology Infrastructure

As a representative of China's "national digital health team," WeDoctor has digitized medical scenarios at scale from an early stage, accumulating a vast trove of valuable health behavior data, electronic medical records, and payment records. These assets provide a strong foundation for downstream applications such as AI-powered healthcare, personalized health management, and insurance underwriting. The platform boasts stable daily active users and high annual return-visit rates, making it one of the few digital health companies in China capable of sustaining high-frequency service interactions within a closed-loop data system.

In addition, WeDoctor has independently developed a range of leading technologies, including its "Health Cloud" system, an integrated API system linking medical care, insurance, and pharmaceuticals, as well as smart triage and post-treatment follow-up modules. This multi-scenario technology stack lays a solid digital foundation for the company's future exploration of tokenization and asset securitization.

1.2 Development Bottlenecks and Capital Pressure

Despite its early advantages in users, data, and technology, WeDoctor faces three major challenges as it seeks sustainable commercialization and access to capital markets:

Complex regulatory compliance and limited growth scalability

The healthcare sector is highly regulated, involving multiple government agencies such as the National Health Commission, the National Medical Products Administration, the National Healthcare Security Administration, and the Cyberspace Administration. As a platform-based enterprise, WeDoctor's functions—such as cross-hospital consultations, electronic prescription transfers, and medical insurance payment integration—must navigate a complex matrix of trial policies and regionally varied regulations, resulting in high compliance costs. Additionally, escalating demands for data security and privacy compliance have placed ongoing pressure on the platform's architecture and operational capabilities.

Unproven business model and volatile platform valuation

Although the platform has a large user base, WeDoctor's core revenue still primarily relies on service commissions from online consultations and a portion of pharmaceutical price margins. A stable revenue loop from SaaS services, transaction processing, or health insurance value-added services has yet to materialize. In the capital markets, the company's unproven business model has left investors without a reliable valuation anchor, resulting in repeated delays to its IPO and significant fluctuations in market valuation.

Lack of long-term capital injection and pivot toward digital finance innovation

Amid a tightening global IPO environment and cautious investment strategies among USD-denominated funds, WeDoctor is in urgent need of new financing models to replace traditional equity-based fundraising. Since 2022, the company has begun working with financial institutions in Hong Kong and Singapore to explore new financing structures, such as **tokenization of healthcare data assets**, **issuance of health rewards tokens**, and **cross-border payments integrated with membership systems**. These efforts aim to convert the platform's health behavior points, service tokens, and insurance profit-sharing rights into tradable digital equity certificates, thereby attracting compliant international capital.

2. Strategic Path: Capital Access and Tokenization Attempts

WeDoctor has pursued a multi-dimensional approach to growth and capital strategy:

• On the capital side, the company successfully attracted strategic investors such as Singapore's sovereign wealth fund, Tencent, and Hillhouse Capital, providing both financial backing and user ecosystem synergy.

• To monetize its digital health data assets, WeDoctor explored blockchain-based token issuance, aiming to certify, price, and tokenize its medical data for qualified investor financing. Though the model was not fully implemented due to regulatory constraints, it pioneered a prototype for the 'RWA + AI + Token' financing structure in the health-tech domain.

• WeDoctor submitted an IPO application to the Hong Kong Stock Exchange but suspended the listing due to valuation disputes and an unclear path to profitability—highlighting structural gaps between its capital model and market compliance expectations.

3. Key Success Factors and Lessons Learned

Success Factors:

• The platform's massive user base and ecosystem layout positioned its data assets as uniquely valuable. Its strategy of data ownership and multi-scenario application made it a strong candidate for tokenized models.
• Through distributed network concepts and decentralized data sharing, WeDoctor attempted to create a collaborative model among patients, pharma, doctors, and payers—demonstrating international potential.

Lessons Learned:

• Without clear regulatory guidance, token structures cannot form a compliant financing loop. Key challenges include cross-border capital compliance, investor qualification, and secondary market liquidity.
• The lack of a robust ESG governance framework—especially regarding data privacy, patient consent, and corporate accountability—limited the platform's appeal to international long-term investors (e.g., LPs, insurers, pension funds).
• An underdeveloped monetization model weakened its pricing leverage in traditional markets like IPOs and PIPEs.

4. Strategic Validation and Warnings from This Playbook

The WeDoctor case validates and contextualizes several core models proposed in this playbook:

• Its tokenized financing attempt affirms the feasibility of the 'RWA (Real World Assets) + AI certification + Token valuation' model for digital healthcare ventures.

• The case also warns of the risks for platform companies lacking an ESG framework, particularly in terms of transparency, sustainability, and regulatory accountability.

• For mid-sized tech companies pursuing international capital integration, WeDoctor highlights the need for balance between compliance, governance, and monetization.

5. Outlook and Replication Strategies

• If clear data governance systems and compliant blockchain architecture can be established, similar platforms may pilot tokenized digital health financing in friendly jurisdictions like Singapore, Dubai, or Hong Kong.

• Platforms should build standardized ESG disclosure systems—especially concerning data ethics, cybersecurity, and patient transparency—to earn the trust of global LPs, family offices, and impact funds.

• For replication, WeDoctor offers a four-step reference path for mid-sized platform companies:

① Real World Asset (RWA) certification;
② ESG integration;
③ PIPE fundraising;
④ Tokenized issuance to enhance valuation and capital agility.

Chapter 29: WuXi AppTec – The Global CRO Leader's Privatization Restructuring and Capital Pathway Exploration

I. Company Background and Development Challenges

WuXi AppTec is a globally influential Contract Research Organization (CRO), providing end-to-end services for new drug development. Its offerings span small molecule synthesis, bioanalysis, preclinical research, cell and gene therapy, and CDMO manufacturing. Since its founding, WuXi AppTec has adhered to its mission of "enabling global healthcare innovation," consistently serving the majority of the world's Top 20 pharmaceutical companies.

In 2007, WuXi AppTec successfully listed on the New York Stock Exchange (NYSE), becoming one of the first Chinese biopharmaceutical companies to go public in the U.S. However, in 2015, the company made a critical strategic decision—to privatize and delist from the NYSE. This move reflected a prudent assessment of U.S. capital market valuations and signaled a comprehensive restructuring of the company's equity structure, business layout, and long-term strategy.

Following privatization, WuXi AppTec's path of strategic restructuring was far from smooth. In particular, its effort to relist on China's domestic capital market presented a series of structural and governance challenges.

Four Core Challenges After Privatization

1. Rebuilding the Onshore Capital Pathway: Balancing Exit for Existing Investors and Entry for New Capital

During its privatization, WuXi AppTec brought in a large number of USD-denominated private equity funds (such as Hillhouse, Gaoling, and Boyu Capital). These funds, driven by return targets, expected to exit within a reasonable timeframe. At the same time, the company needed to introduce onshore RMB capital to support its core operations and achieve domestic relisting. This dual requirement placed high demands on valuation methodology, equity structuring, and capital coordination—balancing the exit needs of early LPs while ensuring sufficient room and protection for incoming investors.

2. Balancing Regulatory Requirements and Global Consolidation Structures

WuXi AppTec operates across multiple jurisdictions including China, the United States, and Europe. Its VIE structure, overseas subsidiary holdings, and global revenue consolidation must comply with a complex array of regulatory frameworks—such as audit standards, data security, antitrust policies, and foreign exchange controls. Especially amid rising geopolitical tensions and tighter cross-border audit scrutiny, explaining and validating its corporate structure clearly and transparently to Chinese regulators becomes a critical challenge in the company's compliance and refinancing efforts.

3. Facilitating Lawful Access for USD Funds to Core Domestic Assets

Although WuXi AppTec's main business operations are in China, its key investors include USD-based funds, which seek exposure to the core domestic business. The company must use compliant structures—such as "contractual control + offshore SPVs + structured funds"—to preserve economic rights for USD LPs while respecting regulatory red lines regarding foreign ownership limits, data sovereignty, and domestic control. This requires a highly sophisticated and forward-looking approach to corporate structuring.

4. Governance and Brand Consistency Amid Spin-offs and Multi-Region Financing

As WuXi AppTec continues to expand its business segments, it has incubated and spun off several subsidiaries, including STA Pharmaceutical (synthesis services), WuXi Biologics (biologics CDMO), and JW Therapeutics (cell therapy), among others. While this "platform + subsidiaries" model enhances value realization and operational focus, it also introduces greater coordination costs, fragmented internal incentives, and risks to unified brand identity. Striking a balance between maintaining centralized control and optimizing subsidiary-level governance, incentive mechanisms, and brand alignment remains an ongoing strategic priority for WuXi AppTec.

2. Strategic Path: A+H Share Dual Platform and Exit Mechanism

WuXi AppTec employed a multilayered capital structure to resolve its challenges and accelerate growth.

• In 2018, the company listed on China's A-share market, enabling partial exit for legacy shareholders. By combining secondary share sales and primary issuance, the company created liquidity while opening new capital channels.

• That same year, it completed a secondary listing on the Hong Kong Stock Exchange (HKEX), establishing an international capital platform. The HKEX listing allowed the company to raise offshore capital and serve as a base for license-out deals and global collaborations.

• WuXi AppTec also set up multiple SPV structures to package assets, allowing USD-based funds to invest in specific projects—especially in early-stage pipelines or international clinical development.

3. Key Success Factors and Lessons Learned

Success Factors:

• The company successfully leveraged a combination of secondary share sales, primary offerings, and platform spin-offs to create an integrated capital structure that bridged domestic liquidity and global valuation.
• The dual A+H share listing improved overall flexibility and reduced exposure to foreign exchange and geopolitical risks.
• SPV platforms allowed customized capital access strategies (e.g., LPs, PIPE investors, strategic partners), supporting layered asset management and risk isolation.

Challenges and Lessons:

• Managing parallel platforms and asset spin-offs increased administrative and operational costs.
• Corporate governance frameworks needed to be harmonized across markets, including audit policies, disclosure rhythms, and board decision mechanisms, to avoid regulatory misalignment.
• Lack of a clear consolidation path for spin-off assets could result in valuation inconsistencies and investor uncertainty.

4. Strategic Validation and Model Refinement

WuXi AppTec validates and enhances several key models presented in this playbook:

• It reinforces the concept of combining 'legacy share exit + NewCo arbitrage structure' to create value leverage and unlock capital trapped in maturing assets.

• It offers a practical model for dual global capital platforms (A+H shares), demonstrating how such a structure can enhance fundraising elasticity, pricing mechanisms, and risk mitigation.

• The SPV structure enables layered project financing, investor customization, and future consolidation—highly applicable for emerging international biotech enterprises.

5. Replication Advice and Future Expansion

• Mid-sized biotech firms can emulate the 'WuXi model' by first setting up offshore SPVs for license-out and PIPE financing, then returning to the A-share or HKEX market after establishing valuation anchors.

• FA institutions can use WuXi's blueprint to design financing packages based on 'legacy exit + new equity + dual platform trading' for clients with strong valuation foundations and cross-border deal logic.

• Government zones and industrial funds should consider building a three-tiered capital deployment framework—RMB parent fund + USD SPV + exit platform—to support internationally scalable enterprises.

• WuXi's structure may evolve into RWA tokenization pilots, facilitating digital capital upgrades, broader investor participation, and ESG-compliant disclosure.

Chapter 30：Ascentage Pharma - Comparative Strategy Between HKEX 18A and PIPE Financing

1. Company Background and Development Challenges

Ascentage Pharma (6855.HK), founded in 2009, is one of the earliest China-based clinical-stage biopharmaceutical companies focused on "first-in-class" innovative mechanisms. The company specializes in the development of globally advanced therapies targeting the apoptosis pathway, with a particular emphasis on Bcl-2/Bcl-xL dual inhibitors aimed at treating various relapsed and refractory hematologic malignancies and solid tumors.

Its core candidate drug, **APG-1252**, is undergoing multiple clinical trials simultaneously in China and the United States. It has demonstrated promising efficacy in indications such as **myelodysplastic syndromes (MDS), acute myeloid leukemia (AML), and small cell lung cancer**. With a novel mechanism of action and no similar products approved in China, APG-1252 holds a clear "first-in-class" profile and represents a flagship product in China's global innovative drug strategy.

As one of the few companies to enter the capital market at the early clinical stage, Ascentage Pharma **went public on the Hong Kong Stock Exchange in 2019** under the Chapter 18A biotech listing regime, gaining considerable market attention.

Three Structural Challenges Facing the Company

Although Ascentage Pharma demonstrates strong potential in mechanism innovation and clinical pipeline development, it also faces three typical structural challenges as a **scientific innovation–driven biotech enterprise**:

1. Unclear Clinical Translation Pathway – Especially Regulatory Limitations in the U.S. Market

While APG-1252 and other pipeline assets are being tested in parallel clinical trials in China and the U.S., they remain in Phase I/II exploratory stages under FDA supervision. The company still lacks comprehensive experience in U.S. clinical operations, regulatory submission, trial design, and communications with authorities. Notably, it has yet to build a robust network of key opinion leaders (KOLs), efficient patient recruitment mechanisms, or strong CRO execution capability—factors that contribute to uncertainty in its global development trajectory.

Moreover, competition in certain indications is intense in the U.S., with major global pharmaceutical players like **AbbVie's Venetoclax** already occupying similar Bcl-2-related target space. Therefore, how Ascentage can achieve regulatory advantages such as **Fast Track** designation or **Breakthrough Therapy Designation (BTD)** through differentiated design will be critical to its registration strategy.

2. High R&D Spending with Ongoing Cash Burn – Pressures on Financing Flexibility

As a pure R&D-driven biotech, Ascentage has yet to generate commercial revenue at scale and relies heavily on capital markets to finance its pipeline. With over **70% of annual expenses allocated to R&D**, the company is in a continuous "cash-burning" mode.

Against the backdrop of tightened global capital markets and suppressed biotech valuations in Hong Kong, its financing windows have narrowed while R&D expenditures remain rigid. This places significant strain on cash flow flexibility. Developing a **diversified financing strategy**—including **upfront payments from license-out deals, convertible bonds, and PIPE private placements**—has become a pressing capital optimization challenge.

3. Limited International Investor Recognition – Weak Valuation Anchors

Despite having the advantage of **global targets and China-U.S. parallel trials**, Ascentage's international visibility among institutional investors remains relatively low. Its core products have not yet entered late-stage registration, leaving it without clear commercial validation to support valuation.

In comparison with other hot mechanisms in global biotech—such as **ADCs** and **bispecific antibodies**, which enjoy strong valuation premiums—the **Bcl-2 inhibitor class** is a relatively underrepresented and complex area. The scientific understanding gap and the difficulty in translating early data into investor confidence result in weak valuation anchors during cross-border fundraising and institutional outreach.

2. Strategic Path: Parallel Use of 18A Listing and PIPE Financing

Ascentage's capital strategy demonstrates a phased and diversified approach:

• In 2019, the company successfully listed on the Hong Kong Stock Exchange under the Chapter 18A mechanism, raising approximately USD 140 million. It became one of the first unprofitable biotech companies with no marketed products to go public, opening the door to international capital.

• In 2021, Ascentage introduced PIPE financing to support pipeline advancement, particularly U.S.-based Phase I/II clinical trials. The PIPE capital brought operational flexibility and enabled refined, stage-based financing tailored to clinical progress.

• Simultaneously, the company advanced global clinical registration in parallel with the FDA and began preparing for license-out opportunities, positioning itself for international partnership and business development.

3. Key Success Factors and Lessons Learned

Success Factors:

• The 18A listing mechanism offered a gateway to public markets for unprofitable biotech firms. Ascentage's IPO validated the viability of early entry, establishing brand visibility and a valuation baseline;
• PIPE financing provided flexible and stage-based capital aligned with R&D volatility, improving predictability and capital utilization efficiency;
• A globally coordinated clinical strategy (China-U.S. dual track) improved market visibility and negotiation power for potential license-out deals.

Lessons Learned:

• 18A listings are constrained by valuation ceilings due to investor caution and distant commercialization, making stock prices sensitive to clinical fluctuations;
• Biotech firms need strong integration between clinical progress and BD strategy to create a data-driven licensing narrative;
• A lack of global BD expertise can delay deal execution and weaken investor confidence—especially among PIPE investors.

4. Validation and Optimization of the Playbook's Strategic Model

Ascentage's path provides critical validation and refinement to this playbook's models:

• It effectively verifies the 'PIPE + license-out + U.S. collaboration' multi-channel exit model—where companies list via 18A, then layer in PIPE financing and global clinical trials, offering exit strategies via licensing, PIPE repurchases, or cross-market M&A.

• It provides a stage-based capital roadmap for pre-revenue biotech firms: start with a public listing to build brand and regulatory capital, then leverage PIPE for precision financing tied to clinical data.

• It reminds companies to align PIPE financing with BD timelines to avoid mismatches that may reduce valuation efficiency or increase volatility.

5. Replication Advice and Strategic Planning

• Biotech firms may adopt a three-phase strategy: '18A IPO → PIPE bridge → pre-embedded license-out' to construct a progressive international roadmap.

• PIPE investors should assess whether companies have a global clinical and BD framework, including clear regulatory milestones and deal readiness.

• HKEX regulators may consider refining policies to better support this model—such as recognizing license-out value in valuation and enabling staged PIPE rounds to stabilize price discovery.

• Companies should consider establishing a dedicated global BD platform (e.g., a NewCo) to handle international trials, licensing, and deal execution—thereby improving PIPE appeal and execution speed.

Summary:

This chapter presents five classic case studies that together represent the five primary internationalization pathways for mid-sized innovative enterprises:

- **Dual Listing** (NASDAQ + HKEX)
- **License-out** (Valuation Anchoring)
- **Token Structures** (Liquidity Innovation)
- **Secondary Share Exit** (Dual-Platform Capital Structure)
- **PIPE Financing** (Flexible Capital Support)

Collectively, these cases validate the core strategy proposed in this playbook: the integration of the **NewCo model**, **capital structure innovation**, and **international collaboration**—offering a set of actionable templates for future companies seeking global expansion.

Chapter 31: Case Studies of Failed International Expansion

This chapter aims to systematically review common failure models encountered by innovative pharmaceutical companies during their efforts to expand globally, enhance valuations, and secure international financing. By analyzing real-world case studies, it extracts lessons that can help prevent mistakes and identifies actionable points for optimization, enabling mid-sized companies to avoid common pitfalls in practice.

Case 1: Failure in Pre-IPO Structuring Led to Investor Withdrawal

InferVision is a company focused on AI-powered medical imaging diagnostics. It possesses leading algorithms for pulmonary nodule detection and CT image analysis. Its clientele is concentrated in top-tier (Class A) hospitals and regional imaging centers. Below is a detailed profile of InferVision:

I. Company Overview and Background

- Established & Positioning: Founded in 2016 and headquartered in Beijing, InferVision is an innovative enterprise specializing in AI for medical imaging. Its vision is "AI for Better Health," and it aims to become a global leader in hospital-wide AI applications.
- Product Coverage: It offers AI diagnostic solutions across multiple domains, including pulmonary, cardiovascular, breast, musculoskeletal, and trauma imaging. Its product line extends to surgical planning, clinical follow-ups, and research support, forming a closed-loop solution from diagnosis to treatment.

II. Core Products and Technological Capabilities

- InferRead Series: A deep learning-driven medical imaging analysis system, now deployed in over 1,000 healthcare institutions for disease screening and diagnostics.
- InferOperate Series: Supports clinical surgical planning and navigation, enabling precise and efficient procedures.
- Research Enablement Tools: Platforms such as InferScholar and InferMatrix offer AI-powered assistance for medical research.

III. Certifications and Global Expansion

- Multiple Regulatory Approvals: InferVision's products have received market

approvals from regulatory bodies including China's NMPA, the U.S. FDA, the European CE, the UKCA, and Japan's PMDA.
- Global Reach: Its products are used in over 30 countries, serving more than 1,000 hospitals, including world-class institutions.

IV. Team Structure and Financial Backing

- R&D Team: Backed by a team of experts in medicine, clinical research, and deep learning, the company has developed proprietary convolutional neural network models.
- Investor Base: Supported by top-tier investors including Qiming Venture Partners, Sequoia China, Huagai Capital, Morningside Venture Capital, Goldman Sachs, and Hillhouse Capital.
- Funding History: InferVision has completed at least seven financing rounds. Its most recent round, in August 2021, raised RMB 700 million, led by Goldman Sachs, valuing the company at approximately USD 1.5 billion.

V. Market Performance and Industry Position

- Revenue: In 2020, InferVision generated revenue of approximately RMB 27.7 million. Despite operating at a loss, its technology has rapidly gained market share.
- Certifications: It was among the first companies in China to obtain Class III medical device certifications for AI medical imaging and has expanded into areas such as neurology, cardiology, and oncology.
- Industry Standing: Widely recognized as a leading player, InferVision is considered one of the few dominant firms ("oligarchs") in China's AI medical imaging sector.

VI. Strategic Planning and Future Development

- "Horizontal + Vertical" Strategy: Horizontally, the company covers a broad range of disease types; vertically, it focuses on the entire diagnosis-to-treatment workflow: screening → diagnosis → therapy → management.
- Internationalization: With regulatory certifications in multiple jurisdictions and active deployments in over 10 countries, InferVision is steadily advancing its global expansion.
- Profitability Outlook: Industry insiders believe InferVision is likely to become profitable by 2025. As the sector enters a phase of natural selection, a handful of AI medical leaders are expected to dominate.

VII. Case Summary

InferVision exemplifies a leading force in the AI medical imaging field. It has built a diversified product portfolio, beginning with early lung cancer screening and expanding into cardiovascular, oncology, and surgical domains, thereby forming a comprehensive AI-powered healthcare ecosystem. With robust technological capabilities, strong financial backing, and global regulatory credentials, its international expansion and profitability prospects are highly promising.

However, during its Pre-IPO phase, InferVision failed to complete proper equity restructuring. Legacy shareholders had unclear rights, and new U.S. dollar-based investors lacked priority protections. This led to conflicts among shareholders. Compounded by delays in IPO timing, some investors ultimately withdrew, causing the company's valuation to plunge by half.

VIII. Lessons Learned

It is essential to design clear equity transfer and exit mechanisms—such as earn-outs, convertible instruments, or mandatory buybacks—and to complete corporate governance optimization before any financing round.

This case highlights how shareholder governance is often neglected when designing Pre-IPO structures. Companies that fail to incorporate provisions like liquidation preferences, disclosure obligations, or mandatory co-investment clauses in shareholder agreements risk creating serious conflict between old and new investors.

Therefore, it is strongly recommended that legal advisors be engaged early in the financing process to draft a detailed Term Sheet (TS) and Shareholders' Agreement (SHA), avoiding reactive patchwork solutions that damage market confidence.

Case 2: Token Structure Non-Compliance Led to SEC Investigation

DataOcean Biotech is a biotech company focused on AI-powered genomic data analysis. It attempted to broaden its financing channels by tokenizing its data assets. Its main products include oncology-focused SaaS diagnostic tools and bioinformatics database services.

I. Company Overview and Background

- Founded: 2018, registered in Shanghai. The company was founded by a team of student entrepreneurs with an AI and biotech background.
- Positioning: Specializes in tokenizing genomic sequencing data and AI analytics services, attempting to convert real-world assets (RWA) into tokenized formats for innovative financing.
- Objective: To digitize patient data and genomic databases into investable assets, offering tokens that combine yield with liquidity. These tokens aim to support both investor returns and scientific research funding.

II. Core Concept and Product Layout

- RWA Token Model: The company bundled the income rights from its proprietary genomic testing database into asset-backed tokens. Investors purchasing these tokens would receive dividend payouts and data authorization income.
- AI Analytics Platform: Connected with hospitals and testing institutions to collect genomic data, the platform used AI models to assess disease risks and generate precision medical recommendations.
- Token Economic Design: The token system included lock-up periods, dividend distributions, and buyback clauses. However, it lacked a clear legal framework. The tokens were offered only to qualified investors, but compliance controls were insufficient.

III. Financing Process and Timeline

- Private Equity Stage: Raised approximately RMB 50 million across angel and Pre-A rounds, with participation from angel investors and institutional funds.
- Token Offering Attempt: In 2022, the company initiated plans to launch its RWA token project to raise approximately USD 20 million. The offering was conducted through private channels without Reg D or Reg S filings, nor was it reviewed by a legal third party.
- Market Reception: While some institutional investors expressed early interest, many raised significant concerns during due diligence, particularly around regulatory risk and the lack of a clear exit path for LPs.

IV. Key Failure Triggers

1. Lack of a Compliance Framework
    - The company failed to report to the U.S. SEC and did not utilize Reg D/S exemption pathways. As a result, the token issuance was considered an unregistered securities offering.
2. Opaque Token Mechanism
    - The whitepaper lacked third-party KYC/AML audits, had vague lock-up and buyback mechanisms, and raised red flags for investors regarding the sensitivity of biomedical data.
3. Regulatory Intervention
    - The offering was halted after cross-border financial regulators in one country flagged it as "unauthorized financial activity."
4. Exit Barrier for Investors
    - The company did not implement its buyback mechanism nor establish any public exchange listing plan. LPs were effectively locked in, creating collective pressure and dissatisfaction.

V. Lessons and Reflections

1. Compliance and Legal Design

- Any token-based financing must clearly define the nature of the asset and its legal standing.
- If the tokens involve biomedical data or carry revenue-generating rights, they likely qualify as securities and must comply with SEC regulations via Reg D/S or other lawful exemptions.
- Legal counsel should be involved early to review and structure the offering properly.

2. Disclosure and Investor Communication

- The whitepaper, contracts, and product design must include transparent details: issuer identity, lock-up periods, dividend mechanisms, buyback terms, and exit strategies.

3. Risk Disclosure and Ethical Responsibility

- For projects involving medical data, privacy, security, and ethics must be addressed upfront. Disclosure and mitigation measures are critical for institutional trust.

4. Pathway Selection

- Dual-track financing approaches should be considered—e.g., combining traditional private placements with compliant security token offerings (STO), or listing on regulated token exchanges.

VI. Conclusion

DataOcean Biotech represents a textbook example of the RWA + Token model in the innovative biotech + digital capital space. The case highlights both the potential and the pitfalls of merging medical innovation with tokenized financing. It illustrates the concurrent challenges of legal compliance, private capital execution, and cross-border financial regulation.

The company's failure to comply with SEC filing requirements under Reg D / Reg S led to the project being deemed an illegal securities offering less than three months after launch. The initiative was ultimately suspended.

VII. Takeaways

Token-based financing must be legally structured in advance and thoroughly reviewed by counsel. Use of whitelist mechanisms, lock-up schedules, and clear exit strategies are essential to remain within regulatory boundaries.

This project failed to distinguish between tokenization of digital assets and issuance of securities, mistakenly offering RWA-backed tokens directly to the public, in violation of U.S. securities laws.

For tokenized fundraising, it is crucial to categorize the instrument as a Security Token and use regulatory exemptions like Reg D / Reg S, along with comprehensive compliance practices including KYC/AML checks, lock-up enforcement, and whitelist-controlled issuance.

Case 3: Post-Acquisition Integration Failure in an Overseas M&A

Below is a comprehensive company profile of BioSciGen, providing an in-depth look at this representative mid-sized innovative pharmaceutical firm, including its founding background, core business, technological pipeline, market performance, and its M&A attempt.

I. Company Overview and Background

- Founded: August 2015, registered in the Zhangjiang National Innovation Demonstration Zone in Shanghai.
- Positioning: Dedicated to the development of ADC (Antibody-Drug Conjugates), biosimilars, and early-stage innovative small-molecule drugs. The founding team has deep roots in both venture capital and pharmaceutical R&D, with a strong emphasis on scientist-led innovation.

II. R&D Pipeline and Technological Layout

1. ADC Dual-Target Platform
    - The company developed a "precision strike" ADC carrier platform. Its ADC candidates, currently in Phase I clinical trials, include therapies for HER2+ breast cancer and multiple myeloma. Features include optimized linkers and highly selective antibody combinations.
2. Biosimilar Production
    - Focused on recombinant humanized antibodies, including biosimilars targeting TNF and PD-1. The first biosimilar completed mid-stage clinical trials by the end of 2022 and is expected to file for China NMPA approval by 2025.
3. Early-Stage Small Molecule Innovation
    - The company is developing kinase inhibitors focused on lung cancer and solid tumor indications. These projects are currently in preclinical stages.

III. Financing History and Strategic Partnerships

- Series A (2016): Led by Qiming Venture Partners, raising several hundred million RMB.
- Series B (2018): Backed by Sequoia China and Legend Capital, raising approximately RMB 300 million.
- Series C (2020): Attracted a German venture capital firm to support global registration strategies.

Strategic collaborations include an ADC project contract with a Hong Kong-based CRO and manufacturing and export agreements with CDMO partners in Germany and Denmark for ADC clinical and commercial material production.

IV. Market Progress and Milestone Achievements

- Multiple pipeline products have received IND approvals in China, including two ADC candidates that have entered Phase I trials.
- The biosimilar project has gained priority review status in several provincial healthcare systems.
- In 2021, the company submitted an IPO application to the Hong Kong Stock Exchange but withdrew in 2022 due to market volatility and valuation concerns. It then pivoted toward listing on the U.S. or dual-listing routes.

V. M&A Attempt and Failure Analysis

In early 2023, BioSciGen announced the acquisition of a mid-sized CDMO based in Berlin, Germany, aiming to rapidly build its European CRO/CDMO infrastructure and expand into the EU and high-end markets. However, the acquisition soon encountered significant challenges:

- Cultural Integration Barriers: Language and communication issues created distance between German employees and the Chinese HQ decision-making process. This led to low retention rates post-acquisition and a sharp rise in management costs.
- Lack of Integration Readiness: No language support or unified financial/IT systems were in place. Post-acquisition, the German subsidiary exceeded its financial budget by 30%, audit timelines were delayed, and promised synergies failed to materialize, resulting in potential goodwill impairment.
- Absence of Operational Leadership: No cross-border Project Management Office (PMO) was formed, nor was a “China-Europe integration liaison” appointed. This caused execution gaps and confusion across teams.

VI. Strategic Recommendations for the Future

- Strengthen Cross-Cultural Governance: Appoint a CFO-level M&A integration lead and establish a dual-leadership structure combining local and HQ managers.
- Prioritize Cultural Due Diligence: Conduct cultural assessments, organizational structure analysis, and employee interviews prior to closing, with both parties agreeing on retention plans for key personnel.
- Build a Dedicated Integration Team: Form a cross-functional PMO with finance,

audit, HR, and IT units to plan resource interfaces and standardized processes in advance.

- Use Performance-Based Incentives: Include retention clauses, milestone-based earn-outs, and compensation mechanisms in the M&A agreement.

VII. Summary

BioSciGen represents a classic case of a mid-sized Chinese innovative pharmaceutical company transitioning from R&D to international expansion. With strong capabilities in ADC and biosimilar development, it sought to accelerate globalization through acquisition while its IND pipeline matured and biosimilars gained market access.

However, due to the absence of a robust integration strategy, the company encountered high operational costs and severe cultural clashes, becoming a textbook M&A failure. If it can improve its cultural, financial, and governance integration mechanisms in future acquisitions, it may still rebuild a viable pathway for EU market registration and international growth.

In this case, BioSciGen acquired a European biotech company in hopes of leveraging its clinical data and drug registration channels to enter the EU market. However, post-acquisition cultural clashes and the inability to integrate financial, audit, and tax operations resulted in massive goodwill impairment and disrupted BioSciGen's overall IPO timeline.

VIII. Lessons Learned

M&A strategies must include a comprehensive consolidation roadmap and a well-defined cultural integration mechanism. Cross-border advisors or M&A-focused investment firms should be engaged early.

The root cause of the integration failure was not the financial model, but the lack of cultural fusion mechanisms. BioSciGen did not establish an integration committee (PMO), nor did it appoint a cultural liaison or bilingual management team. As a result, it experienced talent loss, audit delays, and fragmented communications.

It is strongly recommended that future cross-border M&As begin with cultural due diligence and be supported by bilingual integration manuals and synchronized operational frameworks.

Case 4: ESG Report Fabrication Led to Institutional LP Withdrawal

Zhongyun Health is a digital healthcare platform enterprise focused on chronic disease management, digital prescriptions, and integration with medical insurance reimbursement systems. Its core platform serves over one million users and is connected to multiple regional insurance systems. The following is a comprehensive overview of Zhongyun Health, including its founding, business model, technological innovation, market performance, and key milestones.

I. Company Overview and Background

- Founded: December 2014
- Positioning: A leading one-stop chronic disease management and smart healthcare platform in China, dedicated to the mission of "making health simpler through technology."
- Vision: To empower seamless collaboration among doctors, patients, and healthcare institutions by integrating internet hospitals, SaaS systems, and AI-powered capabilities to form a complete chronic care management ecosystem inside and outside hospitals.

II. Core Business and Product Portfolio

1. Hospital-End SaaS: "Zhongyun Yihui"
    - Launch: 2016, China's first standardized digital SaaS platform for chronic disease management.
    - Function: Digitizes chronic disease workflows, integrates with AIoT devices (e.g., glucometers, vital signs monitors), and facilitates internal hospital data interoperability.
    - Scale: By the end of 2021, deployed in over 2,300 hospitals, including 33 of China's top 100 hospitals, with around 87,000 registered doctors and 23.8 million users.
2. Pharmacy-End SaaS: "Zhongyun Consultation"
    - Launch: 2019, in response to "dual-channel" policies and prescription outflow trends.
    - Function: Enables pharmacies to offer onsite consultations and e-prescriptions, improving medication accessibility for chronic patients.
    - Performance: In the first half of 2023, pharmacy solution revenue reached RMB 206 million, a 58% year-on-year increase.
3. Internet Hospital & Digital Prescription Services
    - Launch: Internet hospital platform launched in 2014.
    - Impact: As of 2023, issued approximately 190 million online prescriptions, significantly improving medical accessibility and reducing paper and

transportation costs.

III. Technology Infrastructure and AI Innovation

Zhongyun Medical Brain (ClouDr Brain)

- Incorporates the ClouD GPT diagnostic model and ClouD DTx digital therapy platform, offering AI-powered support for chronic disease diagnosis and treatment.
- AI technologies optimize business processes, improve diagnostic efficiency, and reduce operational costs. The company collaborates with medical universities for R&D integration.

AIoT (Medical Internet of Things)

- SaaS platforms integrate with hardware such as glucometers and vital sign monitors to unify data between hospital and out-of-hospital environments, creating a closed-loop workflow.

IV. Market Performance and Strategic Partnerships

- IPO: Successfully listed on the Hong Kong Stock Exchange main board in 2022, marking its public market debut.
- Ecosystem: Partnered with over 2,700 hospitals and 229,000 pharmacies.
- Strategic Alliances: Collaborated with major pharmaceutical companies on digital marketing and out-of-hospital care expansion.
- Business Model: Operates under the "AIM" model—Access hospitals → Install SaaS → Monetize via medical device/drug marketing—to create a closed-loop commercial ecosystem.

V. Strategic Path and ESG Commitments

- Chronic Disease Market: Targets China's massive chronic care market (worth ~RMB 4.1 trillion) with a digital adoption CAGR of ~35%.
- Academia-Industry Collaboration: Partners with universities and research institutes to jointly cultivate talent and technology.
- ESG Practices: Promotes environmental responsibility (e.g., paper reduction), reduces travel, supports public welfare clinics, and provides accessible digital healthcare services to underserved populations.

VI. Key Milestones Timeline

Time	Milestone
2014.12	Company founded, began developing its internet hospital infrastructure
2016	Launched hospital-end chronic care SaaS "Zhongyun Yihui" with AIoT links
2019	Released pharmacy-end SaaS "Zhongyun Consultation," closing care loop
2021	Rolled out ClouDr Brain (AI diagnosis & digital therapy modules)
2022	IPO on HKEX, ushering in capital market expansion
2023	Pharmacy revenue surged; online prescriptions exceeded 190 million

VII. Summary

Zhongyun Health has gradually built a robust chronic disease ecosystem through its "hospital → pharmacy → internet healthcare" architecture. Leveraging SaaS and AI technologies, it has strengthened coordination among institutions, users, and partners to create a closed-loop digital business model.

Post-IPO, the company experienced strong growth and remained a market leader. However, rapid expansion and public market scrutiny brought increasing pressure on sustainability, compliance, and valuation stability.

During a fundraising round, Zhongyun Health submitted falsified ESG disclosure materials, exaggerating its carbon neutrality claims and employee welfare policies. These inconsistencies were uncovered during third-party due diligence, leading a Middle Eastern fund to terminate its investment, damaging the company's credibility.

VIII. Lessons Learned

ESG has become a "credit score" for international investors. Companies must disclose truthfully and align with global standards such as IFRS or SASB—cutting corners or fabricating reports leads to severe reputational damage.

This incident highlights a fundamental misunderstanding by domestic firms regarding the importance of non-financial indicators to foreign institutional investors. ESG is not just a trend but a key component of institutional risk assessment.

Zhongyun's case demonstrates the risks of operating without third-party ESG ratings or certified disclosure platforms. The absence of independent validation easily triggers trust crises.

Recommendations:
Adopt internationally recognized ESG frameworks such as SASB.
Engage compliance professionals to prepare authentic, traceable, and auditable ESG disclosures and policy documentation.

Case 5: Market Cap Management Failure and Severe Secondary Market Crash

I. Company Overview

Shukun Technology, founded in 2017 and headquartered in Beijing, was co-founded by Ma Chune (a former IBM executive) and her husband Mao Xinsheng.

- Mission: To create an "AI-powered digital doctor" that helps physicians deliver more efficient, accurate, consistent, and accessible medical services.
- Investor Base: Backed by renowned institutional investors such as Sequoia China, YuanYi Capital, Huagai Capital, 5Y Capital, and Qiming Venture Partners.

II. Founders' Vision and Motivation

- Ma Chune spent over a decade at IBM and witnessed firsthand how patients struggled with appointments and diagnostic inefficiencies. Determined to improve healthcare delivery through AI, she committed to entrepreneurship.
- Mao Xinsheng, with a strong background in computer science and artificial intelligence, provided the technical foundation for the company.

III. Technology and Product Development

- Digital Doctor Product Suite: Core offerings include "Digital Heart," "Digital Brain," "Digital Chest," "Digital Abdomen," and "Digital Musculoskeletal." The company has launched over 37 AI-driven products, deployed in over 3,000 public hospitals, covering more than 80% of China's top-tier hospitals.
- Multimodal Recognition Capabilities: Shukun integrates cutting-edge technologies such as cloud computing, big data, AI, IoT, and AR to build a "Digital Human" platform, deeply integrating medical imaging and textual data.
- Breakthrough in Medical Foundation Models: In 2025, Shukun released "ShukunKun" Multimodal Medical Foundation Model 3.0, capable of processing images, text, audio, and more. It simulates clinical diagnostic reasoning and has demonstrated strong performance in assisting diagnoses of lung and breast diseases.

IV. Certifications and Market Performance

- Certifications: Among the first in China to receive multiple NMPA Class III medical device certifications, including for coronary CTA, breast imaging, head and neck CTA, and ultrasound.

- Clinical Accuracy: Its AI-assisted diagnosis systems for pulmonary nodules and breast cancer demonstrate high sensitivity and specificity, leading the industry in performance.
- Recognition: In 2023, named a sector leader in China's AI medical imaging field, enjoying strong credibility within the industry.

V. Financing History and IPO Journey

- Fundraising: Completed at least 10 rounds of financing since inception, totaling billions of RMB. In 2017, it raised RMB 22 million in a seed round from YuanYi Capital; in 2019, it raised hundreds of millions in Series A, with later rounds led by Sequoia China.
- Institutional Investors: Includes Huagai Capital, 5Y Capital, Qiming Venture, CICC Pucheng, China Re Insurance, Goldman Sachs, and Jane Street, among others.
- IPO Filing: Submitted an IPO application to the Hong Kong Stock Exchange in 2021, with joint sponsors including J.P. Morgan, Bank of America, and BofA Securities.

VI. Globalization and Ecosystem Development

- International Certifications: Obtained EU MDR certification; several medical foundation models and AI-native hardware entered clinical pilot phases.
- Smart Hospital Collaboration: Partnered with institutions like Beijing Geriatric Hospital and Huawei to drive smart hospital transformation.
- Global Partnerships: Collaborated with over 5,000 medical institutions worldwide, amassing vast multimodal medical datasets to support model training and deployment.

VII. Summary

Shukun Technology is a fast-rising star in China's AI medical imaging sector. Its simultaneous advancement in technology and market adoption, along with strong financial backing, has established it as a model enterprise.

With its digital doctor product suite and medical foundation model strategy, it has built a globally leading AI healthcare ecosystem and made steady progress on the IPO path. However, precisely because of its advanced technical capabilities and high valuation, the company also exposed vulnerabilities in post-IPO valuation management and stock stabilization—becoming a cautionary case in SPAC-related IPO failures.

Shukun (also referred to as Deepwise AI in its U.S. operations) went public via a SPAC on the U.S. stock exchange. However, after listing, the company lacked an investor relations (IR) team and a robust stock stabilization strategy. The IPO was priced at a high valuation, triggering institutional sell-offs. The stock subsequently plunged over 80%, significantly damaging its capacity for future acquisitions and fundraising.

VIII. Lessons Learned

SPAC is not the finish line—what follows is even more critical: robust market cap management, continuous investor communication, and a well-structured long-term incentive and buyback mechanism.

Many SPAC-listed companies underestimate the importance of post-IPO valuation management. After its listing, Deepwise failed to assign a dedicated IR head, did not conduct regular roadshows, and lacked an investor engagement mechanism, resulting in waning market confidence.

In addition, the IPO was overpriced, with no lock-up provisions or repurchase plans in place. This led to intense short-term selling pressure and steep valuation collapse.

Recommendations:
SPAC-bound companies should establish a dedicated IR team before going public. They should also pre-arrange long-term stock stabilization mechanisms, including:

- Investor incentive agreements
- Management equity incentive plans
- Buyback reserve pools

Summary: Five Classic Pitfalls in Global Expansion

1. Unclear Equity Structure Led to Investor Exit Pre-IPO
   InferVision failed to restructure equity and lacked exit mechanisms, resulting in conflicts between old and new shareholders, financing collapse, and valuation plunge.
2. Non-Compliant Token Offering Triggered Regulatory Action
   DataOcean Biotech bypassed Reg D/S and launched a token offering without legal review. The SEC intervened and the project was shut down due to compliance violations.
3. Failed Cross-Border M&A Due to Cultural and Operational Gaps
   BioSciGen's acquisition of a European CDMO lacked integration planning. Cultural barriers, poor coordination, and financial overruns derailed synergy and delayed IPO plans.
4. Fake ESG Reporting Caused Institutional LP Withdrawal
   Zhongyun Health submitted exaggerated ESG data, which was exposed during due diligence, leading to the withdrawal of a Middle Eastern LP and reputational damage.
5. Lack of Post-SPAC Valuation Management Caused Stock Crash
   Deepwise AI went public via SPAC but lacked an IR team or buyback plan. Overvaluation and poor communication led to an 80% stock drop, undermining its capital market positioning.

Key Takeaway:

Going global requires more than strong products—it demands comprehensive readiness in compliance, governance, culture, and capital structure. Mid-sized innovators must proactively address these dimensions to avoid preventable failures.

Chapter 32 Smart Capital Formula in Action - IVD MEDICAL (01931.HK)

I. Background and Challenges

IVD MEDICAL (01931.HK) Company Overview

IVD MEDICAL (International Diagnostic Medical Group, Stock Code: 01931.HK) is a Hong Kong–headquartered, Hong Kong Stock Exchange Main Board–listed comprehensive healthcare company. The company's core business covers the R&D, manufacturing, and sales of in vitro diagnostic (IVD) products, while also actively expanding into high-end medical equipment, life sciences, and innovative pharmaceuticals.

Since its establishment, the company has built a robust global supply chain and distribution network through a combination of self-developed products and acquisitions, exporting to multiple countries and regions in Asia, Europe, and the Americas. Its key competitive advantages include:

1. Deep technical expertise and brand influence in the IVD sector;
2. A comprehensive global sales network and distribution channels;
3. Partnerships with top international medical institutions and research institutes;
4. Financing capability and brand credibility as a listed company.

In recent years, IVD MEDICAL has actively embraced global medical innovation trends, initiating strategic transformation by acquiring high-value innovative drug pipeline assets, introducing digital and blockchain technologies, and exploring the RWA (Real-World Asset) tokenization path to optimize capital structure and enhance valuation.

In 2025, IVD MEDICAL launched the world's first "Medical Innovative Drug Stablecoin First Stock" project, successfully integrating the group's innovative drug pipeline assets with the blockchain-based digital capital market, setting a new benchmark for both the Hong Kong and global capital markets.

Before 2025, IVD MEDICAL's Hong Kong–listed operations mainly focused on its IVD business. While it had built strong domestic and international channels and brand recognition, its market cap growth in the global capital market had hit a ceiling:

- **Market Cap Ceiling:** Stuck in the mid-cap range (HK$3–5 billion), lacking a compelling growth story to attract long-term global capital.
- **R&D Shortfall:** Insufficient self-developed innovative drugs, scattered pipeline layout, no flagship product to anchor valuation.

- **Capital Structure Constraints:** Limited Hong Kong market liquidity hindered large-scale attraction of international investors, especially USD LPs and sovereign funds.

This situation closely matches the "valuation bottleneck" of mid-market enterprises described in Chapter 3 of this book: businesses with revenue and cash flow, but lacking premium assets and structured pathways recognized by international capital.

II. Introduction of the Smart Capital Formula

The case of **IVD MEDICAL (01931.HK)** perfectly validates the tremendous potential of the *Smart Capital* formula:

Smart Capital=RWA×Stablecoin×(Tri–Market Listing:IPOs+STO)×(OpCo+NewCo)

Since July 2025, the company has proactively announced its application for a U.S. stablecoin license, acquired a significant amount of Ethereum as digital asset reserves, and partnered with leading institutions such as HashKey to explore RWA pathways. This series of tangible strategic moves has laid the groundwork for its future market capitalization to leap from several billion to tens of billions.

According to projections under the *Smart Capital* formula, if the company successfully tokenizes its innovative drug assets as RWAs and issues a compliant stablecoin, it is entirely possible for it to achieve even greater growth within the next 12–24 months.

Specific breakdown:

1. **RWA (Real-World Assets):** Certify the group's globally acquired high-value innovative drug pipeline assets (NewCo assets), including gene therapy, targeted drugs, and rare disease treatments. These assets enjoy global patent protection and have market potential confirmed by independent third-party valuation agencies.
2. **Stablecoin:** Issue the IVDMed Stable Token (IVDMS), pegged to USD 1:1 and collateralized by tokenized pharmaceutical IP and licensing income rights, to facilitate cross-border financing and circulation.
3. **Tri-Market Listings + STO:** Hong Kong Main Board (existing), Middle Eastern stock exchange, and IVDNewCo Exchange platform (STO component).
4. **OpCo + NewCo Structure:** OpCo manages the diagnostic business; NewCo holds tokenized assets for independent valuation and financing.

III. Implementation Path (T+36-Month Blueprint)

- **T+0 to T+6 Months:** Complete asset valuation and certification, set up BVI/SPV, create smart contract templates, ensure compliance for issuance.
- **T+6 to T+18 Months:** Launch stablecoin private placement (Reg D + Reg S), issue first batch of IVDMS Tokens, list on trading platform, attract Middle Eastern investors.
- **T+18 to T+36 Months:** Gradually tokenize remaining assets, plan listing on Middle Eastern exchange, activate secondary liquidity mechanisms, form a cross-border capital loop.

IV. Results and Impact

On **July 31, 2025**, IVD MEDICAL announced the launch of the world's first "Medical Innovative Drug Stablecoin First Stock" project:

- **Market Cap Growth:** Increased 2.3× in one year, from ~HK$3.5 billion to HK$8 billion.
- **Liquidity Breakthrough:** RWA token secondary market trading volume stabilized at over US$50 million per month.
- **Investor Base Upgrade:** Added 5 Middle Eastern sovereign funds and international medical funds.
- **Global Brand Recognition:** Featured by multiple international financial media outlets as a "benchmark case for pharmaceutical asset digitalization."

V. Comparison with Traditional Pathways

Dimension	**Traditional Biopharma Listing Model**	**IVD MEDICAL Smart Capital Model**
Asset Type	Single R&D pipeline or marketed drug	Multi-project global pipeline + digital RWA assets
Financing Channels	IPO + PIPE	IPO + STO + Stablecoin cross-border circulation
Investor Base	Public funds, retail investors	Global LPs, sovereign funds, qualified token investors

Dimension	Traditional Biopharma Listing Model	IVD MEDICAL Smart Capital Model
Liquidity	Single exchange	HKEX + Middle Eastern exchange + IVDNewCo Exchange
Valuation Elasticity	Tied to industry cycles	RWA pricing + international arbitrage mechanisms amplify valuation

VI. Smart Capital Formula Validation

This case validates three major advantages of the Smart Capital Formula:

1. **Valuation Amplification:** Asset carve-out and independent NewCo valuation make hidden value explicit.
2. **Capital Structure Upgrade:** Stablecoins and tokenized assets enable seamless cross-border financing.
3. **Market Reach Expansion:** Tri-market listings + on-chain trading achieve simultaneous global capital access.

VII. Insights and Replicability

Applicable Sectors: Biopharma, advanced manufacturing, clean energy — fields with IP and long-term revenue rights.
Key Preconditions: Assets must be certifiable, valuable, and tradable in global markets.
Risk Control: Strict compliance with securities and digital asset regulations in relevant jurisdictions.

Conclusion:
The IVD MEDICAL case is not only a successful demonstration of the Smart Capital Formula, but also a milestone in how Chinese enterprises can use RWA + stablecoin to achieve capital globalization, providing a replicable strategic model for other mid-sized innovative companies.

Part VII: Strategic Toolkit of Smart Capital

Offers standardized, bilingual toolkits including PIPE agreements, NewCo formation checklists, RWA+Token compliance workflows, ESG templates, and investor pitch materials—forming a complete operational playbook for global capital strategies.

Chapter 33: PIPE Investment Agreement Template (Bilingual)

PIPE Investment Agreement Structure Template

Investor: USD LP / Institutional Fund
Target: NewCo or Portfolio Company
Investment Amount: USD XX million
Equity: XX% or Convertible Note
Governance: 1 Board Seat + 1 Observer
Rights: Information, Buy-back, Anti-dilution, Liquidation Preference
Exit: 12–24 Months via IPO, Trade Sale or Roll-up

《PIPE 投资协议》

PIPE Investment Agreement

本 PIPE 投资协议（"本协议"）由以下各方于【填写日期】签署：
This PIPE Investment Agreement ("Agreement") is entered into on [Insert Date] by and among:

1. **公司方（Issuer）：**
   【公司名称】，一家根据【注册地】法律设立并合法存续的公司，注册地址为【地址】。（下称"公司"）
   [Company Name], a company duly organized and existing under the laws of [Jurisdiction], with its principal office at [Address]. (hereinafter referred to as the "Company")

2. **投资方（Investor）：**
   【投资人名称】，一家根据【注册地】法律设立并合法存续的公司/个人，注册地址为【地址】。（下称"投资方"）
   [Investor Name], a company/individual duly organized and existing under the laws of [Jurisdiction], with its principal address at [Address]. (hereinafter referred to as the "Investor")

第一条 投资条款

Article 1: Investment Terms

1.1 投资金额：投资方同意以总金额【金额】（“投资金额”）认购公司发行的普通股/可转换优先股/可转换债券。
Investment Amount: The Investor agrees to subscribe for ordinary shares/preferred shares/convertible notes issued by the Company in the aggregate amount of [Amount] (“Investment Amount”).

1.2 认购价格：每股认购价格为【每股价格】（如适用）。
Subscription Price: The price per share shall be [Price per Share] (if applicable).

1.3 交割时间：本次投资交割应于满足先决条件后【填写具体天数】日内完成，或由双方书面约定的其他日期。
Closing Date: The investment closing shall take place within [Number of Days] days after the satisfaction of all closing conditions or on such other date as mutually agreed by both parties.

第二条 股份发行与登记

Article 2: Issuance and Registration

2.1 公司应根据适用证券法规定，向投资方发行上述证券，并确保其依法有效发行及登记。
The Company shall issue the above-mentioned securities to the Investor in accordance with applicable securities laws and ensure valid issuance and registration.

2.2 如为可转换证券，公司应说明转换条款、期限、转换价格及相关权利义务。
If the investment involves convertible securities, the Company shall specify the terms, duration, conversion price, and related rights and obligations.

第三条 陈述与保证

Article 3: Representations and Warranties

3.1 公司陈述并保证其依法设立、具有合法授权签署本协议并履行义务的能力。
The Company represents and warrants that it is duly organized and has the legal authority to execute and perform this Agreement.

3.2 投资方陈述并保证其为合格投资者，具备相应资金来源及合规投资权限。
The Investor represents and warrants that it is a qualified investor with lawful funding sources and investment authority.

第四条 先决条件

Article 4: Conditions Precedent

4.1 投资交割的先决条件包括但不限于:
Conditions precedent to the investment closing shall include but not be limited to:

- 公司通过必要的董事会和股东决议;
  Company's approval by board and shareholders;
- 所需政府/监管备案完成（如适用）;
  Completion of any required governmental/ regulatory filings (if applicable);
- 双方完成尽职调查并无重大不利变动。
  Satisfactory due diligence with no material adverse change.

第五条 信息披露与锁定期

Article 5: Disclosure and Lock-up

5.1 公司应向投资方提供合理信息披露，包括季度报告、重大事项等。
The Company shall provide reasonable disclosures to the Investor, including quarterly reports and material events.

5.2 锁定期安排（如适用）：投资方所持股份应自交割日起【x】个月内不得转让。
Lock-up period (if applicable): Investor shall not transfer the shares within [x] months from the Closing Date.

第六条 违约与争议解决

Article 6: Breach and Dispute Resolution

6.1 任何一方违反本协议条款，守约方有权要求赔偿并/或终止协议。
In case of breach, the non-breaching party shall be entitled to claim compensation and/or terminate the Agreement.

6.2 本协议适用【法律管辖区】法律，并提交【仲裁机构/法院】解决争议。
This Agreement shall be governed by the laws of [Jurisdiction] and submitted to [Arbitration Institution/Court] for resolution.

第七条 其他

Article 7: Miscellaneous

7.1 本协议一式两份，中英文版本具有同等法律效力。
This Agreement is made in two counterparts in both Chinese and English, both versions being equally authentic.

7.2 未尽事宜由双方另行协商签署补充协议。
Matters not covered herein shall be subject to supplemental agreements negotiated and signed by the parties.

第八条 股东权利条款

Article 8: Shareholder Rights

8.1 投资方自交割日起即享有与其他同类股份持有人相同的表决权、分红权与信息权。
As of the Closing Date, the Investor shall enjoy the same voting, dividend, and information rights as other holders of the same class of shares.

8.2 公司应允许投资方派遣一名观察员列席董事会会议（如投资金额超过公司当时估值的5%）。
If the Investment Amount represents more than 5% of the Company's then valuation, the Investor shall be entitled to appoint one board observer to attend board meetings.

8.3 公司应在未来任何新一轮融资中，给予投资方等比例优先认购权（Pro Rata Right）。
The Company shall grant the Investor the pro rata right to participate in any future equity financing rounds.

第九条 退出机制

Article 9: Exit Mechanisms

9.1 回购权（Put Option）：若公司在【36】个月内未完成上市、并购或第三方股权转让退出，投资方有权要求公司以不低于初始投资金额【+8%年化回报】的价格回购其所持股份。
Put Option: If the Company fails to complete an IPO, M&A, or qualified third-party transfer within [36] months, the Investor shall have the right to require the Company to repurchase the shares at a price not less than the original investment plus an annual return of [8]%.

9.2 公司承诺，在回购请求后【90】天内完成回购款项支付，逾期应承担【12%】年利息。
The Company agrees to complete the repurchase payment within [90] days of receiving the notice. A default interest of [12%] per annum shall apply thereafter.

9.3 优先出售权（Tag-Along Right）：如控股股东拟转让其股权，投资方有权按比例随售。
Tag-Along Right: In the event the controlling shareholder intends to transfer their shares, the Investor shall have the right to participate in the sale on a pro-rata basis.

第十条 并购条款

Article 10: M&A Clauses

10.1 若公司进行资产出售、整体并购、控制权转移等重大交易，投资方应享有提前【30日】书面通知权。
In the event of an asset sale, acquisition, or change of control, the Investor shall be given at least [30] days prior written notice.

10.2 在并购交易中，投资方所持股份应优先获得退出或现金清偿安排，优先于普通股股东。
In the case of an M&A transaction, the Investor shall have liquidation preference over ordinary shareholders, with priority in receiving cash or equivalent consideration.

10.3 若并购对价包含股票置换，投资方有权选择退出或跟随换股，并按 1:1.5 比例优先分配换股比例（如 NewCo 结构适用）。
If the consideration includes stock swap, the Investor shall have the option to either exit or participate in the swap, and may be granted preferential terms at a 1:1.5 swap ratio (applicable in NewCo structures).

公司（Company）： **投资方（Investor）：**

签署人：________________ 签署人：________________

日期：________________ 日期：________________

Chapter 34: NewCo Formation Flowchart and Legal Checklist

I. NewCo Formation Flowchart and Key Steps

Flowchart Overview:

Chinese Parent Company / Asset Provider → Project Screening and Asset Evaluation

→ Determine NewCo Structure

→ Register NewCo (BVI/Cayman)

→ Sign Asset Injection Agreement

→ Inject Assets / Licenses into NewCo

→ Compliance Audit and Valuation Benchmarking

→ Launch Fundraising or Token Issuance

→ Token On-Chain / or IPO Channel

Notes and Highlights:

Project Screening and Evaluation: Identify business units or rights suitable for offshore structuring, such as licenses, contracts, or AI models.

Choosing the Place of Incorporation: BVI or Cayman Islands are common due to tax neutrality, flexible equity design, and Token-friendly policies.

Registration Process: Includes KYC, shareholding structure design, obtaining certificate of incorporation and memorandum.

Asset Injection Methods: Can be done via License Agreements, VIEs, Equity Transfers—emphasizing the separation of ownership and control.

Compliance Audit and Valuation: Recommended to engage Big 4 or international accounting firms; prepare whitepaper and tokenomics if issuing tokens.

Follow-up Paths: Token offering, SPAC merger, IPO, etc.

II. NewCo Legal Checklist

Module	Key Legal Points	Recommended Actions
Formation Stage	Jurisdictional compliance, KYC, equity structure design	Engage lawyers, establish dual-share structure
Asset Injection Stage	Define IP/license/revenue rights, tax and FX planning, enforceability	Sign license agreement, issue legal opinion
Shareholder Rights Design	Voting rights, liquidation rights, pre-emptive rights, anti-dilution	Specify in Articles and Shareholder Agreement
Token Structure	Security token classification, risk disclosure, chain selection	Draft whitepaper, design token buyback mechanism
Governance & Control	Board setup, reserved matters, voting mechanism	Create shareholder agreement, include veto rights
Exit Mechanism Design	IPO/SPAC/token listing, preferred liquidation, repurchase terms	Design convertibles, define repurchase pricing
Document Checklist	Certificate, M&A, shareholder agreements, legal opinions	Archive and submit to banks/regulators

Note: Additional materials can be customized for specific projects, including Shareholder Agreements, License Agreements, Token Subscription Agreements, Board Resolutions, etc.

Chapter 35: RWA + Token Compliance Guide (Reg D / Reg S)

This chapter provides a systematic compliance pathway for token issuance based on real world assets (RWA), tailored for companies and funds in healthcare, technology, and digital asset sectors. By leveraging U.S. securities regulations (Regulation D and Regulation S), blockchain tokenization, and offshore legal structures, it aims to achieve a digital capital model that is compliant, auditable, and offers exit mechanisms for qualified investors.

Step 1: Accredited Investor KYC / AML Identification

Before initiating token issuance, issuers must identify and verify the identities of prospective investors to ensure compliance with securities law standards:

• For U.S. investors (Reg D path), they must qualify as Accredited Investors based on income or net worth thresholds and be verified via platforms like Onfido or Jumio.
• For non-U.S. investors (Reg S path), AML checks and sanctions list screenings must be conducted using tools like Chainalysis to evaluate wallet compliance history.
• After due diligence, a whitelist of approved wallet addresses should be maintained for subsequent smart contract restrictions.

Step 2: Issuance Vehicle Setup (Cayman Fund + Token SPV)

A proper legal structure is foundational to compliance. A typical setup involves a Cayman master fund with a separate token-issuing SPV:

• A Cayman Islands Exempted Limited Partnership (ELP) serves as the master fund managing LP relationships.
• The Token SPV, usually formed in Cayman or BVI, is responsible for issuing and managing the token.
• Token-to-fund equity linkage is structured via agreements like a Token Purchase Agreement and a Revenue Sharing Contract.
• All structures must be disclosed in the fund's Private Placement Memorandum (PPM) and reviewed by legal counsel.

Step 3: Token Smart Contract Design (Transfer Restrictions + Whitelist Controls)

Token design must comply with regulatory requirements and enforce legal logic on-chain:

• Smart contracts should include vesting or lock-up logic (e.g., Reg D 6–12 months), anti-concentration alerts, and address whitelisting.
• Tokens cannot be listed on public markets unless they qualify for secondary trading on compliant platforms like Securitize, INX, or TZero.
• On-chain identity protocols (e.g., ERC-3643) should be integrated to bind wallet addresses with verified KYC identities.
• Full audit logs should be maintained to verify each transaction's legality.

Step 4: Private Placement Compliance Filing (Form D & Reg S Disclosure)

• For Reg D offerings, Form D must be filed with the U.S. SEC within 15 days of the first sale, disclosing offering size, number of investors, and any commissions.
• A formal Private Placement Memorandum (PPM) in English should include project purpose, risk factors, lock-up rules, and tax implications.
• Reg S disclosures must clearly state that tokens cannot be sold or transferred within the U.S. market to avoid triggering U.S. jurisdiction.
• A legal opinion is recommended to strengthen trust with investors and support onboarding on secondary platforms.

Step 5: Liquidity Mechanisms (Delayed Transfer, Custody, Buyback Options)

Token liquidity design must comply with regulation while offering structured exit opportunities:

• Delayed transfer logic: allow partial transfers post-lock-up period, or apply daily transfer limits.
• Compliant secondary trading: list tokens on approved digital securities exchanges with KYC-based identity verification.
• Buyback options: Issuers can offer periodic buyback windows (e.g., quarterly or semi-annual), priced based on Net Asset Value (NAV).
• Use of stablecoins (e.g., USDC) as settlement currency reduces FX friction.

Notes

- Reg D applies to U.S. accredited investors only; public solicitation is prohibited unless under Rule 506(c).
- Reg S is intended for non-U.S. investors and emphasizes offshore offering characteristics.
- All smart contracts should be audited by third parties and preferably open-sourced.
- Legal counsel from both U.S. securities and Cayman offshore specialists is highly recommended.

This guide serves as a reference for tokenized fundraising structure design, due diligence, and legal compliance review.

Chapter 36：ESG Integration and Strategies for Accessing Long-Term International Capital

1. Background and Strategic Value

This newly added module is designed specifically for embedding ESG (Environmental, Social, and Governance) principles, with the goal of aligning with the investment preferences of major overseas LPs (such as pension funds, sovereign wealth funds, and long-term institutional investors). It aims to enhance project compliance, accountability, and attractiveness to global capital.

In today's global capital landscape, ESG has become a basic screening threshold for long-term capital institutions (e.g., BlackRock, Norwegian Pension Fund, CalPERS, GIC, etc.). For mid-sized enterprises seeking entry into U.S. or Hong Kong capital markets, it is essential to incorporate the following ESG elements to improve transparency and compliance:

Integration Strategy:

- ESG should not be an auxiliary component, but a core governance element of the NewCo platform.

- Establish ESG disclosure mechanisms and internal quantifiable targets in alignment with USD LP requirements.

2. ESG Core Module Design Recommendations

E – Environment

- Green Clinical/R&D Processes: Reduce animal testing, promote simulation platforms, optimize energy usage.

- Environmentally Responsible Medical Supply Chain: Establish standards for low-carbon emissions and recyclable packaging.

- ESG Data Reporting: Publish annual disclosures aligned with UN PRI, including carbon footprint, energy, and water usage.

S – Social

- Employee Equity and Incentive Mechanism: Set gender ratio goals, offer career training, implement fair ESOP plans.

- Data Privacy and Patient Rights: Ensure AI data processing complies with GDPR/HIPAA to protect data usage rights.

- Inclusive Healthcare: Collaborate with governments, insurers, and NGOs to promote precision healthcare and expand social impact.

G – Governance

- Independent Director Mechanism: Introduce two internationally experienced independent directors and establish an ESG committee.

- ESG-Linked Incentives: Tie a portion of management incentives to ESG targets such as carbon reduction and female executive ratio.

- Anti-Corruption and Transparency: Implement conflict-of-interest disclosure and cross-border compliance risk control protocols.

3. ESG Standards Alignment and Rating Systems

Standard	Application Path
SASB Standards	Align with industry-specific disclosure metrics (Biotech, AI Health)
TCFD Reporting Framework	Disclose climate risk management and emission reduction in ESG annual reports
UN PRI Commitment	Signed by NewCo or ETAO's parent company to align with UN Principles for Responsible Investment
MSCI ESG Rating	Apply for MSCI ESG ratings to enhance PIPE fund investability
Nasdaq ESG Guidelines	Comply with ESG disclosure rules for U.S.-listed companies (Form 10-K/20-F)

4. Business Logic and Value Summary

Value Dimension	Significance

Financing Compatibility	Meets ESG screening criteria for European and American LPs, enhances PIPE/fund investability
Brand Credibility	Strengthens the social influence of ETAO and NewCo in global capital markets and healthcare ecosystems
Risk Management	Mitigates potential ESG litigation, data privacy, gender discrimination, and audit opacity risks
M&A Premium	Generates 'compliance premium' in future M&A deals as ESG ratings gain relevance

Conclusion

ESG is not a burden, but a 'capital passport to long-term value.' Embedding ESG within the NewCo structure not only enhances global investor acceptance, but also gives enterprises greater long-term pricing and bargaining power in capital markets, business development, and global governance.

ESG Disclosure Structure Template (IFRS/SASB)

Core ESG Framework Components:

- **E – Environmental:**
    - GHG Emissions
    - Energy Efficiency & Carbon Reduction
    - Green Procurement Strategy
- **S – Social:**
    - Labor Compliance
    - Workplace Diversity & Inclusion
    - Data Privacy & Protection
- **G – Governance:**
    - Board Composition & Oversight
    - Audit Committee Structure
    - Anti-Fraud & Anti-Corruption Mechanisms

Recommended Reporting Format:

- Quantitative KPIs disclosed per SASB sector-specific metrics
- Risk and opportunity narratives structured under IFRS Sustainability Disclosure Standards

English Summary Format:

- Environmental: GHG Emissions, Energy Usage, Green Procurement
- Social: Labor Compliance, Diversity, Data Privacy
- Governance: Board Structure, Audit Oversight, Anti-Corruption
- Recommended Method: SASB Metrics + IFRS Sustainability Risk/Opportunity Narratives

Here is a **draft IFRS-aligned ESG (Environmental, Social, and Governance) Reporting Template**, designed to help companies disclose material sustainability information in line with evolving global standards such as **IFRS S1 and S2 (from ISSB - International**

Sustainability Standards Board). This template is suitable for integration into annual reports or standalone sustainability reports.

ESG DISCLOSURE TEMPLATE

IFRS-Aligned Format (IFRS S1 & S2 Compatible)

1. General ESG Disclosure (IFRS S1 – General Requirements for Disclosure of Sustainability-related Financial Information)

1.1 Governance

- Description of governance structure overseeing ESG-related risks and opportunities
- Roles of the Board and management in ESG oversight and strategy
- Frequency and method of ESG performance reviews

1.2 Strategy

- Company's short, medium, and long-term ESG goals
- Identification of material ESG risks and opportunities
- Impact of ESG risks/opportunities on business model, strategy, and financial planning

1.3 Risk Management

- Process for identifying and assessing ESG risks
- Integration of ESG risks into overall risk management system
- Scenario analysis or stress testing if applicable (especially for climate risk)

1.4 Metrics & Targets

- ESG KPIs monitored (e.g., GHG emissions, energy intensity, employee diversity)
- Targets set (e.g., net zero by 2050) and performance against them
- Methodologies and assumptions used in measurement

2. Climate-Related Disclosures (IFRS S2 – Climate-related Disclosures)

2.1 Governance (Climate-Specific)

- Oversight of climate-related risks and opportunities
- Roles of Board and executives in climate strategy and decision-making

2.2 Strategy (Climate-Specific)

- Climate-related risks/opportunities identified and timeframe (short/medium/long-term)
- Impact on business operations, value chain, and financial performance
- Resilience of strategy under different climate scenarios (e.g., 1.5°C, 2°C)

2.3 Risk Management (Climate-Specific)

- Identification and evaluation of physical and transition climate risks
- Tools and frameworks used (e.g., TCFD, SASB, CDP)

2.4 Metrics and Targets (Climate-Specific)

- Scope 1, 2, and 3 GHG emissions (with methodology: GHG Protocol, ISO 14064, etc.)
- Climate-related targets (e.g., Science-Based Targets) and achievement status
- Use of carbon credits or offsets (if applicable)

3. Social and Governance Metrics (Supplemental)

3.1 Social Metrics

- Workforce composition (gender, ethnicity, etc.)
- Employee training and retention rates
- Community engagement and human rights practices
- Health & safety performance (e.g., injury rates)

3.2 Governance Metrics

- Board composition and diversity
- Anti-bribery and corruption policies
- Executive compensation linked to ESG metrics

- Data privacy and cybersecurity practices

4. Assurance and Data Quality

- Whether ESG data is audited or assured by third parties
- Limitations or estimation techniques
- Basis of preparation, restatements (if any)

5. Appendices

- Glossary of ESG terms
- ESG performance summary table
- Alignment with other frameworks: TCFD, GRI, SASB, SDGs
- Contact point for ESG inquiries

Chapter 37: Tri-Market Listing Timeline (T+36 Months Roadmap)

Strategic Timeline – A 36-Month Execution Blueprint for Capital Elevation

Strategic Roadmap for the Hong Kong ChenChen Project

Phase 1: T+0 ~ T+6 Months

Core Objective: Initial Structure Setup + Legacy Equity Transfer + Platform Integration

Action	Description
Establish NewCo (BVI/Cayman)	Finalize corporate structure; Inject partial legacy equity from ChenChen, ETAO becomes controlling shareholder or lead strategic partner
Sign Strategic Cooperation Agreement	Framework agreement between ChenChen and ETAO (includes global licensing, capital exit, FA terms, etc.)
Initiate PIPE Round 1 Negotiations	Led by WSHP Capital to introduce USD-based investors and define payout structure for legacy equity holders
Launch AI Empowerment + BD Alignment	Align ETAO's AI platform with ChenChen's R&D pipeline Begin pre-licensing deal packaging
Start Token Structure Design (Optional)	Initiate legal and technical framework for RWA tokenization to prepare for future asset token issuance

Phase 2: T+6 ~ T+12 Months

Core Objective: Capital Infusion + Overseas BD Transaction + Valuation Uplift

Action	Description
License-out or BD Transaction	- Facilitate the first milestone partnership with a global pharmaceutical company - Secure upfront payment or co-development agreement

Pilot Token Issuance (Optional)	- Issue RWA-A/B Tokens under ERC-3643 standard - Complete first-round token financing via private placement
Complete FA Due Diligence	- PIPE investors complete due diligence and inject a new round of USD capital - Uplift NewCo valuation
International Brand Expansion	- Attend global pharma summits such as the JP Morgan Conference and BIO - Enhance the brand visibility of ChenChen and ETAO

Phase 3: T+12 ~ T+24 Months

Core Objective: NASDAQ Consolidation or NewCo Valuation Decoupling

Action	Description
ETAO Acquires or Consolidates NewCo	- ETAO absorbs NewCo via a cash + stock swap - Achieve valuation consolidation and narrative upgrade
Trigger Token-to-Equity Conversion (Optional)	- RWA token holders convert into ETAO shares at a 1:1.5 ratio - Complete liquidity exit
Begin HKEX/STAR IPO Preparation	- Prepare HKEX Chapter 18A or A-share IPO documents under NewCo - Complete three years of historical financial audits
Achieve Valuation Milestone	- Through AI empowerment, license-out deals, and enhanced NASDAQ valuation - Target valuation: USD 500M – 1B

Phase 4: T+24 ~ T+36 Months

Core Objective: HKEX or A-share Listing for Dual-Market Capital Arbitrage

Action	Description
IPO on HKEX or A-share Main Board	- Position NewCo as an 'internationally validated mature subsidiary' - Achieve listing and build a WuXi AppTec-style dual-platform structure
ETAO Retains Controlling Stake	- ETAO retains no less than 15–30% equity - Continues to benefit from capital linkage

PIPE Fund or FA Exit	- Investors exit through IPO, stock swap, or token buyback mechanisms
Achieve Dual Valuation and Liquidity	- Combine local HK pricing and global NASDAQ valuation - Support NewCo's long-term growth with two-market capital support

Summary: 5-Step Execution Logic

1. First 6 Months: Complete structural design, capital readiness, and brand positioning
2. Within 12 Months: Advance BD transactions, initiate tokenized financing, and drive valuation uplift
3. Within 24 Months: Complete NASDAQ consolidation or spin-off; establish capital exit pathways
4. Within 36 Months: Return to HKEX/A-share market as an international platform for valuation re-rating
5. Long-Term Framework: RWA + PIPE + dual-market structure to form a global capital arbitrage loop

T+36 Month Financing–Valuation–Exit Path

Time Phase	Core Actions	Target Valuation at This Stage
T+0	Establish NewCo + PIPE Financing	RMB 2.3 billion
T+6	License-out Transaction + AI Synergy	RMB 3.0 billion
T+12	Prepare for Hong Kong IPO or Initiate M&A	RMB 5.0 billion
T+24	Public Listing Consolidation + Token Buyback Activation	RMB 8.0 billion
T+36	Dual Listing on HKEX Main Board / A-Share Market	RMB 10.0 billion+

Chapter 38: Investor Pitch Scripts and Slide Structure

This chapter provides a structured communication strategy for project owners and fund managers to present to global LPs (especially USD-based PIPE investors), including meeting preparation, materials checklist, suggested English scripts, Q&A tactics, and post-call follow-up.

I. Pre-Meeting Preparation

1.1 KYC & AML Screening

- Confirm LP has completed KYC (passport/ID, proof of address, sanctions list screening)
- Use tools like Onfido, Chainalysis for wallet-level AML compliance
- If LP invests via a fund, request GP-LP documentation or fund certificate

1.2 Investment Terms: Safety Provisions

- Include downside protection in Token Subscription Agreement: • PIPE buyback window (e.g., 5% per quarter) • IPO equity swap rights (e.g., 1 Token = xx shares) • Early unlock clauses (e.g., BD LOI or regulatory milestones)

1.3 Document Checklist

- Investor Deck (PDF, bilingual)
- Token Offering Memorandum (valuation & liquidity)
- Subscription Agreement + Accredited Investor Certificate template
- Exit Rights Memo (buyback, equity swap, secondary transfer)
- Risk Disclosure Memo (with legal summary)
- Team Profiles + Legal Structure Diagram

II. Recommended Opening Script (English)

"Thank you for taking the time. We believe this project represents a unique intersection of China's biomedical innovation and a globally compliant digital capital structure, which could provide an asymmetric upside for early LPs."

Supplemental Talking Points:

- "Unlike most early-stage biotech projects, our model integrates RWA tokenization, structured PIPE terms, and legal clarity through Reg D + Cayman."
- "The value proposition is not only scientific, but financial — we've built mechanisms for optionality, liquidity, and aligned investor interests."
- "We've seen similar valuation anchors used in deals like Tempus, GRAIL, and Sophia Genetics, and our structure offers early LPs better rights with lower entry thresholds."

III. Talking Points by Section

3.1 Project Value & Scientific Basis

- Briefly explain clinical mechanism (antibody/target/data)
- Milestones: IND, Ph1/2, BD LOIs
- Highlight platform capability (not just one product)

3.2 Token Structure Highlights

- Token is not a security; serves as optional exit exposure (see Exit Memo)
- Transfer-restricted smart contracts and KYC whitelisting enabled
- Rights are financial only: no voting, no governance obligations, equity swap optionality

3.3 Compliance & Legal Backing

- Diagram: Token SPV → Cayman Fund → License-out Entity → OpCo
- Legal Team: Ogier (Cayman), Loeb Smith (Reg D), PwC (audit)
- KYC/AML: Chainalysis/Onfido connected; whitelist trading on INX/Securitize

IV. Suggested LP Q&A Tactics

Q1: What's your valuation anchor?

A: "We use a 3-pillar approach: (1) DCF from license revenue, (2) signed BD LOIs, (3) benchmarking listed biotech/token projects."

Q2: How do I exit if the IPO doesn't happen?

A: "Quarterly buybacks, swap rights, and compliant ATS secondary trading are all structured in."

Q3: How is capital safeguarded?

A: "All funds are milestone-gated, escrowed, and legally triggered by regulatory or clinical events."

Q4: Why use Token vs Equity?

A: "Token offers structured liquidity and modular rights; equity is available via optional swap but Tokens avoid governance dilution."

V. Post-Call Follow-Up

5.1 Recommended Email Contents

- Thank-you note + Attachments (Deck, Subscription Agreement, Legal Summary)
- Highlight lock-up terms, exit paths, legal contacts

5.2 Internal Log Sheet

- Interest Level: High / Medium / Passive
- Investment Amount Range
- Response Timeline Estimate
- Next Step: Technical deep dive or family office follow-up?

5.3 Suggested Deal Flow Timeline

1. Initial call + Deck delivered
2. Legal packet sent within 7 days
3. Schedule second Q&A meeting (terms feedback)
4. Execute Subscription Agreement
5. Fund wiring + Token/Investor registry

Appendix: Sample Templates Available Upon Request:

- Meeting Minutes Template
- Legal Opinion Summary
- Token Buyback Term Sheet

Investor Deck Structure Template

This is a standard investor summary deck structure for projects involving RWA tokenization, Web3 medical technologies, or compliant fund offerings. It is suitable for presentations to global LPs, PIPE funds, and strategic investors. Recommended for use in pitch decks, data rooms, and fundraising documentation.

1. Project Summary

- Project Name: [Insert Name]
- Founded: [Year/Month]
- Legal Domicile: [Cayman / Delaware / BVI, etc.]
- Mission: [One-line statement of purpose]
- Core Product or Protocol: [Brief overview of the platform or technology]
- Strategic Positioning: • RWA-driven / ESG embedded / Cross-chain protocol • Target users: Hospitals, data providers, investors, researchers

2. Unique Value Proposition

- Asset Value Points: • Backed by tangible assets (e.g., data rights, compliant licenses, biosamples, algorithmic IP) • Token design includes cash flow or governance mechanisms • Real licensing (BD) deals under negotiation or completed
- Competitive Edge: • Technology barriers: patents / algorithms / federated systems / data integration • Market lead: existing clients, trial hospitals, clinical pilots • Compliance: token issuance structure, legal advisors, audit plans in place

3. Market Opportunity

- Global Trends: • AI + Health / ESG + Token / Data Rights / Federated Computing / Medical RWA
- TAM–SAM–SOM: • Total Addressable Market (TAM): $[X]B • Serviceable Available Market (SAM): $[X]B • 5-year Target Share (SOM): $[X]M
- Benchmarking Table:

Project	Sector	Valuation	Listing/Funding
Tempus	AI Health	$10B	Series D / PIPE

Sophia Genetics	Data Platform	$1.5B	Nasdaq IPO

4. **Investment Terms**

- Current Round: PIPE / Pre-A / Strategic
- Raise Target: $[X]M
- Token Price: $[X] per Token
- Minimum Commitment: $100,000
- Lock-up Period: 12 months
- Subscription Documents: PPM + Subscription Agreement + AI Certificate + Exit Memo
- Post-Deal Capital Structure:

Investor Type	**Ownership %**	**Form of Holding**
PIPE LP	XX%	Token + Exit Memo
Core Team	XX%	Token + Equity
Ecosystem Fund	XX%	Token Only

5. **Valuation Anchors**

- Valuation Methods: • DCF projection based on license revenue • Structured deal terms (milestone-based licensing) • Industry comparables (token benchmarks or biotech IPO precedents)
- Supporting Docs: • FA valuation memo • BD LOIs / Heads of Terms • Excel valuation model (available upon request)

6. **Exit Scenarios**

- PIPE buyback: post-lock-up quarterly buy window (e.g., 5%/quarter)
- Token-to-Equity: If IPO/M&A, allow 1 Token = [X] Shares
- Secondary Liquidity: Whitelisted transfers via platforms (e.g., INX, Securitize, tZero)
- IPO/M&A Pathway: Target exchanges (Nasdaq, HKEX, SGX); timeline [Insert]

7. **Tokenomics Summary**

- Total Token Supply: 1,000,000,000
- Allocation Table:

Category	% Allocation	Unlock Terms
PIPE Investors	15%	12-month lock + 24-month vesting
Founding Team	20%	1-year lock + 3-year vesting
Advisors	5%	6-month lock
Ecosystem Incentives	30%	DAO/community governed
Reserve Pool	30%	Long-term buybacks & incentives

8. Team Credentials

- CEO: [Name], former [Company], background: Harvard/Stanford/PKU
- CTO: [Name], blockchain/AI leader with project X experience
- Legal Advisors: Loeb Smith / Ogier / DLA Piper
- Financial Advisors: Securitize Capital / PwC

9. Legal & Compliance Framework

- Structure: Cayman SPV + Reg D + Reg S + contractual lockups + accredited investor verification
- Controls: Onfido / Chainalysis + whitelist-enabled smart contracts
- Core Docs: PPM, Subscription Agreement, Exit Memo, Investor Q&A

10. Contact Information

- Primary Contact: Zhang San / CEO
- Phone/Email: zsan@example.com / +1-123-456-7890
- Registered Address: Cayman Islands / Central, Hong Kong
- Website / IR: www.projectxyz.com/investor-relations

Chapter 39: Global LP Q&A Playbook

This chapter provides standard English questions and recommended Chinese interpretations for project teams, fund managers, and FAs when communicating with global LPs (especially PIPE investors). It helps ensure professional delivery, legal clarity, and investor confidence.

1. Valuation-Related Questions

Q: How is your token valuation justified without a secondary market price reference?

Suggested Explanation (CN):

DCF Model: Projected discounted future cash flows reflecting real value creation;

License-Out Deal Structure: Valuation anchored by binding BD milestones or buyback agreements with large pharma partners;

Comparable Analysis: Benchmark against similar-stage biotech/tokenized projects.

Sample Answer (EN): "We apply a three-pillar approach: (1) a discounted cash flow projection based on future revenue from licensing and commercialization, (2) structured BD agreements with milestones that provide valuation anchors, and (3) comparable benchmarking against peer-stage biotech platforms."

2. Legal Structure & Compliance

Q: Is the SPV Cayman-based and is the token issued under Reg D or Reg S?

Suggested Explanation (CN): • Issuer is typically a Cayman SPV for token issuance, investor governance, and legal insulation; • Reg D for U.S. investors, Reg S for non-U.S. investors; • KYC/AML compliance enforced via platforms like Onfido/Chainalysis; • Legal teams include Ogier, Loeb Smith, DLA Piper.

Sample Answer (EN): "Yes, the issuer is a Cayman-based SPV. Tokens are offered under Reg D for U.S. investors and Reg S for non-U.S. persons. We enforce strict KYC/AML procedures and the smart contract includes built-in transfer restrictions. Legal counsel includes Ogier (Cayman) and Loeb Smith (Reg D)."

3. Liquidity & Exit Scenarios

Q: What are my liquidity options if there is no IPO in 2 years?

Suggested Explanation (CN):

Scheduled PIPE buyback window post-lock-up;

Equity swap right if IPO or M&A occurs;

Secondary trading access on platforms (e.g., INX, Securitize) for whitelisted investors.

Sample Answer (EN): "We offer three potential liquidity paths: (1) scheduled token buybacks, (2) equity swap rights in case of IPO or acquisition, and (3) secondary trading via whitelisted ATS platforms like INX or Securitize after regulatory lock-up."

4. Risk Mitigation

Q: How do you ensure investors' funds are safeguarded in case of clinical or regulatory delay?

Suggested Explanation (CN):

Funds are held in escrow by licensed financial institution;

Milestone-based disbursement aligned with regulatory approvals;

Token buy-back clause in case of severe delay.

Sample Answer (EN): "We utilize a multi-layered risk control framework: (1) investor funds are held in escrow, (2) drawdowns are milestone-based with regulatory triggers, and (3) a token buy-back clause is in place to provide protection in case of unexpected clinical delays."

Investor FAQ (Bilingual)

This appendix compiles the key questions most frequently raised by investors (LPs) during PIPE private placements, token financing, and international compliance alignment. It also provides standard bilingual Q&A suggestions, suitable for use in Investor Memos, Offering Deck appendices, or IR rehearsal sessions.

1. Legal Structure

Q: Is the token Reg D compliant?
A: Yes. We operate through a Cayman or BVI SPV and issue tokens under Regulation D Rule 506(c), targeting accredited U.S. investors only. All participants undergo KYC/AML screening via providers such as Onfido and Chainalysis, and legal opinions are issued by Loeb Smith and Ogier.

Tips:

- Provide a screenshot of Reg D Form D submission / SEC filing number.
- Attach legal classification note explaining that the token does not constitute a security.

2. Exit & Redemption Options

Q: What are the redemption options for LPs?
A: Our token includes a structured exit mechanism:

1. Quarterly buyback rights from a treasury-backed pool.
2. Equity conversion options at pre-defined ratios upon IPO or acquisition.
3. Whitelist-based secondary trading on platforms such as INX or Securitize.

Suggested Add-ons:

- Token Exit Memo diagram.
- Buy-back execution schedule.

3. Regulatory Risk Mitigation

Q: How do you mitigate regulatory risk in multi-jurisdictional offerings?
A: We engage experienced legal counsel in the U.S., Cayman, and Hong Kong to design dual-path compliant structures (Reg D + Reg S), apply for appropriate licenses (VASP where applicable), and conduct quarterly legal reviews. All investor materials include audited disclosures and are reviewed for securities law classification.

Additional Suggestions:

- Provide a legal pathway diagram.
- Include a compliance responsibility checklist.

4. Valuation Methodology

Q: What drives token or equity valuation in your offering?
A: We apply a multi-anchor model:

1. Projected license-out cash flows modeled via DCF.
2. Benchmarking against comparable public and private biotech valuations.
3. Asset-backed NAV calculations where applicable.

These models are audited and included in the Offering Memorandum.

Suggested Materials:

- Comparative chart of the three valuation models (DCF vs NAV vs Peer Comp).
- Valuation opinion letter issued by an FA or law firm.

Recommended Uses of This Appendix

- As Investor Relations (IR) FAQ material.
- As an appendix in the Offering Memo or a supplement at the end of an Investor Deck.
- As a communication tool for legal and financial advisors when engaging with LPs.
- As a standardized bilingual Q&A template for cross-border transactions.

Common Strategic Q&A for Founders and Investors

This chapter compiles frequently asked strategic questions from USD LPs, PIPE funds, family offices, broker-dealers, and founder teams. Each question includes the original English version, a simplified Chinese translation, and standardized bilingual responses. It is designed for use in investor pitches, due diligence sessions, private placement meetings, and international presentation settings.

1. Secondary Share Transfers and Dilution

Q: How do you transfer secondary shares without hurting valuation?
问： 如何在老股转让中避免影响整体估值？

A: We embed value-added mechanisms (strategic NewCo share swap or asset-based anchoring) to preserve upside and ensure alignment.
答： 我们通过战略性 NewCo 换股或资产锚定机制，保证估值稳定、同时增强整体项目的协同增值空间。

Further Notes:

- Delivery terms can be structured via token-equity swap mechanisms or license-out revenue earn-outs.
- SPV acquisitions + PIPE-based buyback strategies help manage market expectations and liquidity rhythm.

2. Token Pricing and Valuation Logic

Q: What governs your token pricing model?
问： 你们 Token 定价依据是什么？

A: Dual-anchored by comparable equity valuation and projected license-out revenue; disclosed in the offering memo with redemption terms.
答： 定价锚定同行股权估值与 License-out 收益预测，已在 Offering Memo 中披露，含退出与回购条款。

Further Notes:

- Pricing model integrates DCF discounts, peer comparables, and blockchain circulation prices.
- Valuation anchors are clearly defined in formulas for buybacks or token-to-equity

conversion ratios.

3. Compliance Pathways and Legal Disclosure

Q: Is the token offering compliant with SEC/Reg S requirements?
问： Token 私募发行是否符合美国 SEC 及 Reg S 规定?

A: All offerings are conducted under Reg D (506c) or Reg S frameworks with third-party KYC/AML providers and legal counsel involved.
答： 所有发行均基于 Reg D 或 Reg S 框架完成，配合 KYC/AML 审查与法律团队审核，确保全面合规。

Further Notes:

- Reg D (506c) applies to U.S. investors; Reg S for non-U.S. offshore LPs.
- Legal opinions from firms such as Loeb Smith and Ogier validate the token structure.
- KYC providers include Onfido, Chainalysis, and Securitize Passport.

4. Listing Pathways and Geographic Strategy

Q: Why dual-listing instead of focusing on HKEX?
问： 为何不直接赴港上市，而选择双地挂牌?

A: We target U.S. IPO first for higher tech-driven valuation, then arbitrage upside via Hong Kong to capture local liquidity.
答： 我们优先选择美国上市获取更高的科技类估值，再通过香港实现流动性套利，形成中美资本联动效应。

Further Notes:

- Nasdaq in the U.S. offers premium valuations for AI and HealthTech sectors.
- Hong Kong enables RMB-denominated secondary liquidity and access to GBA (Greater Bay Area) investors.
- A dual-layer structure (Token + Equity) can be established pre-IPO to support cross-border circulation.

Supplementary Questions (Optional Add-ons)

Q: What safeguards are in place if clinical or regulatory delays occur?
A: Funds are milestone-controlled, placed in escrow accounts, and tied to performance-based release schedules.

Q: How do you balance token utility with long-term equity planning?
A: Tokens offer optional liquidity and programmable governance, while equity remains the foundation for long-term alignment and exit.

Recommended Use Cases for This Chapter:

- Investor due diligence Q&A simulation
- IR training materials for founders and team
- Offering Memo appendix: strategic bilingual Q&A manual
- Reference script for bilingual responses in FA/legal meetings

Investor Pitch Roleplay – Founder vs LP

This chapter uses bilingual dialogue simulations to present common interaction scenarios between investors (LPs) and entrepreneurs (Founders/CEOs) at different fundraising stages. Topics include valuation anchoring, token structure, exit mechanisms, and compliance disclosures. Each scene is accompanied by annotation tips, suggested presentation materials, and supporting visuals, making it ideal for IR training, lawyer-accompanied meetings, or pre-roadshow rehearsals.

Scene 1: Valuation and Exit Mechanism

Investor (LP): You claim a valuation of USD 100M. What's the anchor?
Founder (CEO): It's anchored on a signed ADC license-out at USD 20M upfront and a 3-year PIPE-backed relisting roadmap.

Chinese Prompt:
LP 问：贵公司如何得出 1 亿美元估值？
创始人答：我们已签署一个价值 2 千万美元的 ADC License-Out 协议，同时搭配 3 年 PIPE 融资+美股重新上市路径。

Suggested Visuals:

- Valuation structure comparison chart (DCF/Comparables)
- Key terms of the license-out agreement (amount, milestones, payment structure)
- PIPE financing roadmap (timeline + investor types)

Scene 2: Token Mechanism Explanation

LP: Will your token be liquid?
Founder: 12-month lock, then quarterly redemption via treasury-backed pool. We also allow swap into equity post-IPO.

Chinese Prompt:
LP 问：你们的 Token 是否具备流动性？
创始人答：我们设定 12 个月锁仓，之后每季度开放回购窗口，并在 IPO 后允许 Token 按比例换股。

Suggested Visuals:

- Token unlock diagram (lock-up period + buyback schedule)

- Token-to-Equity swap mechanism (trigger conditions, conversion ratio)
- Liquidity platform pathways (e.g., Securitize, INX)

Scene 3: Compliance and Legal Pathway

LP: Are your offerings legally compliant under U.S. law?
Founder: Yes. We issue under Reg D (506c) for U.S. investors and Reg S for offshore LPs, with KYC/AML handled by Onfido and legal opinions from Ogier and Loeb Smith.

Chinese Prompt:
LP 问：你们的融资是否符合美国证券法？
创始人答：是的。美国投资人适用 Reg D（506c），非美投资人适用 Reg S；我们使用 Onfido 完成 KYC 审查，并由 Ogier 与 Loeb Smith 出具法律意见函。

Suggested Visuals:

- Compliance structure diagram (Cayman SPV → Token issuance)
- Legal opinion summary (e.g., non-security status, accredited investor definitions)
- Form D filing screenshot (draft)

Scene 4: Financial Projections and ESG Strategy

LP: What's your long-term revenue plan and ESG positioning?o
Founder: We project license revenue exceeding USD 50M within 5 years, and our ESG disclosure aligns with IFRS S1/S2 including climate metrics, board oversight, and data transparency.

Chinese Prompt:
LP 问：贵公司未来收入预期与 ESG 策略如何？
创始人答：我们预计 5 年内 License-Out 收入超 5000 万美元，ESG 报告参考 IFRS S1/S2 披露框架，涵盖气候指标、治理结构、数据透明机制。

Suggested Visuals:

- Revenue projection model (annual license income + token operation yield)
- ESG disclosure table template (bilingual)
- Board ESG responsibility chart

Scene 5: Exit Mechanisms and Downside Protection

LP: If no IPO happens, how can I exit?
Founder: We offer three options: (1) quarterly buybacks up to 5%, (2) equity swap at defined valuation, (3) regulated secondary trading on whitelist-based platforms.

Chinese Prompt:
LP 问：若未来无 IPO，投资人如何退出？
创始人答：我们设计了三类路径：1）季度回购（限额 5%）；2）按协议估值换股退出；3）通过合规白名单平台二级转让。

Suggested Visuals:

- Token Exit Memo diagram
- Buyback window + execution process flow
- List of live/planned secondary trading platforms (e.g., INX, tZERO)

Recommended Use Cases:

- Investor pitch rehearsal scripts
- Entrepreneur IR training materials
- Simulated sessions for FA/legal due diligence meetings
- Supplementary "Common Q&A" slide in the investor deck

Regulator Interaction Scripts – HKEX / SEC Scenarios

This chapter uses a Q&A simulation format to illustrate typical interaction scenarios when innovative biotech companies or token issuance projects respond to inquiries from the Hong Kong Stock Exchange (HKEX) or the U.S. Securities and Exchange Commission (SEC). It covers five major themes: 18A clinical development disclosure, token compliance structure, offshore bridging mechanisms, pricing justification, and risk factor supplements.

Scenario 1: HKEX 18A Inquiry – Clinical Bridging Strategy

HKEX Reviewer: Has your ongoing Phase I/II trial in China been considered as part of an international bridging strategy?
Applicant (CMO): We have partnered with global CROs to design a supplementary clinical data package, which we plan to submit in Q4. This data package complies with the technical standards required for joint review by the FDA and EMA.

Recommended Exhibits:

- Bridging trial design diagram (synchronized trials in China, U.S., and EU)
- Summary of statistical analysis plan (PK/PD comparisons, patient inclusion criteria)
- Communication records or meeting minutes with the FDA/EMA (if applicable)

Scenario 2: SEC Inquiry – Token Structure Legality

SEC Reviewer: Please clarify if any part of the offering constitutes a security under the Howey Test.
Applicant Counsel: The offering is structured under Regulation D Rule 506(c), targeting accredited investors only. The token represents a right to participate in future revenue, not equity. All relevant offering materials—including the PPM, AI Certificate, and Token Exit Memo—have been disclosed. Legal opinion letters from Loeb Smith and tax counsel are also on file.

Recommended Exhibits:

- Token structure diagram (rights mapping, equity conversion, post-investment pathway)
- Table analyzing the four elements of the Howey Test
- Key excerpts from legal opinion (whether it constitutes a security and registration obligations)

Scenario 3: HKEX Second Round Inquiry – Valuation and Fundraising Reasonableness

HKEX Reviewer: The proposed fundraising amount appears disproportionately large compared to your current asset base. Please explain your pricing rationale and use of proceeds.
Applicant (CFO): We used a three-anchor valuation approach:

1. A DCF model based on projected revenue from license-out agreements;
2. Comparable pre-IPO valuations of peer companies over the past two years;
3. A third-party FA-issued NAV report.
   Funds will be used in phases for Phase III trials, international regulatory filings, and simultaneous commercialization in the Middle East and Hong Kong.

Recommended Exhibits:

- Use of proceeds chart (broken down by stage/region)
- Cover page and summary formula from the NAV valuation report
- Comparable transaction valuation references (e.g., Hua Medicine, CStone Pharmaceuticals)

Scenario 4: SEC Inquiry – Risk Disclosure Supplement

SEC Reviewer: Please expand the section on liquidity and marketability risks, especially regarding token transfer restrictions.
Applicant (General Counsel): We have revised the Risk Factors section to clarify that tokens are non-transferable within the first 12 months and may only circulate post-lock-up via ATS platforms approved through a whitelist mechanism. We've also added disclosures regarding smart contract enforcement, redemption limits, and secondary trading uncertainties.

Recommended Exhibits:

- Redline comparison of the Risk Factors section (before/after)
- List of secondary market platforms (e.g., INX, Securitize) and related compliance filings
- Screenshots summarizing smart contract terms (lock-up logic, whitelist mechanism)

Scenario 5: HKEX Inquiry – ESG and Corporate Governance

HKEX Reviewer: Please explain how your company meets ESG disclosure requirements, especially whether an ESG oversight mechanism exists at the board level.
Applicant (IR Head): We have adopted the IFRS S1/S2 disclosure framework. We regularly update Scope 1–3 carbon emission data, employee diversity metrics, and governance

practices. An ESG Committee under the Board reviews these and disclosures are made with the annual report. We've also launched an ESG blockchain pilot, where selected data is verified on-chain.

Recommended Exhibits:

- Outline of ESG report (bilingual) and summary of audited data
- Board structure chart + ESG responsibility matrix
- Screenshot or demo link of the ESG blockchain disclosure module

Applicable Use Cases for This Chapter:

- Pre-IPO inquiry preparation for HKEX 18A listings (initial and second review phases)
- SEC Regulation D filings and Comment Letter response drafting
- Mock sessions with financial advisors or legal counsel before regulator meetings
- Internal simulation scripts for IR or CFO teams preparing for roadshows or disclosures

Risk Scenario Scripts and Strategic Response Toolkit

This chapter focuses on typical crisis scenarios that may arise during cross-border financing, token private placements, and PIPE transactions. It provides bilingual (Chinese-English) response scripts, legal/financial structure suggestions, and actionable crisis management checklists. The aim is to help teams maintain investor trust and project momentum under pressure.

Scenario 1: Token Price Drop Triggers LP Panic

Issue: Token price falls below the private placement cost, causing LP anxiety or potential withdrawal.

Suggested English Response:
"We maintain a redemption pool and have buyback authority through BD proceeds. The token is not purely speculative but represents real-world license revenue claims. In addition, secondary liquidity is managed through whitelist-based venues only."

中文回应建议：
我们已设定回购池，并授权使用 BD 交易收入进行回购操作；该 Token 并非纯投机性资产，而是锚定了真实 License-Out 收益的权益凭证，具备稳定现金流支撑。

Action Checklist:

- Launch the **Buy-back Window** and disclose execution details.
- Share updated **financial forecasts** and **Token Exit Memo**.
- Organize **closed-door LP Q&A sessions** or monthly update meetings.

Scenario 2: Media Questions Overseas Valuation Bubble

Issue: Financial or social media outlets challenge token valuations or transparency of offshore pricing.

Suggested English Response:
"Our valuation is backed by signed license-out transactions, audited DCF models, and cross-market listing arbitrage mechanisms. We are committed to transparent disclosures, and all figures are supported by legal counsel and financial advisors."

中文回应策略：

我们的估值基础清晰可证，包括 1）已签署 License-Out 交易协议；2）FDA/EMA 路径下的境外临床推进数据；3）美股/港股双市场套利机制。所有数据可提供审计支持，合作方亦包含国际 FA 与律师事务所。

Recommended Actions:

- Publish **Token Pricing & Exit Logic FAQ**.
- Draft a **Media Response Template**, citing legal opinions.
- Release a bilingual **"Valuation Anchors Explained"** PDF with visuals for data room use.

Scenario 3: PIPE Investor Withdrawal or Payment Delay

Issue: PIPE fund withdraws or delays disbursement due to internal shifts or market fear.

Response Strategy:

1. Activate a **Dual-LP Pool**: Prepare backup LP list with pre-agreed transfer terms.
2. Enable **Phased Buyback Structure** with embedded swap clauses (refer to Token Buyback Schedule).
3. Introduce **Bridge Financing Plan**: Engage FA for short-term facility to maintain transaction momentum.

Suggested English Script:

"We understand market volatility concerns. We've activated our dual-LP contingency structure and initiated bridge financing to ensure continued runway. In addition, our Token includes built-in buyback clauses to stabilize investor confidence."

Legal and Operational Actions:

- Prior to buyback triggers, issue **IR notice** and obtain LP **written consent**.
- Amend **Subscription Agreements** to include substitution clauses.
- Sign **Memorandum of Exit (MOE)** with original PIPE party including force majeure waiver provisions.

Optional Scenario 4: FX Control or Cross-Border Compliance Delays

Issue: Delays in domestic-to-offshore fund transfer, token equity swap, or HK SPV account opening.

Suggested Mechanisms:

- Use **HKD Internal Loop + RMB Reinvestment** model to avoid large single-point forex conversion.
- Set up a **Middle East SPV settlement pool** (e.g., Abu Dhabi Free Zone + VASP license).
- Open **custodial sub-accounts** with Hong Kong brokers for secondary token buyback and settlement.

Key Tip:

Prepare **legal structure flowcharts** and simulate worst-case contingency pathways.

Chapter Use Cases:

- IR/COO/CFO **training manual** for offshore teams
- Investor communication scripts and **Data Room FAQ**
- **PIPE legal clause emergency protocols**
- Source material for lawyers drafting **"Crisis Management Memorandum"** for token offerings

This chapter emphasizes a practical logic of "Clear Answers, Transparent Narratives, and Performable Scenarios," serving as the final execution layer of your outbound financing strategy—aligned with earlier chapters on agreements, valuations, and structure design.

Risk Disclosure Standard Statements (Bilingual)

This chapter compiles standard risk disclosures commonly used in digital assets, tokenized financing, PIPE investments, and medical technology sectors. Applicable in whitepapers, PPMs, Subscription Agreements, and Investor Memos, these bilingual statements aim to ensure legal clarity and global compliance.

1. Regulatory Disclosures / 合规豁免相关

EN: "This offering is limited to accredited investors under Regulation D and is not registered with the SEC."

中: 本轮融资仅面向合格投资人，依据 Reg D 豁免，不构成公开发行，也未向美国 SEC 注册。

EN: "Securities offered under Regulation S are not available for U.S. persons and are subject to resale restrictions."

中: 根据 Reg S 发行的证券不得向美国人士出售，亦受转让限制。

EN: "The token is not intended to be a security in any jurisdiction unless explicitly acknowledged under local law."

中: 除非法律明确认定，本项目 Token 不构成任何司法管辖区下的证券。

2. Liquidity and Exit Risks / 流动性与退出风险

EN: "There is no guarantee of future liquidity or IPO exit. Investments may result in partial or complete loss."

中: 项目无法保证未来可流通或上市退出，投资者需承担部分或全部损失风险。

EN: "Secondary trading, if any, will only be conducted through whitelisted platforms and compliant addresses."

中: 如有二级市场流通，亦仅限于通过合规平台与完成白名单认证的钱包地址。

EN: "Buyback or swap options are discretionary and may be adjusted or suspended without notice."

中: 项目设立的回购或换股机制属于非强制条款，可能根据实际情况调整或中止。

3. Token Holder Limitations / 投资人权利与限制

EN: "Token holders shall not have any equity rights unless otherwise specified in a conversion clause."

中: 除非协议中另有规定，Token 持有者不自动拥有股权权益。

EN: "Holding tokens does not entitle the investor to dividends, voting rights, or board representation."

中: Token 本身不赋予投资者任何分红、表决或董事会席位权利。

EN: "Token utility is subject to platform implementation and shall not be construed as guaranteed performance."

中: Token 的使用权取决于平台实际部署，不构成承诺性权益。

4. Forward-Looking Statements / 前瞻性声明与模型预测

EN: "The financial projections are forward-looking and subject to change based on clinical or market conditions."

中: 所提供财务预测属于前瞻性信息，可能因临床进展或市场条件调整。

EN: "Statements regarding future milestones, regulatory approval, or market entry are subject to material uncertainty."

中: 关于未来里程碑、监管批准或市场进入等表述均存在重大不确定性。

EN: "Any valuation model provided is for illustrative purposes only and does not represent a fair market value guarantee."

中: 所提供估值模型仅作参考，不构成项目真实价值或投资回报的保证。

5. Legal and Contractual Risk / 合同法律责任提示

EN: "Participation in this offering is voluntary and subject to final acceptance by the Issuer."

中: 投资人认购本项目属自愿行为，最终认购需经发行方确认。

EN: "This document shall not be deemed a solicitation, advertisement, or public offering under any jurisdiction."

中: 本文件不构成任何司法辖区内的招揽、广告或公开发行行为。

EN: “The issuer reserves the right to amend terms or cancel the offering at its sole discretion.”

中: 发行方保留随时修改融资条款或取消发行的全部权利。

EN: “Investors are advised to consult independent legal, tax, and financial advisors before participating.”

中: 建议投资人在参与本项目之前咨询独立法律、税务与财务顾问。

Note: These risk disclosures should be consistently reflected across the Token Offering Memorandum, Investor Q&A Handbook, Accredited Investor Declaration, and Subscription Agreement appendices to avoid any cross-border compliance misunderstanding.

Chapter 40: Strategic Cooperation Agreement (Bilingual)

战略合作协议 Strategic Cooperation Agreement

本战略合作协议（“本协议”）由以下双方于【签署日期】在【地点】签署:

This Strategic Cooperation Agreement (the “Agreement”) is entered into by and between the following parties on [Date], at [Location]:

甲方 / Party A：

医道国际有限公司（ETAO International Co., Ltd.）
注册地址 / Registered Address: [填写]
代表人 / Authorized Representative: [填写]

乙方 / Party B：

香港晨晨有限公司（Alpha Biopharma HK Limited）
注册地址 / Registered Address: [填写]
代表人 / Authorized Representative: [填写]

第一条 合作背景

Article 1 – Background

鉴于乙方为江苏晨晨医药有限公司（“江苏晨晨”）的控股母公司，江苏晨晨拥有创新药物其产品在中国大陆的全部商业化权益，并于最近一轮融资中以投前估值人民币 20 亿元成功融资人民币 3 亿元，由香港上市公司西藏药业完成投资，投后估值为人民币 23 亿元。

Considering that Party B is the controlling shareholder of Jiangsu Alpha Biopharma Co., Ltd. (“Jiangsu Alpha”), which owns full commercialization rights of Its product in mainland China, and recently raised RMB 300 million from Tibet Pharmaceuticals (HK listed) at a pre-money valuation of RMB 2 billion, resulting in a post-money valuation of RMB 2.3 billion.

第二条 合作内容

Article 2 – Scope of Cooperation

1. 甲方将担任乙方及其附属公司在全球资本市场上的**独家财务顾问（FA）**，全面协助乙方推动其核心产品其产品的全球（除中国）市场战略拓展与资本运作。

Party A shall act as the **exclusive financial advisor (FA)** to Party B and its affiliates, and shall fully support the global (ex-China) development and capital market expansion strategy of Its product.

2. 甲方负责引入战略及美元资本，帮助乙方以人民币 23 亿元的估值完成 60%老股东股权转让融资，即目标为人民币 13.8 亿元，投资方拿走香港晨晨老股东 60%股权，当然也对应子公司江苏晨晨投 60%的股份。

Party A is responsible for introducing strategic and USD capital to assist Party B in completing a financing round based on a valuation of RMB 2.3 billion, targeting the acquisition of 60% equity from the existing shareholders, i.e., RMB 1.38 billion. The investors will acquire 60% of the equity held by the existing shareholders of Alpha Biopharma HK Limited, which also corresponds to a 60% stake in its subsidiary Jiangsu Alpha Biopharma.

3. 为了吸引机构投资人，双方同意在美国共同推动设立 NewCo，NewCo 将获得其产品及其他相关管线在全球（除中国）市场的独家开发、注册、商业化及再授权权益。

In order to attract institutional investors, both parties agree to jointly facilitate the establishment of a U.S.-based company, which shall receive exclusive rights to develop, register, commercialize, and sublicense Its product and other related pipelines globally (excluding China).

第三条 医道国际融资佣金

Article 3 – Financial advisory fee

作为独家财务顾问，医道国际（ETAO）有权就成功募集的总资金金额收取等值于 **7%** 的财务顾问服务费，以体现其在整个交易过程中所承担的全面职责，包括但不限于：投资人引入、结构设计、交易文件准备、管理层咨询以及未来并购协调等工作。

As exclusive financial advisor, ETAO shall be entitled to a financial advisory fee equal to 7% of the gross proceeds successfully raised, in recognition of its full-scope responsibilities including investor sourcing, structural design, transaction documentation, management advisory, and future M&A coordination.

为作为本次融资的独家财务顾问，甲方有权就成功融资部分从乙方处收取等值于**融资金额 7%**的财务顾问服务费（FA 佣金），该费用应在融资金额到账后十（10）个工作日内一次性支付。上述费用不含增值税、银行手续费等其他相关成本，乙方应予以承担。

As the exclusive financial advisor for this financing transaction, Party A shall be entitled to receive a financial advisory fee equal to 7% of the total amount of funds raised, payable by Party B within ten (10) business days following the receipt of investment proceeds. This fee is exclusive of any applicable taxes, bank charges, or other transaction-related expenses, which shall be borne by Party B.

第四条 医道国际未来并购权

Article 4 – ETAO's Future Acquisition Rights

1. 在甲方完成纳斯达克主板上市后，甲方享有优先并购香港晨晨全部或部分股权的权利，方式包括但不限于现金、股份交换或两者组合。

Upon successful Nasdaq uplisting, Party A shall have the **right of first refusal** to acquire part or all of Alpha Biopharma HK Limited's equity by means of cash, stock swap, or a combination thereof.

2. 该优先权的具体价格、估值机制、付款安排等将在后续并购意向书或正式协议中另行明确。

The specific pricing, valuation mechanism, and payment terms of such acquisition shall be further agreed upon in a separate acquisition term sheet or definitive agreement.

第五条 双方责任分工

Article 5 – Roles and Responsibilities

甲方（ETAO International）	**乙方（香港晨晨）**
担任独家 FA，引入融资	提供全球授权及资料支持
设立 NewCo 并主导治理	配合设立、股权安排与技术交接
建立国际管理团队	协助 BD 及国内与海外衔接
推动未来并购整合	参与谈判并享换股等权益

第六条 保密义务

Article 6 – Confidentiality

双方须对本协议内容及相关合作信息严格保密，未经另一方书面同意不得向任何第三方披露，除非依照适用法律法规或监管要求。

Both parties shall keep the contents of this Agreement and all related cooperation information strictly confidential, unless required by applicable law or regulatory authority.

第七条 法律适用与争议解决

Article 7 – Governing Law and Dispute Resolution

1. 本协议适用美国纽约州法律。

This Agreement shall be governed by the laws of the State of New York, USA.

2. 因本协议引起的或与之相关的任何争议，双方应首先友好协商解决；协商不成的，提交纽约国际仲裁中心（NYIAC）进行仲裁。

Any disputes arising from or in connection with this Agreement shall be first resolved through amicable negotiation. If such negotiation fails, either party may submit the dispute to the New York International Arbitration Center (NYIAC) for final and binding arbitration.

第八条 生效与其他

Article 8 – Effectiveness and Miscellaneous

1. 本协议自双方签字盖章之日起生效，初步有效期为 12 个月。

This Agreement shall become effective on the date of signature and seal by both parties and remain valid for an initial period of 12 months.

2. 双方可根据需要进一步签署补充协议以推进融资、授权、并购等具体事务。

The parties may enter into supplemental agreements as needed to advance financing, licensing, and acquisition matters.

甲方：**医道国际有限公司**
签字人：______________
签署日期：____________

乙方: **香港晨晨有限公司**

签字人: ______________

签署日期: ____________

FA Fee Analysis

This memo outlines the role of the financial advisor (FA) across the full project lifecycle, including strategic planning, structural design, valuation guidance, and investor engagement:

- Scope of FA Services:
  Financing strategy, project packaging, investor negotiation, structural advisory
- Recommended Fee Rate:
  7% based on the total amount successfully raised
- Optional Fee Structure:
  Cash + equity combination and/or milestone-based payment
- Success Criteria & Arbitration Clause:
  Suggest including clear definitions of "successful financing" and dispute resolution terms

I. Benchmark Reference: Wall Street FA Fee Practices

Deal Size	Typical FA Fee Range (Cash / PIPE)	Remarks
<$10M	7%–10%	Early-stage / high-risk startup deals
$10M–$50M	5%–7%	Common for VC / PIPE / convertible deals
$50M–$200M	3%–6%	Fee percentage decreases as deal size increases
>$200M	1.5%–3%	Large M&A or structured deals (e.g. convertibles)

Conclusion:
A 7% fee on a $200M deal is above market average.

II. Key Factors Affecting FA Fee Justification

Factor	Supports Higher Fee?	ETAO Evaluation
Early-stage financing / high risk	Yes	Yes – Pre-IPO and early outbound stage
Complex structure / cross-border / biotech	Yes	Yes – Chinese parent, IP license, NewCo involved
Difficult capital sourcing	Yes	Yes – Targeting USD LPs and cross-border compliance
FA provides execution + structuring	Yes	Yes – ETAO assumes role of FA + post-deal integration
Exclusive mandate	Yes	Yes – Agreement clearly states ETAO as exclusive FA

Conclusion:

If ETAO is responsible for full-cycle services—deal sourcing, structuring, investor execution, strategic advisory, and post-deal integration—a 7% fee is reasonable and arguably modest.

III. Market Comparables

Case	Deal Size	FA Fee	Type	Notes
Lazard raises $50M for early-stage biotech	$50M	5% + tail	PIPE financing	Early-stage private placement
Goldman Sachs leads $200M PIPE	$200M	2.5% + equity warrants	PIPE + pre-M&A	Blue-chip transaction
Mid-size FA supports SPAC PIPE ($20M)	$20M	6%–8%	PIPE after SPAC	Similar to ETAO structure

IV. Overall Judgment

Item	Assessment
$200M × 7% = $14M total fee	Above average, but reasonable if structuring & post-deal services included
If FA only introduces investors	Suggest limiting fee to 3%–5%
If FA also leads structuring, team building, license execution, M&A	7% is justifiable and well-supported
Suggested Structure	5% base fee + 2% back-end success bonus (or equity incentive with lock-up)

V. Suggested Agreement Clause (Bilingual)

English:
"As exclusive financial advisor, ETAO shall be entitled to a financial advisory fee equal to 7% of the gross proceeds successfully raised, in recognition of its full-scope responsibilities including investor sourcing, structural design, transaction documentation, management advisory, and future M&A coordination."

Chinese:
作为独家财务顾问，医道国际（ETAO）有权获得相当于成功融资总额 7%的财务顾问费，以体现其在整个过程中所承担的全面职责，包括投资人对接、结构设计、交易文件编制、管理咨询以及未来并购协调等服务内容。

Chapter 41: Smart Contract Audit and On-Chain Governance Mechanism Recommendations

In RWA tokenization, DeFi protocols, and Web3 fund structures, smart contracts and on-chain governance mechanisms function as the "operating system" of the digital asset environment. This chapter outlines best practices for smart contract auditing and governance design to ensure project security, transparency, and scalability.

1. Smart Contract Audit Tools and Process

Smart contracts are immutable once deployed, making their security and vulnerability prevention critical.

• Recommended Tools:
  - Certik: Offers formal verification, static analysis, security scoring, and real-time monitoring (Skynet).
  - Quantstamp: Specializes in security audits for DeFi and NFT-related smart contracts.
  - SlowMist: A leading Chinese blockchain security firm offering a hybrid of automated and manual audits.

• Suggested Audit Process:
  1. Submit initial codebase with project documentation;
  2. Conduct static analysis and fuzzing (Fuzzing + Formal Verification);
  3. Issue preliminary audit report and feedback;
  4. Developer revises and submits the updated version for review;
  5. Final audit report is published, preferably uploaded on-chain or via GitHub.

• Additional Recommendation: Perform dual audits with two separate firms for enhanced credibility.

2. Governance Mechanism Design Recommendations

Once the project is live, token governance should manage critical functions such as fund usage, protocol upgrades, and proposal execution. Recommended mechanisms include:

• Vote-Locking Mechanism:
  - Require participants to lock tokens for a period (e.g., 7–90 days) to gain voting or proposal rights;
  - Prevent airdrop attacks and short-term manipulation;

- Inspired by Curve's veToken model.

• Multisig Wallet Oversight:
  - Important assets and admin privileges should be controlled by a multi-signature committee (e.g., 3-of-5 or 4-of-7 scheme);
  - Use platforms like Gnosis Safe for permissions and transaction history transparency;
  - Mitigates single-point-of-failure and centralization risk.

• On-Chain Annual Report Disclosure:
  - Upload annual audit reports, asset summaries, and financial disclosures on-chain or via IPFS with hash on-chain;
  - Increases investor transparency and enhances regulatory readiness.

• Governance Incentives:
  - Provide long-term governance participants with annual rewards like vote rebates, governance points, or dividend bonuses.

3. Recommended Governance Platforms and Frameworks

The following are widely used governance platforms in the Web3 space, suitable for token issuance, DAOs, and protocol governance:

• Snapshot (Gas-Free Voting System):
  - Voting occurs off-chain, reducing gas costs;
  - Easily integrated with community platforms like Discord and Discourse;
  - Supports weighted voting, delegated voting, and proposal filtering.

• Aragon (Modular DAO Governance Toolkit):
  - Offers a full suite for DAO creation, voting, treasury management, and contract administration;
  - User-friendly UI supporting hybrid on-chain/off-chain governance;
  - Allows custom roles and governance rules.

• SafeDAO (Built on Gnosis Safe):
  - Focused on asset security and multi-sig authorization;
  - Suitable for fund-style DAOs and investment-token projects;
  - Can integrate with token vesting and payroll systems for smart compensation governance.

As token structures grow in complexity, project teams must not only ensure smart contract security but also build a transparent, auditable, and censorship-resistant governance framework. Leveraging trusted audit firms and governance platforms builds confidence with investors, partners, and regulators alike.

Financial Audit and Tax Planning for Tokenized Projects

With the development of blockchain technology, an increasing number of enterprises are tokenizing real-world assets (RWA) for financing, profit-sharing, and income rights transfer. However, this introduces unprecedented challenges to traditional financial auditing and tax processing.

This chapter aims to provide practical accounting, auditing, and tax planning strategies for enterprises engaged in tokenization, ensuring that such projects are financially auditable and tax compliant, thereby laying a foundation for future fundraising, regulatory filings, or IPOs.

1. Accounting Challenges: How to Recognize Revenue for Tokens Representing Future Rights?

Tokens often represent some form of future economic benefit, such as dividends, net income sharing, or asset-backed yield, rather than revenue that can be realized immediately. This creates a mismatch between the time of token issuance and revenue recognition.

Key accounting issues include:
• Should token proceeds be treated as deferred revenue?
• Are tokens equity instruments or financial liabilities?
• Should token issuance proceeds be booked as operating revenue or as capital reserves?

2. Recommended Practice: Use Variable Interest Entity Accounting under US GAAP / IFRS

According to leading audit firms (e.g., PwC, Deloitte), the following approaches are commonly adopted:
• If token holders have residual rights or governance rights, classify them as Variable Interest Entities (VIE).
• If tokens merely represent future cash flows, treat them as contract liabilities or deferred revenue, to be recognized as income upon maturity.
• Tokens should be disclosed as separate line items, with clear documentation of issuance price, quantity, associated rights, and contractual obligations.
• Detailed disclosures should be provided in the notes to annual financial statements, covering token structure, responsibilities, valuation models, and material uncertainties.

3. Audit Process: Big Four Audit + Token Valuation Report + Contract Alignment

Auditing a tokenized project requires not only traditional financial statement audits but also on-chain asset valuation and protocol logic verification:

• Engage auditors with crypto asset experience, such as PwC Crypto or EY Blockchain departments.

• Require the financial advisor (FA) to provide a Token Valuation Report, including model assumptions, market benchmarks, and risk disclosures.

• Auditors must validate smart contracts and compare them to the white paper/token agreements to ensure that price, vesting, and restrictions are correctly executed.

• If tokens are linked to fund/company equity, the audit must extend to operational financials and supporting documentation.

4. Tax Planning: Segregated Accounting + Dividend vs. Capital Gain Classification

Tax treatment of tokens varies significantly across jurisdictions. Enterprises should separate their onshore and offshore activities:

• Separate accounting is advised for onshore operating entities and offshore token issuers (e.g., Cayman or BVI SPVs).

• If token income is classified as 'dividend-like', it should be treated similarly to equity dividends with applicable withholding tax.

• If classified as 'capital gain-like' (e.g., platform credits, data access fees), it should be reported as taxable business income.

• Different countries (e.g., U.S., Hong Kong, Singapore) interpret token taxability differently; tax residency must be determined for global income reporting.

• Engage international tax advisors to ensure compliance with CRS, FATCA, and BEPS frameworks.

Tokenized financing, as an emerging capital tool, can boost investor confidence and pave the way for IPOs, M&As, and fund registrations if supported by compliant accounting, auditing, and tax structures.

Enterprises should proactively build cross-border accounting and tax systems to meet evolving regulatory and transparency requirements in the digital asset space.

12 Steps from Valuation Bottlenecks to Global Capital Elevation

Designed for Chinese mid-sized tech companies, AI healthcare ventures, and outbound innovators; covers full-cycle financing, valuation, compliance, and exit strategies

Phase 1: Restructuring & Valuation Anchoring (T -18 to T -12 months)

Step 1: Asset Mapping & Core Value Confirmation (RWA)
Identify and categorize core technologies, licensing rights, AI models, and future income streams as Real-World Assets (RWA) to anchor valuation.

Step 2: Set Up NewCo Structure (BVI/Cayman)
Establish an offshore NewCo entity to hold RWA assets and rights, forming the basis for compliant cross-border fundraising and token issuance.

Step 3: Equity Reorganization & Governance Clarity
Streamline shareholder structure, finalize legacy shareholder exit mechanisms, and define board governance to remove barriers for institutional investors.

Phase 2: Financing Readiness & Capital Access (T -12 to T -6 months)

Step 4: Design PIPE Financing Structure (with Protection Clauses)
Bring in USD PIPE capital with preferred shares, convertible notes, or token-linked instruments; embed investor protections such as buyback, liquidation preference, and anti-dilution.

Step 5: Tokenization Design & Digital Capitalization
Tokenize future income/licensing rights, introduce programmable assets linked to stablecoins, and connect to Web3 funds or global LP liquidity pools.

Step 6: On-Chain Audit & ESG Disclosure Framework
Implement auditable blockchain-based data disclosures and integrate ESG metrics (IFRS/SASB aligned) to meet global investor expectations.

Phase 3: Cross-Border Compliance & Filing (T -6 to T -3 months)

Step 7: Register Offshore Entity & Compliance Pathways
Complete offshore filings for NewCo/SPV, select proper legal channels (e.g., Reg D, Reg S, 506(c)), and prepare investor offering documents.

Step 8: Prepare Audit Reports & Legal Opinions (US + HK Dual Track)
Obtain 3-year US GAAP audits and legal due diligence reports to support either SPAC/M&A or Hong Kong 18A listing track.

Phase 4: Multi-Market Listings & Exit Strategy (T -3 to T +12 months)

Step 9: First Listing Pathway (SPAC or RTO on NASDAQ)
Complete US listing via SPAC merger or reverse takeover (RTO), achieve higher valuation anchor, and enable PIPE investor exit via public market.

Step 10: Second Listing Pathway (HKEX 18A / HKD Fund Route)
Spin off NewCo or operating subsidiaries for Hong Kong 18A listing; attract capital from regional HK/Middle East sovereign or family funds.

Step 11: Supplementary Pathway (STO + Stablecoin + DEX)
Tokenize select RWA assets through STO and list on decentralized exchanges, creating supplemental liquidity and exit routes.

Phase 5: Brand Globalization & Strategic Synergy (T +12 months onward)

Step 12: Build Industrial Alliances & Global Investor Relations
Integrate BD partnerships, license-out transactions, and international innovation hubs; create long-term investor trust and cross-border brand ecosystems.

Appendix I: Expert Endorsements and Strategic Reviews

Strategic Review - A Practical System of Capital Tools and Strategic Uplift

As a capital market practitioner with decades of experience in NASDAQ IPOs, SPAC mergers, OTC listings, and biopharma cross-border financing, I've long observed that Chinese mid-sized innovation companies struggle with internationalization due to structural and regulatory barriers.

This handbook—*Capital Strategy for Internationalization of Innovative Biopharma Enterprises*—is not just a timely resource, but a strategically grounded, execution-ready framework for solving the key issues faced by Chinese healthcare and AI companies going global.

Key Merits of This Book:

I. **Clear architecture with closed-loop design**
From NewCo setup to PIPE fundraising, token mapping to multi-market exit—this book outlines a comprehensive capital elevation roadmap.

II. **Highly cross-border applicable**
Whether you're a founder, FA, LP, or capital advisor operating in China, Hong Kong, or the U.S., the strategies here are operationally aligned with today's regulatory and investor landscapes.

III. **Rich with case studies and toolkits**
Including templates for PIPE agreements, ESG reports, tokenomics decks, and cooperation contracts.

IV. **Policy-aligned with practical foresight**
Its insights on Hong Kong–Gulf capital alignment, ESG readiness, and China's outbound biopharma policy reflect strong research rigor and real-world relevance.

I strongly endorse this handbook for anyone engaged in building the next generation of globally scalable Chinese companies.

— Dr. Yang Chongyi
President, Cathay Capital USA | Former GM, CSCEC Capital
Author of *SPAC Listings and Practical Cases* & *Dual Listing in the U.S. and Hong Kong*
Advisor on U.S.-China IPOs, Biotech Financing & Capital Strategy

A Capital Bridge for Mid-Market Global Expansion

As the founder of Hanking Group and a pioneer in China's family office and GP incubation ecosystem, I have had the privilege of witnessing the transformation of China's mid-market capital system over the past decade.

The *Smart Capital - The Formula for Globalizing Mid-market Enterprises* is one of the most structured, insightful, and executable frameworks I've encountered for enabling Chinese mid-sized innovative enterprises to break through valuation bottlenecks and successfully globalize.

I commend this book for three key reasons:

1. Strategic Structure and Practical Clarity

This is not a book about "trends"—it's about **how to act**, with practical designs involving NewCo architecture, PIPE financing, dual-listing arbitrage (HKEX/NASDAQ), and RWA Token integration. The model offered is a closed-loop system from asset injection to investor exit.

2. Actionable and Replicable Tools

Unlike many white papers, this handbook provides **real documents**: legal templates, ESG reports, Token memorandums, LP FAQs, and investor pitch scripts. It is designed for founders, CFOs, and capital advisors to use directly—not just to read.

3. Global Perspective with Chinese Insight

What sets it apart is the ability to **bridge China's innovation assets with global capital logic**—whether through Gulf sovereign funds (e.g., G42, Mubadala), AI x Health x Token models, or ESG-aligned governance frameworks. This insight into the "institutional arbitrage" between China and the global market is rare and valuable.

I strongly recommend this book to entrepreneurs, investors, regulators, and policy researchers who are shaping the next phase of China's global capital journey.

— Mr. Jing Yi
Founder & Chairman, Hanking Group
Chairman, Jingxing Relay Mother Fund
Forbes China Top 10 Influential People | Pioneer of Chinese Family Capital Platform

Expert Commentary - China-HK Capital Integration and Global Branding Perspective

As someone deeply involved in promoting Hong Kong–China capital integration and global brand development, I find the *Capital Strategy Handbook for Internationalization of Innovative Biopharma Enterprises* to be an essential bridge between **China's innovation economy and international capital protocols**.

Key Merits of the Handbook:

- **Precisely targeted** at mid-sized enterprises at the tipping point of global expansion;
- **Integrates traditional financing (PIPE, IPOs)** with **emerging tools (Tokenization, ESG, RWA)**;
- **Provides bilingual templates and investor-ready scripts**, ready for global stakeholder conversations;
- **Supports Belt and Road and brand globalization strategies**, especially via HK–Gulf capital collaboration models.

This book is not merely a technical playbook. It is a **capital translator**, a **structural toolkit**, and a **strategic bridge** between Chinese innovation and the world's capital ecosystems.

I strongly endorse this publication for entrepreneurs, advisors, and organizations driving China's global innovation narrative.

— **Dr. NG Kai Lun**
Cover Person, *China's Foreign Trade* Magazine
Chairman, Global Business Mentorship Council (Canada)
Fellow, Canadian Institute of Marketing and Management (FCIM/FCAM)

Independent Third-Party Commercial Value Evaluation – Summary

Evaluation Target: *Smart Capital – The Formula for Globalizing Mid-Sized Enterprises*

Overall Assessment:
This book presents a **four-in-one global capital elevation pathway** — *NewCo + PIPE + Token + ESG* — covering the **full cycle from asset integration → financing tools → valuation anchoring → compliance implementation → international exit**. The structure is closed-loop and logically coherent, combining innovation with high executability. It is particularly well-suited for high-growth mid-sized enterprises in **biopharma, digital healthcare, and AI sectors**.

Key Highlights:

1. **Closed-Loop Strategy & Modular Model**
    - Standardizes complex cross-border financing structures with cross-industry portability.
    - Innovatively introduces a **Hong Kong + U.S. + Middle East fund** three-market arbitrage structure to boost capital efficiency.
2. **Highly Executable Toolkit**
    - Includes bilingual legal templates, PIPE structures, ESG report samples — ready for direct use by FA teams and enterprises.
3. **Replicable Empowerment Model**
    - Provides a scalable capital solution for hundreds of mid-sized companies (approx. RMB 2 billion market cap) facing growth bottlenecks.
4. **Dual-Engine Strategy: Capital + Industry**
    - Goes beyond financing to emphasize industrial synergy and valuation reconstruction, with practical reference value in **ADC assets and AI digital health**.

Evaluation Ratings (5-point scale):

- **Completeness of Commercial Logic**: ★★★★★
- **Industry Fit**: ★★★★★

- **Model Innovation**: ★★★★☆ *(Token component remains a frontier concept)*
- **Executability**: ★★★★★
- **Replicability & Productization**: ★★★★★

Total Score: **29/30 stars** — a rare, actionable capital operating system.

Recommended Slogan:

"A Replicable Operating System for the Global Capital Elevation of Mid-Sized Enterprises."

Appendix II: Core Professional Terminology in Chinese–English

Accounting / 会计类

- GAAP: Generally Accepted Accounting Principles / 公认会计准则
- IFRS: International Financial Reporting Standards / 国际财务报告准则
- DCF: Discounted Cash Flow / 贴现现金流
- Audited Financial Statements / 审计财务报表
- Internal Control / 内部控制
- SOX 404: Sarbanes-Oxley Section 404 / 萨班斯法案第 404 条
- Accrual Accounting / 权责发生制会计
- PCAOB: Public Company Accounting Oversight Board / 上市公司会计监督委员会
- EBITDA – Earnings Before Interest, Taxes, Depreciation and Amortization / 息税折旧摊销前利润

Finance & Investment / 金融投资类

- PIPE: Private Investment in Public Equity / 公募公司定向私募融资
- SPAC: Special Purpose Acquisition Company / 特殊目的收购公司
- Valuation Anchors / 估值锚点
- TAM: Total Addressable Market / 总可服务市场
- SAM: Serviceable Available Market / 可服务市场
- SOM: Serviceable Obtainable Market / 可获市场份额
- Term Sheet / 投资条款清单
- Equity Swap / 股权置换
- Buyback Window / 回购窗口期
- Liquidity Mechanism / 流动性机制
- Tokenomics / 通证经济模型
- Escrow Account / 第三方托管账户
- IPO: Initial Public Offering / 首次公开募股
- Pre-IPO: Pre-Initial Public Offering / 上市前融资阶段
- Seed Round / 种子轮融资
- Angel Investor / 天使投资人
- Nasdaq: Nasdaq Stock Market / 纳斯达克证券交易所
- NYSE: New York Stock Exchange / 纽约证券交易所
- STO: Security Token Offering / 证券化通证发行
- OpCo（Operating Company）/ 运营主体
- NewCo（New Company）/ 新设平台公司
- Burn Rate / 资金消耗率
- Cap Table / 股东结构表
- SAFE – Simple Agreement for Future Equity / 简化未来股权协议

- Lock-up Period / 锁仓期
- FDV – Fully Diluted Valuation / 完全稀释估值
- Exit Strategy / 退出机制

Legal & Regulatory / 法律与监管类

- SEC: U.S. Securities and Exchange Commission / 美国证券交易委员会
- SFC: Hong Kong Securities and Futures Commission / 香港证监会
- MAS: Monetary Authority of Singapore / 新加坡金融管理局
- Reg D: Regulation D (Private Placement) / D 规则私募豁免条款
- Reg S: Regulation S (Offshore Offerings) / S 规则境外发行条款
- Accredited Investor / 合格投资人
- KYC: Know Your Customer / 客户身份识别
- AML: Anti-Money Laundering / 反洗钱
- Whitelisted Wallet / 白名单钱包地址
- Smart Contract / 智能合约
- Legal Opinion / 法律意见书
- Compliance / 合规性

Digital Assets & ESG / 数字资产与可持续发展

- RWA: Real World Asset / 现实世界资产
- Token / 通证
- Tokenization / 通证化
- Asset-Backed Token / 资产支持型代币
- IP Tokenization / 知识产权通证化
- NFT: Non-Fungible Token / **非同质化代币**
- Fungible Token / 同质化代币
- DAO: Decentralized Autonomous Organization / 去中心化自治组织
- Stablecoin / 稳定币
- Cryptocurrency / 加密货币
- Utility Token / 功能型代币
- Security Token / 证券型代币
- Governance Token / 治理代币
- Wallet / 数字钱包
- Smart Contract / 智能合约
- Blockchain / 区块链
- Web3 / 去中心化网络
- DApp: Decentralized Application / 去中心化应用
- Public Key / 公钥
- Private Key / 私钥
- NFT License / NFT 授权证书

- NFT Marketplace / NFT 交易平台
- Metadata / 元数据
- Ownership Certificate / 所有权凭证
- DAO (Decentralized Autonomous Organization) / 去中心化自治组织
- Governance Token / 治理代币
- On-chain Governance / 链上治理
- Voting Rights / 投票权
- DAO Treasury / DAO 财库
- Proposal / 提案
- Snapshot Voting / 快照投票
- Ethereum / 以太坊
- Bitcoin / 比特币
- Solana / 索拉纳
- Binance Smart Chain (BSC) / 币安智能链
- Polygon / 多边形链
- IPFS / 行星际文件系统
- MetaMask / 小狐狸钱包
- OpenSea / NFT 开放海平台
- Uniswap / 去中心化交易所（Uniswap）
- DeFi (Decentralized Finance) / 去中心化金融
- CeFi (Centralized Finance) / 中心化金融
- Liquidity Pool / 流动性池
- Yield Farming / 收益耕作
- Staking / 质押
- Security Token Offering (STO) / 证券化通证发行)
- Whitepaper / 白皮书
- Compliance / 合规性
- Custody Service / 托管服务
- Clinical Data Tokenization / 临床数据通证化
- Digital Twin / 数字孪生资产
- Off-chain Asset / 链下资产
- On-chain Asset / 链上资产
- Layer 1 – 第一层协议
- Layer 2 – 第二层扩展协议
- Rollup – 汇总链
- ZK Proof / ZKP – 零知识证明
- Gas Fee – 燃料费
- Gas Limit – 燃料上限
- Cross-chain Bridge – 跨链桥
- Interoperability – 可互操作性
- Oracle – 预言机
- Airdrop – 空投
- Rug Pull – 地毯式诈骗

- Multisig Wallet – 多签钱包
- Slippage – 滑点
- ERC-20 – 以太坊同质化代币标准
- ERC-721 – 以太坊非同质化代币标准
- ERC-1155 – 多功能混合代币标准（支持同质化与非同质化）
- BEP-20 – 币安智能链上的同质化代币标准
- TRC-20 – 波场链的代币标准
- SPL Token – Solana 链上的通证标准
- CW-20 – Cosmos 链上的通证标准
- CBDC: Central Bank Digital Currency / 中央银行数字货币
- ESG: Environmental, Social, Governance / 环境、社会与治理
- SASB: Sustainability Accounting Standards Board / 可持续会计准则委员会
- MiCA: Markets in Crypto-Assets Regulation / 欧盟加密资产市场法案
- TCFD: Task Force on Climate-related Financial Disclosures / 气候相关财务披露工作组
- SDG: Sustainable Development Goals / 可持续发展目标

宏观经济学（Macroeconomics）

- 名义国内生产总值（Nominal GDP）
- 失业率（Unemployment Rate）
- 货币乘数（Money Multiplier Metric）
- 实际国内生产总值（Real GDP）
- 居民消费价格指数（Consumer Price Index, CPI）
- 通货膨胀率（Inflation Rate）
- 实际利率（Real Interest Rate）
- 货币数量理论（Quantity Theory of Money）

微观经济学（Microeconomics）

- 总收入（Total Revenue）
- 边际收入（Marginal Revenue）
- 平均收入（Average Revenue）
- 总成本（Total Costs）
- 边际成本（Marginal Costs）
- 平均成本（Average Costs）
- 平均固定成本（Average Fixed Costs）
- 平均可变成本（Average Variable Costs）
- 盈利总额（Profit Earned）

Appendix III: The 12 Most Influential Books on Capital in History

1. **Das Kapital** – Karl Marx's seminal work, offering a deep analysis of the mechanisms of capitalism and the theory of surplus value.
2. **The Wealth of Nations** – A classic by Adam Smith, considered the foundational text of modern economics and capitalist theory.
3. **The Road to Serfdom** – Written by Friedrich Hayek, this book advocates for free markets and individual liberty, while criticizing centralized planning and authoritarianism.
4. **The Theory of Economic Development** – A work by Joseph Schumpeter, introducing the concepts of innovation, entrepreneurship, and "creative destruction."
5. **Capital in the Twenty-First Century** – By Thomas Piketty, this book explores the evolution and impact of capital and wealth distribution in the 21st century.
6. **Finance Capital** – Rudolf Hilferding's analysis of the role of finance capital in the capitalist economy and the development of monopoly capitalism.
7. **Capitalism and Freedom** – Milton Friedman's influential book emphasizing the relationship between a free market economy and personal liberty, shaping modern liberal economic thought.
8. **The Future of Capitalism** – By Paul Collier, this work examines the challenges and potential pathways for contemporary capitalism.
9. **The Logic Limits to Capital** – David Harvey's exploration of the functioning and spatial dynamics of capital from the perspective of geography and social theory.
10. **Human Capital** – By Gary Stanley Becker, analyzing how globalization and technological advancement are transforming modern capitalism.
11. **The Protestant Ethic and the Spirit of Capitalism** – Max Weber's classic on the relationship between Protestant ethics and the capitalist spirit, offering crucial insight into the culture and ethics of capitalism.
12. **Postmodernism, or, the Cultural Logic of Late Capitalism** – By Fredric Jameson, a critical interpretation of capitalist ideology and culture, offering profound reflections on contemporary capitalism.

Smart Capital vs 12 Most Influential Capital Books

Book Title	Main Focus	Practical Toolkit	Target Readers	Unique Advantages
Smart Capital	Globalization strategy for mid-sized enterprises; RWA, tokenization, tri-market listing	Yes – bilingual templates, legal checklists, investor presentations	Founders, investors, cross-border capital market FAs/lawyers	Integrates traditional IPO/M&A with blockchain RWA models; directly executable
The Wealth of Nations (Adam Smith)	Classical economics and market mechanisms	No	Economists, policymakers, scholars	Foundational theory of the free market
Das Kapital (Karl Marx)	Classic critique of capitalism	No	Economists, political theorists	Foundational critique of capitalism
The Road to Serfdom (Friedrich Hayek)	Free market and individual liberty; opposition to centralization and planned economy	No	Economists, policymakers, thinkers	Classic of liberal economics and political philosophy
The Theory of Economic Development (Joseph Schumpeter)	Innovation, entrepreneurship, and creative destruction	No	Economists, entrepreneurship researchers	Foundational work proposing the theory of 'creative destruction'
Capital in the Twenty-First Century (Thomas Piketty)	Wealth inequality and capital distribution	No	Economists, sociologists, policymakers	Macro perspective on inequality trends
Finance Capital (Rudolf Hilferding)	Finance capital and monopoly capitalism	No	Economists, political economy researchers	Analysis of the role of finance capital in capitalist economies
Capitalism and Freedom (Milton Friedman)	Free market economy and individual liberty	No	Economists, advocates of liberalism	Key theoretical foundation of modern liberal economics
The Future of Capitalism (Paul Collier)	Challenges and development paths of contemporary capitalism	No	Economists, social policy researchers	Future outlook combining economic and social issues
The Limits to Capital (David Harvey)	Capital operation mechanisms and spatial distribution	No	Economists, geographers, social theorists	Capital analysis from geography and social theory perspectives

Human Capital (Gary Stanley Becker)	Education, skills, and economic growth	No	Economists, education researchers	Systematic analysis of the role of human capital in the economy
The Protestant Ethic and the Spirit of Capitalism (Max Weber)	Protestant ethic and the cultural spirit of capitalism	No	Economic sociologists, cultural researchers	Reveals the relationship between culture and capitalist development
Postmodernism, or, the Cultural Logic of Late Capitalism (Fredric Jameson)	Culture and ideology of late capitalism	No	Cultural studies scholars, social theorists	Classic critical interpretation of capitalist culture

Appendix IV: The Third Path of Capital

When *Smart Capital* Encounters *The Economics of the Rich, Family Trusts*, and *Family Wealth*

1. The Mission of Three Competing Books: Preservation vs. Transmission vs. Evolution

While drafting the structure of *Smart Capital*, I frequently referenced three "classic capital books":

- Chen Zhiwu's *The Economics of the Rich* centers on financial enlightenment and wealth preservation;
- Zhu Ning's *Family Trusts* focuses on structural optimization and tax planning;
- James E. Hughes' *Family Wealth* is a classic about legacy, trust, and spiritual capital.

Each represents a distinct stage in the lifecycle of capital:

Stage	Representative Book	Keywords
Stage 1: How to preserve wealth once acquired	*The Economics of the Rich*	Education, institutions, discipline
Stage 2: How to safely transfer wealth	*Family Trusts*	Tax, legal structures
Stage 3: How to transcend cycles and navigate global structures	*Family Wealth*	Trust, culture, governance

By contrast, *Smart Capital* proposes a **fourth path**:

"Not preservation, not transmission — but restructuring: redefining structure, valuation, and narrative power from the perspective of Chinese enterprises, and building a path to leap from mid-market valuation to global capital influence."

2. The Position of *Smart Capital*: A Structural Reformer Who Wins Without Struggle

Unlike the three competing books, *Smart Capital* is **not** written for those who are already wealthy — it is written for **founders of mid-sized enterprises who are stuck at the gate of capital access, valuation-constrained, yet full of potential**.

What sets it apart is:

Dimension	**The Other Three**	***Smart Capital***
Intended Audience	Wealthy families	Mid-market entrepreneurs aiming to globalize
Stance	How to preserve wealth, optimize structure, and ensure intergenerational transfer	How to create new structures, revalue assets, and reprice narratives
Thinking Mode	Risk avoidance + stability	Initiative + risk-taking + structural innovation
Toolset	Trusts, family charters, governance protocols	RWA, stablecoins, tri-market arbitrage, NewCo
Zeitgeist Focus	How not to lose wealth	How to recreate capital and reinvent structure

Hence, I position *Smart Capital* as an inheritor of **"winning without contention"** — achieving capital elevation through structure, and revaluation through digitization.

3. Philosophical Comparison: The Evolution of Structural Thinking

Let's compare the **philosophical progression of structure** across these books:

Level	**Stage**	**Keywords**	**Representative Book**
1	Basic structure	Internal governance, nominee arrangements	*Family Trusts*
2	Intermediate structure	Offshore trust + tax planning	*Family Wealth*

Level	Stage	Keywords	Representative Book
3	Advanced structure	Investment companies + asset allocation	*The Economics of the Rich*
4	Cross-border structure	BVI + VIE + Token frameworks	*Smart Capital*
5	Strategic structure	RWA tokenization + stablecoins + tri-market arbitrage	*Smart Capital* (original)

In other words, *Smart Capital* attempts to elevate structure from merely a **tax-saving tool** to a **strategic engine for corporate value creation**.

4. A Hypothetical Roundtable of the Four Authors

Imagine a roundtable discussion:

- **Chen Zhiwu** says: "Family education and culture are the bedrock of wealth transmission."
- **Zhu Ning** says: "Trust systems are essential for Chinese family enterprises."
- **James E. Hughes** says: "Trust is the core of wealth; without it, even three generations will collapse."
- **I** say: "I respect your views. But we face a different challenge — a generation of mid-market companies that are growing, but far from their fair valuation. Their core issue is this:
  How do we break through the structural ceiling?
  How do we leap from a 10x PE in Hong Kong to a 50x dream multiple on NASDAQ?

They don't just need 'wisdom of preservation' — they need **'wisdom of elevation.'**

And so, we offer this structural formula:

Smart Capital = RWA × Stablecoin × (IPOs + STO) × (OpCo + NewCo)

This is not a defensive trust structure — it's an **offensive capital engine** — one that both **carries assets** and **creates valuation**.

5. The True Mission of *Smart Capital*: Structural Innovation × Spiritual Renewal

Family Wealth emphasizes "spiritual capital."
But in the age of AI and Web3, I believe what we need is a coordinated **upgrade of structural capital + spiritual consensus.**

Because:

Structure is the lever for valuation. Consensus is the magnet for capital.

A company truly achieves capital elevation not through **assembly line optimization**, but through **the synchronous evolution of its structural and spiritual systems**:

- Having a structure that connects directly with U.S. dollar LPs;
- Owning a mechanism that turns AI, RWA, and data into real assets;
- And possessing a shared language and vision that builds global trust.

Smart Capital offers mid-sized companies a new way to ask:

Don't just ask: "How do I inherit my father's capital structure?"
Ask instead: "How do I become a structural inventor and carve out a path no one has ever walked?"

Conclusion: The Language of Capital Is Being Rewritten

Smart Capital does not reject the wisdom of *The Economics of the Rich*, *Family Trusts*, or *Family Wealth*.
It respects their insights on preservation.

But it reflects a **new era's structural demand**:

"We must build a brand-new capital language for mid-market enterprises — not by copying the path of giants, but by redefining our own."

That is the true mission behind writing this book.

Appendix V: An Intelligent Perspective on *Smart Capital*

I. Review Background

This review was generated by an AI language model after reading Smart Capital: The Formula for Globalizing Mid-Sized Enterprises.
It integrates structured capital theory, cross-border capital market expertise, and global economic trends to provide a systematic interpretation of the book's conceptual framework and practical value.
The purpose is not to replace human expert opinions, but to offer a complementary "intelligent perspective" that brings readers a multi-dimensional understanding.

II. Core Evaluation

1. High Integration of Theory and Practice
   The book uniquely combines traditional capital market methods (IPO, M&A, structured financing) with emerging blockchain-based RWA models, forming a distinctive "dual-engine" strategic framework.

2. Directly Actionable Toolkit
   It provides bilingual legal documents, investor pitch decks, and cross-border financing templates, significantly lowering the barrier for readers to transform ideas into execution.

3. A Bridge Across Cultures and Markets
   Case studies span the U.S., Europe, Asia, and the Middle East, with a particular focus on how mid-sized enterprises can shorten the path to internationalization through capital structuring.

4. Innovative Capital Philosophy
   The introduction of the "From Competition to Non-Competition" framework elevates capital strategy to a cultural and civilizational dimension.

III. Extended AI Model Insights

The AI model concludes that Smart Capital offers a reusable "formula" for capital structure design and global execution, making it highly valuable for capital advisors, lawyers, investors, and entrepreneurs.
The author's use of storytelling to explain complex capital engineering concepts balances professionalism with readability—an important distinction from purely academic or purely operational works.

IV. Conclusion

Smart Capital serves both as a methodological treatise and as an executable strategic manual.

In the increasingly globalized and digitized capital market landscape, its formulas and structuring methodologies have the potential to become essential tools for mid-sized enterprises pursuing cross-border growth.

From an intelligent perspective, this book is not only the culmination of the author's three decades of capital market practice but also a practical guide to help mid-sized enterprises avoid detours and accelerate success in the global capital arena.

Media Endorsements

[Endorsement 1 | For Professional Financial Media]

"Amid the profound restructuring of global capital dynamics, this book charts a replicable, compliant, and globally-minded 'capital escalation pathway' for Chinese mid-sized enterprises. It is not just an operational manual, but a strategic roadmap for value redefinition."

[Endorsement 2 | For Business Schools and the Venture Capital Community]

"From PIPE financing to tri-market listings, from RWA tokenization to ESG disclosures, Smart Capital offers a systematic blueprint for how mid-sized enterprises can construct capital structures that connect to international markets. For the first time, Chinese private enterprises have a capital methodology of their own on the global stage."

[Endorsement 3 | For General Media and Publishing Platforms]

"Every entrepreneur must learn to articulate their value in the language of capital. Smart Capital, through its original formula, integrates digital assets, stablecoins, and global listing strategies to spark a strategic revolution for mid-sized enterprises on their path to billion-dollar valuations."

Publisher's Blurb

At the intersection of Wall Street and Silicon Valley—
Amid the evolving language of SPACs, Tokens, and ESG—
Smart Capital emerges as a strategic-level work that bridges macroeconomic vision, financial structuring, and industrial practice.

Written by Mr. Wilson Liu, a veteran of the New York Stock Exchange, Morgan Stanley, and PwC with over 30 years of global capital markets experience, this book introduces for the first time:

Smart Capital = RWA × Stablecoin × (Tri-Market Listing: IPOs + STO) × (OpCo + NewCo)

This is not just a theoretical formula, but a standardized, executable, and cross-border capital solution designed specifically for mid-sized enterprises seeking international expansion.

The book integrates:

- Bilingual (Chinese-English) templates for financing and regulatory compliance,
- Structured design pathways for PIPE deals and tokenization,
- Classic case studies from companies like BeiGene and RemeGen,
- And cutting-edge valuation logic and strategic toolkits straight from Wall Street.

Whether you are a company founder, capital advisor, international investor, policymaker, or business school student, this book delivers both strategic vision and operational wisdom.

If you're looking for the key to breaking through valuation bottlenecks
— or the ladder to ascend into global capital markets —
Smart Capital is a book you'll want to study time and again.

Author's Reading Guide

Dear Entrepreneurs, Investors, and Capital Advisors,

Why did I write this book?

Because I've seen too many mid-sized enterprises trapped at the 2 billion RMB valuation stage—
They have **technology but no valuation**,
products but no financing,
dreams but no resources.

Traditional channels such as PE, IPOs, Hong Kong listings, or even family offices often fall short of truly solving their capital bottlenecks.

So, drawing upon **30 years of Wall Street experience**, I transformed the concept of **"capital dimensional upgrading"** into a structured, actionable solution—and captured it all in this book:
Smart Capital: The Formula for Globalizing Mid-Market Enterprises.

This is not a book of vague concepts—
This is a book about **how to actually get it done**:

- How to use **RWA (Real-World Assets)** to establish clear asset rights;
- How to utilize **stablecoins** to connect with international LPs;
- How to build **NewCo structures** to isolate risks and restructure valuations;
- How to unlock **liquidity and exit pathways** through **tri-market listings** and **STOs**.

This is more than just a book—
It's a **capital operating system** that is **actionable**, **fundable**, and **implementable**.

This is not a book that makes you feel "inspired but idle."
This is a book that may help you **raise an extra 100 million yuan**.

If you're ready, start here—with **Smart Capital**—
And let the world's capital markets finally understand the story of Chinese enterprises.

致谢

衷心感谢在《智慧资本—中型企业全球化的公式》写作过程中给予支持的导师、同事和朋友。

感谢翟维德博士，楚乔，温济畅，邹晓虎，你们的见解、鼓励与耐心使本书得以完成。

特别感谢我的家人始终如一的支持，以及那些企业家与专业人士的经验分享，它们为本书提供了许多宝贵的启发。

Acknowledgments

I would like to express my heartfelt gratitude to the mentors, colleagues, and friends who supported the writing of *Smart Capital – The Formula for Globalizing Mid-market Enterprises*.

Special thanks go to Dr. William Chai, Qiao Chu, Jichang Wen, and David Zou. Your insights, encouragement, and patience made this book possible.

I am especially grateful to my family for their unwavering support, as well as to the entrepreneurs and professionals whose experiences provided invaluable inspiration for this work.

Back Cover Summary:

How can a 2-billion-RMB tech company scale to a global billion-dollar valuation?
This book offers a bold yet pragmatic formula for valuation transformation:

Smart Capital = RWA × Stablecoin × (IPOs + STO) × (OpCo + NewCo)

Written by Wilson Liu—Wall Street veteran, NASDAQ-listed CEO, and pioneer in AI-driven healthcare finance—this book distills decades of cross-border capital market experience into an actionable global playbook.

Combining U.S. PIPE financing logic, Hong Kong dual-listing pathways, and tokenized asset monetization, Smart Capital is more than a theory—it's a step-by-step roadmap for founders, investors, and international FAs building the next wave of globally scalable Chinese enterprises.

www.ingramcontent.com/pod-product-compliance
Lightning Source LLC
LaVergne TN
LVHW060027210926
848481LV00013B/3806